INTERPRETING TELEVISION

SAGE ANNUAL REVIEWS OF COMMUNICATION RESEARCH

Volume 12

SAGE ANNUAL REVIEWS OF COMMUNICATION RESEARCH

Interpreting Television:
Current Research Perspectives

WILLARD D. ROWLAND, Jr.

and

BRUCE WATKINS

Editors

 SAGE PUBLICATIONS Beverly Hills London New Delhi

For information address:

SAGE Publications, Inc.
275 South Beverly Drive
Beverly Hills, California 90212

SAGE Publications India Pvt. Ltd.  SAGE Publications Ltd
C-236 Defence Colony   28 Banner Street
New Delhi 110 024, India   London EC1Y 8QE, England

Printed in the United States of America

Library of Congress Cataloging in Publication Data

Interpreting television.

   (Sage annual reviews of communication research ; v. 12)
   1. Television broadcasting—Research—Addresses, essays,
lectures. I. Rowland, Willard D. II. Watkins, Bruce.
III. Series.
PN1992.55I54   1984   384.55′4′072   84-17714
ISBN 0-8039-2393-7
ISBN 0-8039-2394-5 (pbk.)

FIRST PRINTING

CONTENTS

PREFACE

OVER THE PAST DECADE the quantity and quality of published literature on the role and meaning of television content has increased notably. That increase has been encouraged through expanded, more sophisticated undergraduate and graduate curricular offerings involving television and media studies, and increased opportunities for conference interchange among those conducting research in this field. We have both been variously involved in such efforts and in conjunction with the series editors felt it was time for a volume of the Sage Annual Reviews of Communication Research to take formal cognizance of the trends in television studies. Accordingly, we examined the programs of the many large and small North American communication, journalism, speech, and film conferences during 1982–83, searching for worthy representatives of current television research. We also reviewed numerous other unpublished papers, as well as various publications in sources we thought not otherwise likely to be seen regularly by the majority of subscribers to this series. One of the 1982–83 conferences, at Ann Arbor, was actually coorganized by one of us, and five of the papers here derive from that gathering. The rest are from the other sources, and together the collection offers considerable insight into the range and depth of contemporary television studies research.

The purpose of this book is to demonstrate how some of the various current approaches have influenced the study of television in society and culture. The effort here is not to represent all aspects of the new and developing approaches to every facet of television. To present only a fair sample of all such work across all the relevant areas of television inquiry would be a herculean task, occupying many volumes. Rather, this effort is the more modest, though nonetheless significant, one of trying to demonstrate how some of the current changes in communication research are helping redefine the issue of television as a cultural institution. The approaches presented in this book focus primarily on television as a creator and conveyor of meaning, as a text through which to interpret the culture and societies in which it exists.

Much of this research rises out of the debates between traditional, mainstream positivistic research and the various conflicting trends in cultural and critical studies. Some of this work tries to resolve those debates, seeking to show how to answer large cultural, interpretive questions within the framework of sufficient "data" and controlled methods. Much of the rest of the work tries to transcend the debate, at least as it is typically posed, attempting simply to get on with interpreting television from the vantage points of differing sociocultural perspectives. While the central concern is with matters of meaning in television, that concern is framed in light of television as a social process, as a medium embedded in crucial environments of content creation, viewing, interpretation, and use among individuals and groups, all in turn interrelated with patterns of ideology, social experience, economic structures, and political interests.

Most of the papers for this volume are speculative, theoretical works in progress, albeit careful and disciplined. While most are grounded in rigorous empirical analysis, there is considerable variance in interpretation of both "rigor" and "empirical." There is no principal method or unified theory at work here. To the contrary, the volume is a celebration of the rich, disputatious diversity in current television research. Indeed, there are a set of multifaceted dialogues and serious arguments among the authors, though not necessarily in terms of the mutual consideration of one another's contributions. The debates are more implicit than explicit, resting in differences over views about theory, method, epistemology, and social reality that are associated with the several emerging strains of contemporary critical and cultural media studies. Some of these arguments even extend to differences with portions of previous volumes in this annual series. To what extent the papers here reflect the most definitive aspects of the current major shifts and disputes in mass media research remains to be seen. At any rate they do represent a solid sample of new directions for research on television and attempts to understand its cultural meanings and resonancies.

By way of acknowledgement we would like to thank the series editors for the opportunity to develop this volume, and we are grateful to them and many of our colleagues at Illinois and Michigan who offered much useful advice and encouragement. We would especially like to thank Diane Tipps for her careful, efficient, and unflappable assistance during the preparation of the final manuscript.

Willard D. Rowland, Jr.
Urbana-Champaign

Bruce Watkins
Ann Arbor

INTRODUCTION
Beyond Mass Culture and Normal Science in Television Research

Willard D. Rowland, Jr. and Bruce Watkins

FOR SOME TIME NOW there has been increasing dissatisfaction with the inability of much American popular and scholarly commentary to describe and explain the role of the mass media, particularly television, among individuals and in society. The problem of self-reflection by the mass press and electronic media themselves is, of course, related to their fundamental economic motives and their concomitantly shallow and spotty capacity for sophisticated cultural analysis. That their performance in matters of popular culture coverage has been at least equally as poor is hardly surprising. More troubling, however, has been the long period of relatively narrow discourse about television within the academy. Here one might have expected that with some isolation from the commercial marketplace there would have been more freedom and capacity for careful, wider-ranging criticism. One might have been particularly hopeful on this score in light of the growth of an increasingly self-conscious, professionally organized field of mass communication research. If anywhere, this ought to have been the place for a strong, convincing source of commentary on television.

However, as it developed communication research was severely constrained by intellectual and structural factors related to its heritage. Emerging on the margins of and in the interstices between the humanities and the social sciences, communication studies had a substantial problem of self-identity and legitimation. To make claims to a place in the academy that would take it beyond the most elementary vocational chores of journalism, broadcasting, and advertising training, and in many cases just to protect turf dearly won in those realms, communication research had to make a series of accommodations with its forebears that were to be more costly than it could imagine.

With regard to the humanities, the compromise was to buy into the traditional aesthetic analyses of content that led it far too deeply into the mass culture debate. In retrospect this commitment may have been inevitable. As Lowenthal (1957), Williams (1958), Hall and Whannel (1964), and Smith (1973) have shown, the roots of the debate over popular art and mass culture are variously as old as the social and economic dislocations of the renaissance, enlightenment, and industrial eras and the associated adjustments in the nature and process of culture. The then contemporary controversies over Elizabethan drama, Montaigne's fascination with the positive possibilities of diversion in commercial entertainment, Pascal's despair over it, Arnold's hopes for the spread of a middle-class morality, and Progressivist anxieties over dance halls and motion pictures, all suggest how the rise of commodity culture engendered a series of arguments whose terms remained remarkably common over three or four centuries. It should therefore not be surprising that mid-twentieth-century American intellectual commentary on film, radio, and, finally, television—the latest stage in the development of a highly technologized and commercial popular culture—should adopt a debate framework of such longstanding. In the 1950s communication research was barely a recognizable field and as a loose amalgam of various other disciplines and traditions it could do little more at the outset than inherit their perspectives, errors and all.

In drawing in part from the standard humanities syllabus, one of the costs for communication studies was to accept the traditional distinction between high and low culture in which the classics of literature, art, and music were taken as given and as the former, while television and other mass media were clearly associated with the latter. Since the newly developing programs in communication had no clear disciplinary conventions of their own and yet required some literature on television, they found themselves turning to collections of commentary that grew out of the traditional literary curricula (Rosenberg and White, 1957, 1971; Jacobs, 1959; Casty, 1968; Hammel, 1972).

But this strategy had the ironic result of helping undercut the efforts to build a credible foundation to humanities-based media research. For in accepting so much of the high culture perspective—at least its agenda, if not all its conclusions—in television criticism, the field was accepting the very terms of the medium's dismissal. Moreover, dually rooted as it was in a comfortable prewar conservatism and a traditionally optimistic liberal progressivism, such classical humanism carried with it a sociopolitical outlook that turned out to be an argument about much more than the nature of a medium's content. Even those with a somewhat more radical view tended to accept the high culture-low culture dichotomy—well-educated European socialists retained a strong sense of correct aesthetics—and were not overly troubled by the political contradictions.

Throughout the nineteenth century, and all during the rise of ever more specialized curricula, "culture" itself had become associated increasingly with notions of product and artifact, and with the entire problematic structure of industry, commercialism, and the complex processes embedded there. Simultaneously as more and more groups came under the umbrella of the "populus," that term had lost its identity with the venerated Aristotelian notions of the whole polity, particularly as the revisionist attacks on classicism had come to reveal the embarrassing exclusions implicit in its ancient usage. Associated increasingly with images of the Jacobin mob, "popular" shifted steadily into a pejorative cast, to be made synonymous finally with the industrial revolution's "mass." Never strictly denotative, the derogatory connotative aspects of this terminology came to control much of the twentieth century debate about communication. As Raymond Williams saw more clearly and earlier than most, in its strictest sense the high culture critique of television was as much as anything an argument against the audience. He recognized that "there are in fact no masses, there are only ways of seeing people as masses," and that the critique therefore was a class-bound, elitist lament about those who were either contemptuously or patronizingly presumed to be the helpless, rootless victims of the new media, subject to their "politial or cultural exploitation" (Williams, 1958). Although in time the conservative and liberal cultural critics took cognizance of this critique and tried to argue against it (Rosenberg, 1971; Gans, 1974), much of the condescending tone, the missionary sense of uplift, and the rationalization remained.

While the dominant mien of the humanistic approach was socially critical, there was a subdivision of it that was decidedly optimistic. This was the tendency of some not merely to reject the high culture critique, but to take that rejection so far as to embrace indiscriminately all aspects of modern popular culture. From this perspective all products of contemporary cultural production were of essentially equal status and value. Not just situation comedies and game shows, but ashtrays and T-shirts were grist for the popular culture mill. While clearly important as a way of helping broaden the possible range of scholarly discourse about contemporary culture, such approaches frequently tended to be so fervent and all-embracing that in their shock-effect they were often counterproductive. To see significance in every cultural artifact and to celebrate that meaning without any appeal to discipline or some basis for validation was to discredit much of the more cautious, tentative, yet rich analyses of television and popular culture that were otherwise beginning to emerge.[1]

Rising in the spirit of modernism and the new criticism, this form of popular cultural analysis failed to share with those schools much of their control or their serious understanding of that which was being rejected. It also closely paralleled and fostered the rise of the McLuhanesque embrace of the new electronic media and its celebration of the presumedly forthcoming technological and human neuropsychic revolutions. Similarly an heir of the new critical spirit, that enthusiasm likewise failed for its careless dismissal of the more disciplined, cautious historiographies of technology and culture out of which it had also risen, but not before it had done much to help confound the debate over television and the nature of the electronic age, distracting attention from the necessary examination of their origins and continuing realities (Carey and Quirk, 1970; Czitrom, 1982). Further, as much as its subject matter, the lack of empirical rigor in this approach to popular culture caused damage to the emerging field in other ways. Discussions about "meaning" of media symbols often became nothing more than opinion exchanges, and "evidence" nothing more than clever or unique arguments and examples. It made little difference to outside scholars whether the lack of rigor came from theoretical differences of opinion about how to conduct proper social inquiries, or inadequate training of humanists who set foot in areas traditionally the domain of the social scientists. Iconoclasm and aphoristic insights could draw attention to the new field, but alone they could not legitimize it.

Meanwhile, throughout the mid-twentieth century and quite independently from their problems with communication questions, humanistic approaches to the study of human behavior and society were being displaced by the modern forms of positivistic social science. Rooted in the expansive, essentially optimistic American social and economic experience, the new scientific imagination focused on the present and future, on the fact and the importance of "objective" research techniques. America was a series of problems that could and would be solved by the new technocracy that was emerging to control the methods for gathering and analyzing the data. The older, more essentially European traditions for studying the mind, social process, politics, the economy, and even history and language, were being converted into the newer spirits of positivism and pragmatism, with their assumptions about objective reality and the possibilities of validation.

As these sciences came to command greater authority and resources at the heart of the American academy, and as the issues of modern media and communication themselves became more salient, the latter came increasingly under the purview of the former. By the time of the rise of television, communication studies had come to be predominantly the scientific investigation of psychological and social effects. Reflecting the American concern with the individual, the primary group, and their problems of the moment, and being also concerned about practical patterns of causality, much of the first generation of television inquiry was consumed with questions of useful applications, such as its utility as an educator, and questions of impact, particularly the matter of dire consequences for youth. Anxious to secure itself in the academy and uncertain both of its own skills and the more general prospects among the beleaguered humanities, much communication research tended to follow the scientific siren, holding out hope that in synchronization with the expected breakthrough in the social and behavioral sciences, a powerful, general theory of communication action would be found.

Yet for all the appeals to science much of the American work on television was still somewhat constrained by a lack of theoretical and ideological self-consciousness (Hall, 1982). During the early, interwar phase of communication research there had been some brief flirtation with approaches to media content that would take into account social, economic, and political presuppositions as, for instance, in Adorno's (1941) work on popular music at Lazarsfeld's Bureau of Applied Social Research. But, as Adorno himself and several others have noted, the critical research tradition that he and other Marxist émigrés from the Frankfurt School represented simply did not fit well within Lazarsfeld's program of pragmatic administrative research (Adorno, 1969; Lazarsfeld, 1969; Lowenthal, 1957; Morrison 1977). The forms of applied social research being developed at the Bureau and contributing so directly to the central tendencies of postwar American communication research were too closely allied to industrial support and to the general tradition of liberal accommodations with existing media structures to permit lines of inquiry that took as problematic those very economic and social arrangements (Rowland, 1983). Additionally, the research methods being developed were much better suited to testing small hypotheses and measuring easily defined units and effects. Research studies that required that the research method be "turned back on itself" as part of the scientific inquiry were extremely difficult to conceptualize, let alone design. In this sense much mid-twentieth century American social science, and by extension the themes of communication research it was fostering, was theoretically naive.[2]

At the outset this condition was not well recognized by American communication researchers. The initial series of anthologies on communication research, influenced largely by the campaign research programs initiated at the bureau, the Office of War Information, and the few other centers that had received industry and government aid before, during, and shortly after World War II, were highly instrumental in orientation (Schramm, 1949, 1960; Dexter and White, 1964; Berelson and Janowitz, 1950, 1953, 1966). There was some, but only minimal, attention to media structure and process, and matters of content and meaning were largely ignored. The focus was principally on questions of persuasion, audience behavior, and effect. Ironically, to a great extent many in communication research, including the editors of the principal readers, thought they were caught up in serious theoretical disputes, as among direct effects, limited effects, and uses and gratifications models. It has only recently become widely clear how relatively narrow and largely methodological were those disputes. Reflecting the American penchant for emphasizing matters of technique over abstraction, there was little patience or capacity within social science at large, nor communication studies itself, for examining the epistemological roots of American social thought and therefore for recognizing the essentially common world views and cultural models embedded in such ostensibly different theories as behaviorism and functionalism.

Serious matters of theory concerning television were not entirely alien to communication studies, but their pursuit was only occasionally notable within initial communication research programs. To be sure, there was much avowal of theoretical interest in this field, as in the formation of "theory and methodology" interest groups and divisions in its professional organizations. But the practice there was more the operational testing of relatively narrow hypotheses treated outside of any social or historical context. Indeed, for a field to consider a "theory and methodology" division as separate from content-based divisions points to a curious intellectual segmentation. Theory infuses all research, willy-nilly, and important and meaningful findings are seldom encountered without sufficient theoretical bases.

Apart from the initial abortive efforts of the Frankfurt School refugees, the earliest locus of communication and culture theoretical construction in the much deeper ideological and cultural sense implicit here tended to be in film study programs, some of which were associated with broadcasting, speech, and communications departments, but many of which originated in separate theater, fine arts, or literature programs. As one of the initial popular arts, film had also suffered the disdain of traditional literary and cultural criticism. Originally, as the medium of the urban, immigrant, laboring classes and all too clearly the product of an increasingly commercial cultural production process, film was simply dismissed by those intellectual elites who shared with existing educational, religious, and political forces the anxieties about the ability of such media to bypass the traditional institutions for interpreting and handing down values and standards (Jowett, 1976). However, as film persisted and its popularity widened increasingly into and beyond bourgeois realms, some in the academy dared to begin to take it seriously and incorporate it into arts and literature curricula, particularly during the postwar, mid-century expansion of higher education.

At this stage film had begun to escape the low culture opprobrium, but not entirely. The initial terms for film studies legitimation required that it adopt characteristics of aesthetic analysis that embraced the invidious distinctions of the mass culture debate, venerating a few favored films as high classics and dismissing the unworthy rest. As television spread to near ubiquity during the 1950s, it became the new popular culture pariah and film could rise above it. Thus, for instance, in 1958 the *Quarterly Journal of Film, Radio, and Television* (previously, in the 1940s, the *Hollywood Quarterly*) could abandon its broadcast components, rename itself the *Film Quarterly,* and dedicate itself almost exclusively to the study of film as "an art form in itself," and "to the hypothesis that a body of serious critical thought about film is possible," unabashedly appealing to the old French aesthetic standard, *"Ca, c'est du cinema!" (Film Quarterly,* 1958–1959, Vol. 12, Nos. 2–3).

Among the reactions to this claim for traditional art status was support for some of the indiscriminate popular culture celebration noted above, but regardless of the errors of this or that enthusiasm the intellectual reality was that film was finding a place in the academy for regular study and critique. In many instances that instruction was tied to production and professional concerns, not unlike the experience of journalism. But to the extent that film remained the primary province of literature and language programs, and initially in communication within speech departments, it tended to be associated predominantly with traditions of rhetoric, literary criticism, and cultural interpretation that, for all their sociocultural biases, offered a certain protection against the more scientistic, quantifiably empirical approaches to media and interpersonal communication that were otherwise capturing so much of journalism and speech research. Though never intended as such, the value of this protection was that it provided time for at least one area of media content study to come to be influenced by the postbehaviorist debates within the humanities and the qualitative aspects of the social sciences.

This exposure proved to be crucial for television studies, because by and large within the more positivistic realms of communication research the study of television programs and content was being ignored. To the extent the scientific imagination in communication research addressed itself to television content it had begun to do so largely within the frame of a quantitative content analysis. Although appealing in part to questions of change in social and cultural values, this approach primarily attempted to create a formal scheme for categorizing and monitoring trends in television representations of social relations that would be susceptible to statistical analysis. Beginning as part of the scientific effects investigation of television violence—as an index of violent acts and the context of their occurrence—this research aspired to a more general status of cultural monitoring. It sought to create a system of "cultivation analysis" that would extend beyond the narrower concerns over violence and television impact on children to provide a set of cultural indicators that would have a reliability and authority analogous to those mechanisms measuring economic and other social developments for policymaking purposes (see, for example, Gerbner, 1972 and 1980).

The degree to which this effort has been successful remains to be seen. It has come under attack from both humanistic and social science traditions, variously for its assumptions about culture and its methodology (Newcomb, 1978; Hirsch, 1980, 1981a, 1981b; Gerbner, 1981a, 1981b). But the relative merits of the attacks and defenses of cultivation analysis need not detain us here. What is of more immediate significance is that the debate about it reflected a greater awareness within communication research during the 1970s that serious attention to television content and the means for interpreting it deserved far more attention than had theretofore been accorded them.

Other indications of the shifting status and focus of television research came in the period of the late-1960s to mid-1970s with a new series of anthologies presenting on the whole a wider body of discourse on television. The material here could not yet be said to be a product of communication research itself. Much of it still emanated from other disciplines and experiences. Most strikingly, perhaps, its initial medium had been journalistic. During the preceding decade or two a number of magazines and newspapers had begun to offer space for increasingly sophisticated commentary on television. Many scholars in established fields—literature, history, sociology—and a number of others working in interdisciplinary experiments among them, as for example in American studies, had become interested in television content issues, but were as yet unable to present their work in mainstream academic forums. They found an outlet in several of the more serious intellectual periodicals—*Commonweal, Saturday Review, The New Yorker, The New Republic, Atlantic Monthly*—which were searching for ways of incorporating commentary on television as an extension of their traditional coverge of the arts and their more recent reviews of film. Precedent for such coverage lay in the work of Gilbert Seldes and a number of traditional culture critics who had been using the periodical forum to comment on the "popular arts" since at least as early as Seldes' and others' work for *The Dial* and *Vanity Fair* in the 1920s (Seldes, 1956).

Likewise during the 1960s a few newspapers, particularly those with major Sunday or weekly culture feature sections, began to carry television review material that went far beyond the more typical daily press fare of simple schedule listings, Hollywood gossip, and reprints of industry promotional material. For occasional or regular columns, these more elite papers, as with their magazine counterparts, often turned to those scholars who had not yet found fully satisfactory acceptance in the conventional academic process. Attending increasingly to its narrative form, production conventions, and social meaning, the periodical commentators were taking television more on its own terms, and while not necessarily celebrating it, they were not dismissing it out of hand either.

Thus, this next wave of anthologies emerged as a combination of a growing body of scholarship on television, though not yet necessarily from within the expanding field of communication research itself, and a certain expansion of arts and culture coverage within segments of the periodical, popular, and even underground press. Robert Lewis Shayon helped broaden the base and range of commentary about television much earlier than most (1951, 1962) and indeed his reviews in the *Saturday Review* from the early 1950s set much of the standard for scholarly and popular criticism of television for nearly two decades. His 1971 collection includes much of that work and his self-reflections on the craft of criticism. Harlan Ellison's books (1969, 1975), in a decidedly more counterculture vein, reprint his columns from the Los Angeles *Free Press*. Michael Arlen's collections (1969, 1976) are from his service as *The New Yorker's* television critic. Horace Newcomb, having already authored one book (1974) and having spent some time as television critic for the *Baltimore Sun*, put together a compendium of essays (1976) by several academics, regular critics (including Arlen and Shayon), and freelance writers, covering a range of issues in television interpretation and meaning. That collection, now in a third edition (1982), has come to be a principal sourcebook for the growing number of college courses on television content and programming.

Another feature of this wave of publications was the entry of a few foundations and even federal agencies. While most such support had gone to the scientific side of communication research, particularly in the effects areas, there had developed some concern about redressing the balance. Accordingly, as in the grants by the National Endowment for the Humanities and the Markle Foundation to the Aspen Institute, there emerged workshops and symposia that brought together a number of academics, critics, foundation officials, and media professionals for a series of conferences in 1974–75 that led to three Aspen/Praeger collections (Cater and Adler, 1975; Adler and Cater, 1976; and Adler, 1981).

These many anthologies served as a watershed for television studies, giving it greater legitimacy in the academy and opening up the possibility for a richer, wider range of inquiry into the field. Still somewhat denigrated within many traditional disciplines and still dominated by positivistic approaches in many journalism and speech programs, television studies nonetheless had now begun to attract a sufficient amount of informed scholarly attention from these several fields to permit it to survive in something other than purely vocational or effects-oriented modes.

Meanwhile the field of communication research had begun to experience a series of paradigmatic tremors and readjustments that were to further enhance not only its general intellectual status, but also its specific value as a forum for television inquiry. All during the postwar rise of positivism in the behavioral and social sciences and the concomitant pressures for professionalized specialization and research technique improvement in the humanities, a certain countercurrent had been flowing. At its base this new direction reflected the general mid-twentieth century process of fundamental epistemological reconsideration common to the sciences and philosophy. During an intellectual era that in effect had begun with the special theory of relativity and the uncertainty principle, it had become increasingly difficult to have confidence in simple notions of uniform, objective reality and truth. Initially slow to take full cognizance of the implications here, social science more recently had finally begun to pay wider attention to problems of the "terministic screen" and the "social construction of reality"—to the ways in which human agency, with all its variable individual and group factors of cognitive frames, knowledge, perceptive capacity, experience, and institutional constraints, significantly shapes the data, the instruments, the event, and therefore finally the observations and conclusions about social and behavioral phenomena. Among the many ways in which the social sciences expressed the new epistemology was the diverse work of such scholars as C. Wright Mills (1959), Noam Chomsky (1968), Robert Nisbet (1971), and Clifford Geertz (1973) with their various concerns about the "cloudy obscurantism" of "abstracted empiricism," the false promises of behaviorism, the ignorance in social science about symbolic action, and the intellectual dangers of academic entrepreneurship tied too closely to the demands of industry and government. In the humanities the debate centered around the disputes over the "irrelevant syllabus" and the class-bound nature of classical instruction.

Nurtured in the ferment of the civil rights, antiwar, and consumer protests of the 1960s and 1970s, these disputes did not necessarily create a sea change toward progress throughout the academy. Indeed, as in aspects of the new curricula in so many social science and humanities departments, the coursework and research often gravitated toward embarrassingly simpleminded and trivial material. But the turmoil permitted aspects of the established fields to make contact with older, long suppressed traditions of inquiry in their own fields and to establish ties across disciplines, to find those who were also in the process of reexamining their respective normal perspectives and key theoretical and methodological frameworks. Those cross currents in turn came to the attention of many working in various aspects of communication research where in their own way they had begun to develop a certain range of dissenting questions themselves. As a result there began to emerge a series of approaches and disputes in communication that centered around such matters as structuralism, phenomenology, and semiotics in film; institutional studies and political economy in media structures; interactionist theory and qualitative methods in communication uses research; neoidealism and symbolic analyses in cultural studies; revised social and political history in technology studies; and generally more iconoclastic trends in interpretation of all aspects of communication research—theory, method, process, and meaning.

In many important ways these approaches were quite disparate and theoretically incompatible. Nonetheless they pointed to a certain maturation and new-found significance for communication studies. Having begun as a vehicle for pursuing professional education around such obviously new and important institutions as the media, the field was now showing promise of perhaps being able to do something more, of becoming a means for helping focus and advance the general epistemological debate. Nowhere yet near capable of making expansive claims in this regard, there nonetheless was a growing sense among many in communication research that in its concerns about such fundamental issues as symbol creation and use, knowledge gathering and framing, and the general process of cultural formation and maintenance, it had something significant to contribute to the intellectual questions of the age.

A principal feature of the general crosscurrent and its strengthening rise in communication research has been its partial dependence upon various aspects of European social thought and cultural studies either to illuminate and help recast aspects of existing, though often overshadowed, American traditions of thought, or to introduce substantially fresh or newly restated perspectives. Such east-to-west transfer is an old and contentious issue in the American academy and arts, reflecting all the fears of provincialism, the love-hate, envy-disdain relationships of American reactions to things European—the debates and insecurities expressed in the charges and countercharges about such contrasting poles as style versus substance, ethereal versus real, manners versus morality, grace versus rudeness, hierarchy versus classlessness, control versus freedom, and theory versus practice. Americans have historically been of multiple minds about the necessity, value, and costs of the transfer. Having depended heavily on the French and English enlightenment literature to express much of the basis for the independence struggle and constitutional formation of the republic, there was great relief, and lingering amazement, at discovering an indigenous, powerful school (or schools) of early and mid-nineteenth century American letters—Hawthorne, Melville, Poe, Emerson, Thoreau, Whitman. Yet in the later rise of social science and its struggle for place in the twentieth-century academy, there was a steady parade to the lectures of the European masters—Weber,

Durkheim, Simmel—and a strong compulsion to legitimize the American social sciences principally as their outgrowth. Lately, as in the critique of positivism, we have come to better understand the substantial reinterpretation of the meaning of science, theory, and method that were associated with those initial Watsonian and Parsonian definitions. The lessons here, particularly in the social and cultural sciences, are important, for there was much in the native American instinct, as in early Chicago School sociology, that was unique in spite of substantial German and French influence, and the suppression or redefinitions of which cost American intellectual thought dearly. Nonetheless, in recent years it has become clear that in the debates about culture, ideology, power, symbol, and meaning the particular scientism of American thought has often been an inhibiting factor. To a considerable extent the interpretation of television offered in this volume and others in recent years is profiting from a greater awareness and receptivity to those strains of cultural theory that have been doing much to redefine the cultural and media studies agenda.

But the flow of valuable thought has never been simply one way. From Paine onward, much European, particularly English, social thought has been both broadened and sharpened by confrontation with the west-to-east influence of American thought. This has been so even for social science in the postwar period of positivism. To read much of the good recent articulations of British critical cultural studies (Curran et al., 1977; Hall, et al., 1980; Gurevitch et al., 1982) is to encounter a series of arguments between European and American styles of thought that would have far less power if they were solely intramural documents and that are, in fact, continuing to be pushed on key issues that the American traditions will still doggedly raise. So, for instance, the pragmatic empirical tradition will continue to press for attention to matters of specificity, reliability, and validity, and while theoretical discourse will correctly attend to the ideological articulations here, it will also have to come to better grips with problems of data gathering and use. This is no less a concern for television studies than for the social sciences at large, and several of the essays in this volume raise it.

Perhaps one way of further pursuing the issue here is to consider the problematic nature of the labels being used to categorize the newly dominant schools of thought. In much American and British communication or cultural studies there has been a tendency to try to label the countercurrent as "critical" research. This rubric is convenient because it invokes the Frankfurt School side of the prewar administrative-critical dichotomy and it suggests commonality with the emerging "critical" schools in various disciplines—sociology, anthropology, history, law. The difficulty here, however, is that such a term is so over-general as to ignore important distinctions within it. So, for instance, in discussing contemporary British media studies Curran et al. (1982) present a three-way split among Marxist traditions alone—structuralism, political economy, and culturalist studies. This typology provides a useful analysis of the basic tenets and serious differences among its components, as over such fundamental issues as base/superstructure, ideological articulation, and relative media power in cultural signification. Yet even this discussion is based on a problematic bipolar typification that pits these British critical/Marxist traditions against American liberal, pluralistic empiricism. Again, this formulation is not without value, for it adds to the understanding of the nature and ideological realities of the social science tradition in American positivism. Further, Curran et al. are aware of some of the difficulties in the distinction, and they provide a useful discussion of the misunderstandings of the oppositions between them. They seek to show how the image of those oppositions "tends to obscure both the internal differences within each of these traditions and the reciprocal influence which each has exerted upon the other" (p. 15). But while proceeding to articulate the differences within British critical studies, they oversimplify both the British and American traditions and the complex, crosspolar nature of the reciprocal influences among the subcategories. For one thing, the use of the American liberal tradition in such a uniform way provides a useful whipping boy that distracts not only from the seriousness of the internal splits in British Marxist cultural studies, but also from the continuing existence of other not strictly Marxian traditions in British criticism. At the very best there needs to be some attention to the long lineage of British empiricism and the extent to which its ideological structure is similar to or different from American empiricism. For another, this strategy treats American social and cultural thought in far too uniform a manner, leaving little room for recognizing the wider extent of views that are variously sympathetic and opposed to the particular British traditions being touted here.

Of course, it should not be surprising that British scholars have been unable to develop those distinctions within the American communication academy, for to a great extent Americans have not much recognized and grappled with them themselves. There has been as great a tendency here to see the matter in the same critical/European versus liberal/American terms, as for instance in discussing the "ferment in the field" (*Journal of Communication,* 1983). The difficulty with that approach is that it too readily tends to cede to the European side too much of the credit and responsibility for the theoretical debate in social thought and communication studies. For the fact of the matter is that the traditions of American communications and cultural discourse are far more varied and seriously contentious than the liberal/pluralist typology recognizes. To be sure, as noted above, there have been dominant positivistic forces and associated liberal central tendencies in the American social science tradition, but the critique of their sway has tended to obscure the variety, breadth, and longstanding themes of dispute within that tradition. In just the matter of critiques of positivism and behaviorism, further theoretical discourse is simply going to have to take far better account of formalist linguistics (Chomsky), literary and rhetorical criticism (Burke, Duncan), interactionist, qualitative sociology (Mead, Blumer), and neo-verstehenism in cultural anthropology (Geertz, Bateson), all cast in notably American idioms. Similarly in communication one finds in the domestic political economic (Smythe, Schiller) and cultural studies (Carey) approaches strong, native critiques of the normal science approaches. Moreover, one finds in these efforts many of the initial formulations of such things as the dependency attacks on the dominant paradigm in international communication research or the distinctions between ritual and transmission models of communication process.

In the end, of course, there are important mutual cross-Atlantic influences in all these lines of argument. The general conclusion soon must be that in a world of international academic conventions and transoceanic joint faculty appointments it is becoming increasingly difficult to speak about any pure national or even regional tradition of thought, especially in communication and cultural studies. But as can be seen in portions of this and other recent volumes on television (Himmelstein, 1981; Newcomb, 1982; Kaplan, 1983; Marc, 1984), there is and has been considerable diversity of thought on the western side of the Atlantic that, while certainly open to and in dialogue with British and continental influences, is not simply the derivative creature of them.

Concurrent with the ongoing philosophical arguments, changes in a technology of communication had a significant impact on the way research has been conducted since the 1940s. Following the end of World War II, many advances in electronics and microprocessors allowed social science researchers to use computers to store and analyze large amounts of data. In an important way, the notion of "mass" was again reflected in research; this time, referring to the large number of respondents whose opinions (on politics, media habits and preferences, and so forth) could be collected, analyzed, and compared. This also increased the rapidity with which new communication scholars could conduct research, and of course publish their results. Some have suggested that this rapidity also had a consequent effect on the time that could be devoted to reflection on research problems. Additionally, the increasing reliance on such technology meant that research questions, and in particular answers to research questions, must be "codeable." This need to reduce issues "to numbers," combined with the more rapid churning out of communication studies, led to what many considered to be incredibly sophisticated and complex answers to very small and trivial problems. This in turn contributed to an often-defensive posture taken by many of the "quantitative" communication scholars, who felt pressured to justify their membership in the fraternity of "real social scientists."

Perhaps in some ways measurement accuracy has replaced intellectual discipline. In its attempts to be taken seriously, communication may have made mistakes common to those made early on by other social sciences; by modeling themselves after those in the physical sciences, eager researchers have focused more on developing and fine-tuning the techniques of research design and analysis than on thinking through and selecting appropriate problems for inquiry. New graduate programs in communication feel the necessity to include measurement and design components into the curriculum, yet often assume that the theory will come of its own. There does not seem to be an awareness that good design, indeed good measurement and analysis, comes only from good theory. Academic experimentation that is atheoretical or untheoretical provides very little of the "building blocks" of social science. Many studies currently published in mainstream communication journals seem filled with sophisticated treatments of trivial data, which, while showing effects significant at $p < .05$, make slight contributions to what we really know about human mass-mediated communication.

SCOPE OF THE BOOK

By and large the papers here rise out of the debates about the merits of critical and cultural approaches and their challenges both to the mass culture debate and to normal science traditions in media research. If the last decade of film and television studies has stood for anything it has been to find improved ways of describing social and cultural meanings in media content and by extension to expand the capacity for communication research to theorize about human behavior and culture. As such, this effort has come to emphasize the study of television in context, to see it in intimate relationship with all other principal institutions, expressive forms, and patterns of meaning in society.

In the first section of the volume the authors present a variety of theoretical models for examining the meanings in television. In part as a preface to that modeling and to help interpret the intellectual confusions in the debates about televison, Kreiling's essay shows how American social thought has tended to react to and frame the possibilities for the communication media. Focusing on the early Chicago School of social inquiry, with its expectant faith in the capability of technology to foster a rise of material abundance and enlightenment, he demonstrates the way in which liberal scholars, journalists, reformers, and professional managers, searching for their own professional identities and sociopolitical sway in the twentieth century, perceived in the new media, and eventually television, a key means for "creation of their envisaged new communities." While critiquing the Chicago School failure to recognize the contradictions in their hopes for the new media, Kreiling uses their own methods to show how the illusions in their views and the more recent expressions of them are related to the status conflicts of the new professional middle classes and elites of which they were principal spokesmen early in the American century. He goes on to portray how the recent debates about the media, and particularly television, have been wrapped up in the struggles and contradictions among key interests in the rise of the variously defined post-World War II "New Class." The story of television, then, is as much as anything else the story of the intellectual hopes for and struggles over it. How we have come to think about television and how that thinking is related to our own socioeconomic and professional affiliations and aspirations defines much of its role and our political response to it.

Newcomb and Hirsch attempt to articulate a model of television as "cultural forum"—as society's primary storyteller—in which they take as central the problem of how audiences and others "use" and interpret programming. Their approach is based on the American cultural studies' notion of communication as symbolic, ritual process and their concern is with "the sociology of interpretation," how individuals and groups negotiate meaning and arrive at definitions of significance in television programming. This interest in the audience is part of a broader effort to link the current problem of interpretation with the traditional issues of uses. Acknowledging the limitations of functionalist models, Newcomb and Hirsch are nonetheless concerned that the matters of how people think about, perceive, and react to television not be dropped entirely from the analysis. They acknowledge and seek to incorporate into their frame the British cultural studies interest in the way in which television content expresses dominant ideological forms, but they insist that the problem of interpretation extends beyond the textual analysis by the researcher or critic to the "inventory that makes possible the multiple meanings extracted by audiences, creators, and network decision makers." Reflecting aspects of the American empirical heritage, the questions here touch back upon the pesky problem of validity—asking how, in fact, we know what we say we know about audience interpretations.

Similar concerns, but in a less prescriptive and more theoretically conscious way, are expressed in Streeter's essay. He discusses the origins, trends, distinguishing characteristics, and dilemmas of the research in the Centre for Cultural Studies at the University of Birmingham. Particularly under the influence of its long-time director, Stuart Hall, the work at the Centre has reflected and led much, though certainly not all, of the developments in British cultural studies. Its work has grown out of a series of encounters with and disputes among literary criticism, American positivism, symbolic interactionism, ethnomethodology, Western Marxism, and structuralism. A review of aspects of that research history and continuing debates gives insight into much of the current agenda on television and media studies. Streeter shows how cultural studies as framed at Birmingham tend to reject distinctions between the theoretical and empirical realms, seeing them as inseparably intermingled in intellectual work. That view in turn is closely related to the notion that "cultural studies sees itself as engaged with and part of a series of cultural and historical developments and processes . . . as embedded in society, not outside society looking in." From this perspective, then, the program-audience distinctions tend to fall away and the study of television implies the simultaneous analysis of the myriad social, cultural, and historical conditions in which the medium and its audiences are enmeshed.

Attending to that portion of communication involving media or message production, Jensen proposes a substantial reorientation of the burgeoning "production of culture" literature. She reviews aspects of the mass culture debate, suggesting ways in which, while exhausting itself, it nonetheless left unresolved certain issues that production perspectives might yet illuminate. The difficulty Jensen sees, however, is that, in part due to that mass culture heritage and

its links to positivist approaches in social science, the dominant pro-
duction-of-culture literature tends to see culture too much as a product of an industrial-like transmission process, a container of messages
in a linear transfer of information, standing for something else, "reflecting only the structure and process of its production." As a cor-
rective here she argues for an "interpretive" approach that, building
on the ritual view, sees communication as a central "constructive"
act, "a process that actively constitutes the world," and that therefore
leads to a redefinition of cultural production in terms of experience
"centered on [shared] expressive material." This approach implies
studying "symbolic material from within the interpretive world of the
participants" and, as suggested in other cultural studies approaches
discussed above, seeing the process of communication creation in
reflexive relationship to its consumption, to the practices, conditions,
and beliefs of all those sharing in the various facets of its emergence
and use.

Hartley takes issue with current definitions of media effects, arguing that many of the analytical categories that have been used to
describe television and its "effects" are ill-conceived. He presents a
case for reexamining the dialogue between television content and
audience interpretation. He argues that television has supplanted the
power of speech in modern societies, presenting texts with "no inherent
meaning," yet requiring interpretation and sense-making by the variety
of audiences who are exposed to them. Since the meaning of any
television presentation is not bounded by the program itself, and rather
assigned to it by viewers, interpreters, or critics, it is essentially a "dirty"
category for analysis. "Readers" of such texts are likewise difficult to
categorize, since interpretation is often affected by past experiences,
mood swings, and so on. Hartley notes that, as a producer of
meaningfulness, television must over-present the ideology of the dominant society. It does so by continually juxtaposing representatives from
various social categories—usually composed of socially desirable:un-
desirable opposites. He suggests that it is the fine line between
ideologically opposite social categories that actually constitutes the text
for further analysis of the medium of television.

Turow examines a related issue. He begins by noting that, on a
very practical level, audiences derive certain meanings from television's symbolic portrayals. Often these derived meanings are contrary
to values held by certain segments of society. These segments then
act to provide feedback to, and ask for changes from, the producers
of television text. How does this feedback affect the text? What is
the process by which such organized groups are able to communicate

with the creators—or with the institutional representatives of the television industry—who are guided less by creative symbolism, and more by financial solvency? Turow looks in particular at the role of special interest and pressure groups on decisions made about television entertainment. His argument is based on a "resource dependence" framework, which asserts that industry executives have competing conceptions of "audiences" and "publics," and often will try to respond to one (audiences) at the expense of the other (publics). Audiences, Turow notes, are groups composed of people "in terms of categories and concerns that networks and advertisers designate as important." Publics are instead composed of persons organized around issues that they themselves designate as important. Since the resources of television—the programming—are finite, and must be allocated by the institutional representatives, decisions are often made in response to audiences rather than publics. Turow analyzes the ways in which the three American broadcasting networks respond to these dilemmas by examining selected instances in which networks have responded to publics. He outlines what he believes are four goals of the networks in these situations: (1) to limit the influence of various publics; (2) to keep the issues out of the public regulatory arena; (3) to minimize the disruptive influence of any programming changes made; and simultaneously (4) to deter any other publics from exerting new pressures.

The second section of the volume explores specific examples of how several of the various interpretive approaches can be applied, and Fiske provides the book's first example of text interpretation. He examines the cultural meanings of *Doctor Who,* the most durable fictional program ever aired by the British Broadcasting Corporation. Fiske interprets the meanings that *Doctor Who* might hold for its audience by examining its various discourses—politics, morality, economics, and individualism—and by comparing its message of "reality" to the realities of its audience. The chapter argues that there are certain parallels between how humans make sense of symbolic texts and their own realities. He further argues that one of the functions of texts and of discourses is to enable readers to use them as metaphors of their own similar, but more complex, real-life experiences. *Doctor Who* provides for Fiske the perfect example of a television text that portrays the strengths of many of society's strongly held traditional values. Through analysis of the metaphorical presentations of the discourses of good and bad, democratic and autocratic, and so on, Fiske proposes a unique system for understanding the process between the text, the reader, and the culture from which both spring.

Text and social experience are made understandable—for both the "reader" and the scholar—only through analyses of such discourses.

Robinson chooses to examine reality portrayal a bit closer by examining news—rather than "fictional"—programming. She focuses on the Canadian news coverage of the 1980 Quebec referendum. Robinson is sensitive to the entire range of television's symbolic capacities. Thus, both the content of the news coverage—the quotes that are chosen, the pictorial material that is used—and the form of the coverages (production-moment decisions, the television work situation itself) are considered by the author to be proper data for the semiotician. The chapter makes the point that the success or meaningfulness of such television texts is not simply in terms of how closely the stories match reality. Rather, it is in terms of how well the entire portrayal of events expresses underlying and widely-accepted social values.

At one level Atallah's essay is an analysis of "genre theory" and its application to a single television series (*The Beverly Hillbillies*). Explicitly adapting a method from cinema studies, he argues for the "sociological resonance" and the "relative autonomy" of genres, seeing them as a logical framework for television interpretation. He discusses some of the difficulties in this approach and offers suggestions for transcending them, principally through folding into the analysis the nature and imperatives of television not only as a technological industrial and economic institution, but also as a set of narrative forms and mental practices. Television "is an institution constituted at the site of the intersection among several discourses, strategies, positions, and interests, but also inflecting these and producing its own."

At another level Atallah extends the argument throughout this volume about the need to consider the significance of virtually all of television. But in choosing a therefore doubly "unworthy" subject—situation comedy, and a much-maligned example at that—he is attempting to broaden the range of interpretive discourses. He focuses particularly on that notion of unworthiness, suggesting that the critical tendency to ignore or demean some television is an integral part of the discourse about it. Interpretive approaches to television must examine the history and context of our own popular and academic inquiries (including the intersections therein), recognizing that those statements and debates are part of the reality of television and the worthiness of its study.

Zynda discusses the concept of "community" as it has come to be used in framing television experience. He examines the power and mythology of the concept, paying particular attention to its roots in preindustrial American life and thought and the terms of its association with communication and society in the Chicago School tradition. The ties there emphasize a process-notion of society, a view that, as opposed to more structuralist, ideologicist approaches, sees community as a progressive social experience. Within that model, communication is taken as "the means of creating a country of communal sharing of values which obviates questions of class, power and privilege . . . the American answer to politics. . . ."

The attraction of this view is so strong, Zynda argues, that in spite of its evident contradictions it retains a strong grip on the American social imagination. That pattern manifests itself in television where many of the varied and inconsistent notions of community—rural versus urban, family versus profession, social versus economic, individual versus group—have regularly surfaced in post-Vietnam television. As in other examples of interpretive culturalist analysis the implication here is that to understand American television, one must at least attend to the history of American experience with and ideas about such notions as society, community, and, by extension, communication itself.

Lidz discusses television from the perspective of the sociology of religion. He notes the extent of the longstanding though often confused distinctions in American thought between religious moral order and secular moral culture, demonstrating how television has tended to grow up in the latter. We have a civic religion that is tied to traditional Puritan roots but that over time has become detheologized and so brought into the middle class secular context that its morality and values are associated more with traditions of experience that, while having strong aspects of ritual, myth, and faith, are essentially areligious in any traditional sense.

Such confusions about religion and morality, common to so many modern institutions, have led to fundamental conflicts and misunderstandings about television. Many of the concerns about it are framed in terms of moral degeneracy and attendant deleterious impact. But because American culture has developed in such a secular mode, wherein religion is taken more as one of several social institutions rather than as a pervasive, all-informing force, the particular power of religious forms of imagination to raise fundamental issues of values, principals, and existential dilemmas is markedly muted. The debate over television is often cast in terms of morality, but with such a relatively shallow, diverse, and weak religious consciousness much of that debate is enervated and reduced to the problematic realms of aesthetic critique or effects catalogues.

As Lidz suggests the content of primetime television is almost totally secular. To the extent religion intercedes in dramatic television it does so rarely and then only as that separable social institution, not as an enveloping faith and experience. In this light the moral concerns expressed in television are framed and resolved in the more secular aspects of the family and workplace experiences (the sort of communities Zynda discusses), the formal political process covered by the news, or the sporting event, rather than through the conflicts of belief cast up in disputes over scriptural interpretations and ways-of-life practices associated with traditional religious discourse.

As is evident in these summaries, it would be difficult to categorize the essays in this volume in any satisfactory framework. The approaches and topics explored here reflect a strong admixture of interlayered theoretical influences and, while it might be tempting to try to pigeonhole the papers in light of the bipolar, European/critical versus American/liberal dichotomy discussed above, the inadequacy of that scheme should become quickly evident in any careful comparisons among these contributions. To be sure there are marked differences of emphasis among the papers. These are a collection of analyses that rise variously out of interests in how to perceive and comprehend meaning in symbolic creation, analyze ideology and politics in culture, and generally broaden the grounds and improve the methods for interpreting television. Pressed on certain questions the authors of some of these papers might fall back into one or more of the conventional theoretical categories. But what is more interesting is the evidence of cross-ruffing and maturing mutual theoretical interchange that is at work here. There are important contradictions both within and among these essays, dilemmas that will continue to frustrate those seeking a unified, consistent body of cultural and communication theory. But that interest reflects an aspiration for communication studies that is probably fruitless and diversionary anyway. The value of cultural inquiry is not that it settles questions about social reality, but that it helps provide the forum for an ongoing, regularly readjusting process of interpretation.

NOTES

1. For examples and discussions of the strengths and weaknesses of this approach, and particularly the effort to overcome the latter, see Nye (1972), Fine (1977), and Browne (1980), plus various issues throughout the checkered history of the *Journal of Popular Culture*.

2. It is common now to say "atheoretical," but as Curran et al. (1982) suggest, the liberal social science tradition has clear theoretical biases, though its tendency has been to leave them unstated and unexamined.

REFERENCES

Adler, Richard P. [ed.] (1981) Understanding Television: Essays on Television as a Social Cultural Force. New York: Praeger.

Adler, Richard and Douglas Cater [eds.] (1976) Television as a Social Force: New Approaches to TV Criticism. New York: Praeger.

Adorno, Theodor W. (1941) "The radio symphony: an experiment in theory," in P. F. Lazarsfeld and F. Stanton (eds.) Radio Research, 1941. New York: Duell, Sloan & Pearce.

Adorno, Theodor W. (1969) "Scientific experience of a European scholar in America," in D. Fleming and B. Bailyn (eds.) The Intellectual Migration: Europe and America, 1930–1960. Cambridge, MA: Harvard Univ. Press.

Arlen, Michael (1969) Living Room War. New York: Viking.

——— (1976) The View from Highway 1: Essays on Television. New York: Farrar, Straus and Giroux.

Berelson, Bernard and Morris Janowitz [eds.] (1950, 1953, 1966) Reader in Public Opinion and Communication. New York: Free Press.

Browne, Ray B. (1980) Rituals and Ceremonies in Popular Culture. Bowling Green, OH: Bowling Green University Popular Press.

Carey, James W. and John J. Quirk (1970) "The mythos of the electronic revolution," Parts I and II. The American Scholar 39 (2,3): 219–241, 395–424.

Casty, Alan [ed.] (1968) Mass Media and Mass Man. New York: Holt, Rinehart & Winston.

Cater, Douglass and Richard Adler [eds.] (1975) Television as a Social Force: New Approaches to TV Criticism. New York: Praeger.

Chomsky, Noam (1968) Language and Mind. New York: Harcourt, Brace and World.

Curran, James, Michael Gurevitch, and Janet Woolacott (1982) "The study of the media: theoretical approaches," in M. Gurevitch et al. (eds.) Culture, Society, and the Media. New York: Methuen.

——— [eds.] (1977) Mass Communication and Society. London: Edward Arnold.

Czitrom, Daniel J. (1982) Media and the American Mind: From Morse to McLuhan. Chapel Hill: Univ. of North Carolina Press.

Dexter, Lewis A. and David Manning White [eds.] (1964) People, Society, and Mass Communications. New York: Free Press.

Ellison, Harlan (1969) The Glass Teat. New York: Ace.

——— (1975) The Other Glass Teat. New York: Pyramid.

Film Quarterly (1958–1959) "Editors notebook." Winter-Spring, 12 (2–3).

Fine, Gary Alan [ed.] (1977) "In-depth section" (a symposium on popular culture and the social sciences). Journal of Popular Culture 11 (2): 379–526.

Fleming, Donald and Bernard Bailyn [eds.] (1969) The Intellectual Migration: Europe and America, 1930–1960. Cambridge, MA: Harvard Univ. Press.

Gans, Herbert (1974) Popular Culture and High Culture: An Analysis and Evaluation of Taste. New York: Basic Books.

Geertz, Clifford (1973) The Interpretation of Cultures. New York: Basic Books.

Gerbner, George (1972) "Violence in television drama: trends and symbolic functions," in G. A. Comstock and E. A. Rubinstein (eds.) Television and Social Behavior. Reports and Papers, Vol. I: Media Content and Control. Washington, DC: DHEW.
—— et al. (1980) "The 'mainstreaming' of America: Violence Profile No. 11." Journal of Communication 30 (3): 10–29.
—— (1981a) "A curious journey into the scary world of Paul Hirsch." Communication Research 8 (1): 39–72.
—— (1981b) "Final reply to Hirsch." Communication Research 8 (3): 259–280.
Gurevitch, Michael, Tony Bennett, James Curran, and Janet Woollacott [eds.] (1982) Culture, Society and the Media. New York: Methuen.
Hall, Stuart, Dorothy Hobson, Andrew Lowe, and Paul Willis [eds.] (1980) Culture, Media, Language. London: Hutchinson.
Hall, Stuart (1982) "The rediscovery of 'ideology': return of the repressed in media studies," in M. Gurevitch et al. (eds.) Culture, Society, and the Media. New York: Methuen.
—— and Paddy Whannel (1964) The Popular Arts. London: Hutchinson Educational.
Hammel, William [ed.] (1972) The Popular Arts in America: A Reader. New York: Harcourt Brace Jovanovich.
Himmelstein, Hal (1981) On the Small Screen: New Approaches in Television and Video Criticism. New York: Praeger.
Hirsch, Paul (1980) "The 'scary world' of the nonviewer and other anomalies: a reanalysis of Gerbner et al.'s findings on cultivation analysis, part I." Communication Research 7 (4): 403–456.
—— (1981a) "On not learning from one's mistakes: a reanalysis of Gerbner et al's findings on cultivation analysis, part II." Communication Research 8 (1): 3–37.
—— (1981b) "Distinguishing good speculation from bad theory: rejoinder to Gerbner et al." Communication Research 8 (1): 73–95.
Jacobs, Norman [ed.] (1959) Culture for the Millions. Princeton: D. Van Nostrand.
Journal of Communication (1983) "Ferment in the field." 33: 3.
Jowett, Garth (1976) Film: The Democratic Art. Philadelphia: University of Pennsylvania Press.
Kaplan, E. Ann [ed.] (1983) Regarding Television: Critical Approaches—an Anthology. AFI monograph series, Vol. 2. Frederick, MD: University Publications of America.
Lazarsfeld, Paul F. (1969) "An episode in the history of social research: a memoir," in D. Fleming and B. Bailyn (eds.) The Intellectual Migration: Europe and America, 1930–1960. Cambridge, MA: Harvard University Press.
—— and Frank Stanton (1941) Radio Research, 1941. New York: Duell, Sloan & Pearce.
Lowenthal, Leo (1957) "Historical perspectives of popular culture," in B. Rosenberg and D. M. White (eds.) Mass Culture: The Popular Arts in America. New York: Free Press. Free Press.
Marc, David (1984) Demographic Vistas: Television in American Culture. Philadelphia: Univ. of Pennsylvania Press.
Mills, C. Wright (1959) The Sociological Imagination. New York: Oxford University Press.
Morrison, David B. (1977) "The beginnings of modern mass communication research." Centre for Mass Communication Research, University of Leicester, England.
Newcomb, Horace (1974) TV: The Most Popular Art. New York: Anchor.
——(1976) Television: The Critical View. New York: Oxford University Press.

_____ (1978). "Assessing the violence profile of Gerbner and Gross: a humanistic critique and suggestion." Communication Research 5 (3): 264–283.

Nisbet, Robert A. (1971) The Degradation of the Academic Dogma: The University in America, 1945–1970. New York: Basic Books.

Nye, Russell B. [ed.] (1972) New Dimensions in Popular Culture. Bowling Green: Bowling Green University Popular Press.

Rosenberg, Bernard (1971) "Mass culture revisited," in B. Rosenberg and D. M. White (eds.) Mass Culture: The Popular Arts in America. New York: Free Press.

_____ and David M. White [eds.] (1957) Mass Culture: The Popular Arts in America. New York: Free Press.

_____ (1971) Mass Culture Revisited. New York: Van Nostrand Reinhold.

Rowland, Willard D., Jr. (1983) The Politics of TV Violence: Policy Uses of Communication Research. Beverly Hills, CA: Sage.

Schramm, Wilbur [ed.] (1949, 1960) Mass Communications. Urbana: University of Illinois Press.

Seldes, Gilbert (1956) The Public Arts. New York: Simon & Schuster.

Shayon, Robert Lewis (1951) Television and Our Children. New York: Longmans, Green.

_____ (1971) Open to Criticism. Boston: Beacon Press.

_____ [ed.] (1962) The Eighth Art. New York: Holt, Rinehart & Winston.

Smith, Anthony (1973) The Shadow in the Cave. Urbana: University of Illinois Press.

Williams, Raymond (1958) Culture and Society, 1780-1950. London: Chatto & Windus.

PART I

EMERGING APPROACHES TO INTERPRETING TELEVISION

Chapter 1

TELEVISION IN AMERICAN IDEOLOGICAL
HOPES AND FEARS

Albert Kreiling

AS THE NEWEST and seemingly the most potent communications medium on the scene in the period of growth and modernization following World War II, television has been the subject of a great deal of debate—with views ranging from the highly alarmist to the highly optimistic—about its role in American life. The debate has reflected some long-standing hopes and fears of Americans and also some standing tensions among social groups, whose struggles with their rivals may center upon the control of a communications medium.

Paralleling the hopes and fears surrounding television in recent decades were the responses to the expanded mass press in the Communications Revolution of the late nineteenth century. As Michael Schudson (1978: 88–120) has shown, one development was a separation of the newspaper-reading public into the workers and common people, who flocked to the Yellow Press, and the educated upper middle class, which turned to such respectable papers as the *New York Times* and scorned the common man and his flamboyant press. Thus, the enlarged urban public organized itself around the expanding press, and the history of the press was interrelated with the formation of separate taste groups and the development of their respective sensibilities.

Like Ferdinand Toennies (1971: 251–265), some Americans regarded the mass press as a dangerous influence upon the enlarged

AUTHOR'S NOTE: An earlier version of this chapter was published in *Qualitative Sociology*, Vol. 5, No. 3 (Fall 1982). Copyright © 1982 by Human Sciences Press, Inc., New York, NY.

urban "crowd." Toennies pointed to public opinion as a powerful emergent force when people left the web of custom of *Gemeinschaft* villages to enter the "big world" of *Gesellschaft,* and he saw the press as a powerful agency for molding public opinion and shaping the sensibilities of the newly released population.

Some American intellectuals, however, saw the new communications technologies as potential agencies for the spread of a new culture of enlightenment for a progressive Great Community. One illustration of the hopes was a short-lived newspaper, *Thought News,* published by John Dewey, Robert Park, and Franklin Ford. The three men deplored the Yellow Press of their day, but saw in its technology the potential for spreading knowledge and establishing rational standards of judgment in an enlarged democratic public (Carey and Sims, 1976: 4–22). Their hopes, like those of others of the time, were a characteristic expression of the tendency of Americans to interpret their history around the development of technologies, and to look expectantly toward a future community to be made through new technologies.

Dewey was prominently identified with the broader intellectual movement of the reform Darwinism rising to challenge the reigning conservative social Darwinism of such figures as Herbert Spencer. The reform Darwinists shared with their conservative foes an organic image of society, as well as a faith in technology and progress and the expectation that the rising levels of abundance would be endless. With the end of economic problems in sight, the reformers thought, society could turn its attention to "human" and "social" problems, including the redeployment of the expanded media for the creation of a new culture of enlightenment. In the period of the growth of television, a similar myth of endless abundance contributed to the hope among proponents of change that the medium could be freed of its dependence upon the commercial system.

The hopes of the reform Darwinists need to be understood in relation to some long-standing patterns of American imagination. As Joseph Featherstone (1979: 7) noted, there are two recurrent views of the social transformations of modernization:

> the "long revolution" and the "lost community." The first sees the progress of the West since the seventeenth century as a long revolution, a march toward greater social and political equality. The other interprets modernization in terms of a vision of lost community. Proponents of the long revolution speak of gains in equality, autonomy, and the standard of living, and proponents of the lost community speak of

alienation, disenchantment, the collapse of authority, and anomie, pointing to the human cost of progress.

As Featherstone added, Dewey was a characteristic example of the American "fusion ticket," with his hope that the benefits of the "long revolution" could be achieved but the costs of the "lost community" avoided by the construction of a new Great Community.

Dewey and other reform Darwinists typically welcomed the economic and technological progress of their time, but underscored the need for concomitant cultural progress. In their view, economic and technological change had made outmoded the small-town Protestant culture of the communities in which they had grown up. They typically celebrated their liberation from the provincial towns, in a characteristically modern posture of heralding people's emancipation into a wider world of open horizons. However, as Jean Quandt (1970: 75 passim) has shown, at the same time they looked to the wider progressive culture of enlightenment as a replacement for the waning religious and small-town customs and thus, like many Americans in the midst of secularization, attached religious significance to secular cultural realms.

Underlying the hopes for a wider community was the assumption, so typical among Americans, of a consensual rather than a conflict model of society. From this standpoint, the differences among people appear to be remediable matters of misunderstanding and ignorance rather than fundamental differences of interest or value. The assumption, evident in so many social movements, makes the means of social change a task of moral education and contributes to the faith in such agencies of education and persuasion as schools and communications media.

As Dewey and other young scholars were challenging the orthodoxies of their elders, similar trends were under way among young journalists, including the college-educated professionals who scorned the uneducated reporters of the past, and the reform-minded muckrakers. Like numerous young scholars who looked to the European universities, many of the young journalists rejected the dominant lifestyles and career paths of the nineteenth century and sought to assume new identities and public roles. As these groups sought to assert themselves in the expanded media of their time, and saw the media as agencies for the creation of their envisaged new communities, so would the most visible new medium of a later time, television, become the imagined agency of new communities and the stage on which various groups would struggle for legitimacy.

TELEVISION AS PUBLIC RITUAL

The expansion of the media in the Communications Revolution occurred in the midst of the rapid change and development attending the emergence of an urban-industrial order. Similarly, television was the most conspicuous new medium on the scene during the wave of growth and change following World War II. As some observers in the earlier period thought that the expanded press possessed enormous power for good or ill, numerous later observers ascribed great power to television. Consequently, as Jeff Greenfield (1978: 297) noted in a review of several alarmist attacks, "Each of them, to one degree or another, suggests that what has happened *since* the advent of television has happened *because* of television."

In a show of the persistent individualist faith of Americans, many of the alarmist views regarded television as a threat to the individual, in what I will call the "institutional domination" argument. This perspective pictures television as an omnipotent power that manufactures an illegitimate culture, which robs people of their freedom, spontaneity, and individuality. Among the most popular recent writings on the media have been the attacks upon subliminal advertising by Wilson Bryan Key (1973, 1976), who charged that media manipulation posed a threat to people's ability to govern their lives in accordance with their own free will. Thus, like the attacks on "institutional racism," "institutional sexism," and "stereotypes," the "institutional domination" arguments about television expressed the attempts of a middle-class population to keep open the opportunities for the individual in an increasingly organized society.

In many versions of the "institutional domination" argument, Americans have talked about the media partly as a way of indirectly talking about various other things. As Key's writings illustrate, the "institutional domination" argument often employs a radically individualistic language to describe what might better be regarded as power relationships and social developments.

One development registered in the concerns about television was the expansion of "media power," not only as a source of psychological manipulation, but also as a bastion of institutional power. The recent fears about television and other media arose amidst the vast expansion, concentration, and intensified industrialization of the media. As concentrations of power have always frightened Americans by threatening our commitment to individualism, the local community, and

the open society, the media joined political machines, large corporations, and other wielders of concentrated power as villains in the
American imagination. In contrast to the political power of the party
machine or the economic power of the corporation, the media represented knowledge-making or culture-making power, and conservative critics like Kevin Phillips (1975) saw the media as part of the
emerging knowledge industry of the Post-Industrial Society.

Contributing to the concerns about "media power" was television's
role as an agent in and a conspicuous symbol of the increasing na-
tionalization of American life. "We have become in the past thirty
years, because of the revolutions in transportation and communication, a national society," Daniel Bell (1978: 37) observed. The eclipse
of distance, Bell (1980: 261) noted, has made possible the rise of a
national "mobilization politics," long characteristic of the more concentrated European countries, and now carried out before the eyes
of millions of Americans on the enlarged stage of the national media.

Television has also been a stage for the increasingly visible national
culture and status order that have progressively displaced regional
cultures and local status orders. As C. Wright Mills (1956: 253) pointed
out, since the 1920s the local status orders in American communities
have progressively weakened with the rise of a national status market,
populated by the celebrities who have attained prominence in radio,
motion pictures, and television.

The concerns about television also have reflected the process of
modernization and the tensions between modernistic and tradition-
alist sectors of the population. Historians looking back upon the turn-
of-the-century period see as one principal development the modernization of sensibilities among people moving from the genteel ethos
of the nineteenth century into the stepped-up rhythms of the industrial
age (Kennedy, 1975; O'Neill, 1975; Wiebe, 1973). Americans have
again widely embarked upon a general process of change, speed-up,
and modernization of their sensibilities and life-styles, and that development has been registered in the pace of television programming.
Consequently, television has provided another arena for the long-
standing conflict between the adherents of traditional and progressive
tastes, which has resulted in controversy over numerous forms of
entertainment, including jazz and motion pictures.

Coincident with the rise of television was the dislocation, physical
and psychic mobility, and social disorganization among vast sectors
of the population, with the suburban migration, the move to the

Sunbelt, the appearance of a mass college-educated public, and other shifts. In this context, vast sectors of the population felt detached from older models of conduct and sought new models with which to identify and new psychic worlds in which to dwell. Various sociological studies of suburban life in the fifties and sixties pictured suburban youth as turning to peer groups and the mass media when they found a paucity of relevant models for conduct among their parents and other adults in the community. In the same period, communications researchers and political scientists noted a new group of politically independent but interested voters, who might be susceptible to the influence of television in political campaigns. Underlying the enormous power sometimes ascribed to television, then, was the rise of new publics that found the established media of older publics unrepresentative of their own sensibilities.

Consequently, Americans' conceptions of television have been interrelated with the formation of social worlds and taste publics. For years, social psychologists have talked about the abstract groups and worlds formed through the mass media (Horton and Wohl, 1956; Klapp, 1962, 1964; Shibutani, 1955, 1966: 37-46). The media may become arenas in which people find imaginative worlds to inhabit, appealing styles of life, and compelling images linked with the social dramas of those new-found worlds. The population organizes itself into various media publics—the *New York Times* readership, the fans of Fellini films, the Johnny Carson audience, and so forth—that become worlds of social experience in which people find expressions of their sensibilities.

It is facile to point an accusing finger at the media for imposing worlds of sensibility upon their audiences, for the process depends as much upon people using a medium as a springboard for some psychic voyage. The roots of the seeming potency of the media lie deep in the American temper and in the history and social structure of America. Long ago, such observers as Alexis de Tocqueville and Michel Chevalier saw America as standing in the vanguard of modernization, with such bonds of social identification as class and tradition overshadowed by a set of looser, more fluid status groups— "the varied and shifting sectors of society which, in the absence of true class, become the theaters of the unending and agonizing competition among individuals for the attainment of the marks of status" (Nisbet, 1966: 183). Chevalier (1961: 380-385) noted the broad divide between the Yankees and "the democracy," as well as the status coteries that created "certain fashionable distinctions." De Tocqueville (1969: 470–475, 517–520) noted the role of newspapers in supplying the shallow bonds of an ephemeral and accessible literature, to tie together and express the sensibilities of social worlds whose members lacked the deep fund of shared tradition of a class.

The tendency of Americans to forge shifting status groups, already evident in the early nineteenth century, has been further fueled by later developments, and the increasing presence of the mass media has made them ever more available to supply the social bonds and expressive symbolism for the groups so formed. Moreover, with the routinization of bureaucratized work roles, Joseph Gusfield (1979: 43, 57, 59) pointed out, people have become ever more attracted to identifications severed from social structural roles and played out instead in the dramatic world of mass culture. Similarly, Klapp (1964: 250–264) noted how the amorphous social worlds anchored in the public dramas of a media environment have displaced local groups at the center of people's allegiances.

As the media serve as stages for the ritual life of social worlds, they may also serve in discourse as metaphors by which the members of the worlds talk about one another and register their mutual antagonisms. Much of the criticism of television in its early years could be described as the resistance of the "newspaper public" or the "book-reading public" to the rising "television public," just as the attack on tabloids by the readers of respectable newspapers registered the hostility of upper-middle-class people to the masses. In each case, the attack upon the medium is partly an attack upon the people who read or watch it. Behind the public controversies about the media, then, lie conflicts between social groups possessing different sensibilities and inhabiting different mental worlds.

In contrast to the optimists who have heralded the media as instruments for building a wider community, Park (1952: 153, 261 passim) saw that mass communication did not necessarily bring about consensus, but as often exacerbated tension, as latent discord was ever more rapidly transformed into conscious conflict. With the continued growth of the media, the status conflicts long endemic in American life have increasingly been fought around the channels and forms of mass communication. With the progressive dissolution of older repositories of meaning, Murray Edelman (1964, 1971, 1977) argued, politics has become a form of expressive behavior, a dramatic passion play for modern populations. Much the same has happened with the media, another major forum of public drama and conferrer of legitimacy in the modern secular world.

THE NEW CLASS
VERSUS MIDDLE AMERICA

As late as the 1930s, Arthur Marwick (1980: 150–155) noted, Hollywood films pictured the American social landscape as dominated by a small elite, consisting of a "shadow aristocracy" and the Republican business elite. However, by the 1920s, a new middle class of managers and professionals already was rising in American institutions. With the prosperity following World War II, the new upper-middle class or "success elite" increasingly sought to enter or topple the old elite. Consequently, Marwick (1980: 316) noted, in the postwar period the old elite increasingly shared status and influence with the expanding "college-educated professional and managerial class."

With the social transformations of industrialization, Robert Wiebe (1967) showed, the localistic, small-town people, who had dominated American life in the nineteenth century, lost status and power to the rising urban-based, cosmopolitan, bureaucratic-minded new middle class. As the occupants of managerial, bureaucratic, and professional roles, the new middle class lacked the badge of membership of the old middle class—property—and made education a badge of membership. By the 1920s, observers were noting a new shape in the American social order—with mobile, ambitious, cosmopolitan upper-middle-class manipulators attempting to orchestrate the lives of local, traditional lower-middle-class people.

As the new middle class took up new career paths, its members also pursued new life-styles and cultural realms. Detached from the bulwarks of conduct and meaning of nineteenth-century small-town life, the new middle class looked for new models of conduct, new faiths, and new sources of meaning. The paths taken up varied widely. Among many, a new individualism of "self-expression" or "self-realization" developed in place of the old individualism of "self-discipline" and "self-restraint" (Potter, 1965). By the 1920s, a marked separation was evident between the cosmopolitan life-styles and codes of behavior of progressive urban groups and the ways of small-town America. From the time of the First World War, a new "cultural radicalism" was evident on the urban scene, and from about the same time, Lawrence Chenoweth (1974: 4 passim) noted, a new ethic of liberal humanism struggled for legitimacy against the older moralism.

The new middle class sought meaning in the realms of art, literature, science, and intellectual culture. As Hannah Arendt (1961: 44–45) noted, the dominant sector of the nineteenth-century middle class did not employ art and intellectual culture as a public feature

of its status life. In the twentieth century, however, increasing numbers of Americans, often self-consciously borrowing European models of "culture" and "good society," made art and elite culture central
features of their status worlds. As Joseph Bensman and Arthur Vidich
(1971) showed, this practice was common among the new middle
class in the expanding "public" sector—educators, health workers,
psychologists, planners, some communicators, and so forth. One result, noted by Gifford Phillips (1966: 4–5), was the tension between
the older "neo-elitist" culture defenders and the swelling ranks of
"democratic optimists"—the "culture consumers," as Alvin Toffler
(1964) called them—who promoted cultural institutions in the midst
of postwar prosperity.

Out of the rhetorical struggle between "the people" and "the interests" invoked by Progressives at the turn of the century came the
role model of the "disinterested" professional. In their search for new
identities, Theodore Greene (1970: 169–282) showed, many Progressives were attracted to such "heroes of justice" as Theodore Roo-
sevelt. In the recent past, the same role model, now personified by
such figures as Ralph Nader, won widespread admiration in another
rising wave of the educated middle class. Peter Schmitt (1969) showed
how the conservation movement supplied an identity for new urban-
ites at the turn of the century, and that pattern was repeated in the
recent environmental movement. The Progressives' struggle for disinterested professional government also was widely taken up again
in the "new politics" movement, whose "independent," "critical,"
and "issue-oriented" members clamored for "change," sometimes in
the name of a "public philosophy" to overturn the politics of interest-
group pluralism.

Some of these trends are seen as traits of what numerous analysts
call the New Class. However, different writers have different people
and different trends in mind in using the term. The difficulties with
the term result partly from the attempts of writers to link the New
Class with ideas, attitudes, or beliefs, whereas erratic shifts, as issues
and ideas assume the form of fads, often are more characteristic of
the New Class activist style. The ambiguity of the term also results
partly from the increasing separation of divergent status worlds in
recent decades, in contrast to the greater apparent cohesiveness of
American culture in earlier times. By the middle of the twentieth
century, Bernard Bailyn and his colleagues (1977: 1155–1156) noted,
the clash among several rival models of individualism rising in American life was on the verge of explosion. Russell Lynes (1950) identified
eight new forms of "snobbery" of various status worlds, including

the intellectual, the emotional, the sensual, and the political.

In the sense of what the term "class" usually implies, the New Class is not a class, in my view. However, the term may be apt, not as an objective characterization of a group of people, but as an index of people's subjective perceptions of the social landscape. As Marwick (1980: 14 passim) argued, class as a set of objective characteristics of a group is not the same thing as the subjective perceptions of class that people hold and act upon. The idea of the emergence of a New Class captures the perceptions of numerous Americans and thus serves, however imprecisely, to represent the social imagery around which conflicts have formed.

The debate about the appearance of a New Class registers the fact that various segments of the educated new middle class, whose ranks have swelled in the postwar period, have rejected the pieties of traditional America to worship instead, as Michael Novak (1974a: 125) wrote, at the "Shrine of Enlightenment, wherever Americans read journals of opinion, speedread books, line up for the communal mysteries of cinema and theater, struggle valiantly to stay 'in touch' and be 'informed.'" Paralleling the strife between the Yankees and "the democracy" observed by Chevalier, a conflict has emerged between the educated, cosmopolitan New Class and "Middle America" or "the populists" or "the yahoos."

From the populists, who formerly attacked the Wall Street "fat cats" of the business elite, has come a crescendo of sniping at federal bureaucrats and at the liberal universalists of the media and the universities. In turn, some strata of New Class professionals have been embroiled in struggles with the business elite and with various political elites, managers, and bureaucrats who constrain their autonomy. Consequently, as Alvin Gouldner (1979: 61–62) noted, within the American "establishment" there has been something like a civil war as various New Class strata have sought to join or displace older elites. The struggles have assumed the form of both interest-group bartering over tangible issues like wages and working conditions and the more subtle battles for legitimacy (Kristol, 1978: 25–31). Liberal professionals have condemned the "conservative bias" of media content for years, and some of the media professionals have assumed the defiant pose of the "adversary culture."

Television and other media have served as a stage for various conflicts between New Class strata and Middle America, as well as between and among various sectors of each camp, for neither is a unified bloc. As Novak (1974b, 1975) argued, television programming is produced by the upper middle class, and the cosmopolitan, change-oriented, vaguely liberal tone of much of it arouses animosity among less affluent, less educated, less mobile persons.

The conflict over the national media had been building for some time, as revealed by the enthusiastic response to President Eisenhower's gibe at columnists and commentators at the Republican convention in 1964. By the late sixties, Theodore H. White (1969–1970) thought that the mounting hostility of many Americans toward the national media reflected the increasing separation of the nation into "two cultures." As the positive reception in much of Middle America to Vice President Agnew's attacks on the "effete eastern liberals" in the media revealed, regional rivalries were an element in the divide. There was some truth in Kevin Phillips' (1975: 24–38) charge that, like the Yankee entrepreneurs of an earlier time, a new knowledge industry and its allied strata of professionals rising in the Northeast were creating a sectional conflict between that region and the rest of the country.

Although television programming is created by the upper-middle class, the bulk of the audience belongs to Middle America. Consequently, as Novak (1975: 18) charged, much of the programming "represents the educated class' fantasies about the fantasies of the population." Hence, much of the New Class scorns television, or large parts of it, in a show of antagonism toward Middle America much like that shown by the upper middle class toward the readers of the Yellow Press and tabloids in earlier times.

TELEVISION IN THE "BIG WORLD"

The varied enthusiasms of the reformers of the late nineteenth and early twentieth centuries collapsed in the World War I years, to be followed by the frivolity of the twenties and the despair of the Depression. With postwar prosperity, however, a new optimism was dawning in parts of the enlarged new middle class, whose ideologues and activists often were called "liberals," and now are sometimes called the New Class in one of several uses of the term. Like the earlier reformers, many of the liberals were eager promoters of the bureaucratic institutions and professional activities that have expanded markedly in recent decades. And like the earlier optimists who saw the mass press as a potential agency for the creation of a new culture, some of the liberals looked to television to spread a new culture of enlightenment.

The liberals' hopes and programs for television varied. The artistically minded wanted drama and cultural events. Educators and others called for educational programming. Some New Class leaders—rallying under the banner of rationalism, science, progress, and optimism—called for the expanded use of television for the rational critique of society and the debate of political issues. Others wanted to use television for the modification of American attitudes, customs, and life-styles. Nicholas Johnson (1970), former FCC commissioner, and Erik Barnouw (1978), emeritus professor at Columbia University, faulted not only the power structures behind the medium but also the values and life-styles it celebrated, and called for change in the direction of their preferred alternatives.

The television reformers tried various avenues to change. Some looked to public television as the arena for a televised world more to their liking than commercial programming. Change in the commercial system through regulation by the FCC and other government agencies found favor with others. Challenges to station operators at license renewal time by public interest groups seeking to take a license or to force demands upon the operator were tried, often with the help of idealistic young public interest lawyers.

Scientific research to show the dangers in programming as an impetus to change was another tactic. Like the Progressive reformers who set up municipal research bureaus to marshall facts in the service of social change, the Kerner Commission and other public bodies called for the surveillance of the nation's media system (National Advisory Commission on Civil Disorders, 1968: 386–389). Some social scientists looked to the Surgeon General's report on smoking as a possible model for a similarly definitive attack upon televised violence. With the scientific optimism among proponents of change, scientifically defined standards of health and harm became the chief legitimate standards for judging programming.

Initially, the interest in television centered on the local level, with enthusiasm for the educational and public stations opening in the fifties. The aspirations of the liberals surged dramatically onto the national stage in the sixties, with the appointment of Newton Minow as FCC chairman in 1961, a Court of Appeals decision that the public had a right to representation in FCC proceedings in 1966, and the Carnegie Commission's call the following year for a national program of action on public television. Now, in the amorphous constellation that might be called the "public interest television reform movement," enthusiasm for nationally based action seems to have abated. A conference of persons interested in media reform called by the Aspen

Institute in 1976 favored a transfer of responsibility to local groups (Schneyer and Lloyd, 1976: 17). Similarly, numerous former advocates of various reforms at the national level have turned to local action or to internationalism, or have abandoned "the movement."

In television as in its other targets, the movement often scored limited successes as a result of tactical failings. Moreover, like other generations of reformers, the activists often appeared elitist to other people, who saw the liberals' agendas as remote from their own concerns. Like the Progressives, the liberal reformers presumed to speak and act for "the public," and only belatedly discovered that the public was not with them. Much of the public lost interest, or never had any, in the rationalist critique of society and its ills, and the indifference surfaced widely in the turn to mysticism, eastern religions, and other recent trends.

Perhaps most devastatingly, the movement lacked consensus in its own ranks. As Jeane Kirkpatrick (1979: 44) pointed out, New Class activists tend to share "a rationalistic, moralistic, and reformist approach to politics," but differ in the substantive goals they seek. In part, the Aspen Institute conference recommended a turn to the local level because the reformers discovered that they shared only a dissatisfaction with present television performance, not any consensus on the alternatives they wanted (Schneyer and Lloyd, 1976: viii).

Another show of New Class action in television and other media was the rise of adversary journalism. Like the young professionals who entered journalism in the late nineteenth century, a new wave of college-educated reporters in the sixties, who often scorned their elders, sought to give a more intellectual and critical tone to journalism (Grant, 1979). Consequently, as Anthony Smith (1978: 163) noted, "the new television teams of the 1960s, moving from riot to battlefield, demonstration to sit-in," brought to the screen the zeal of the reform-minded British reporters of the mid-nineteenth century who were in the vanguard of the engine of British social change.

Yet, to the journalists' surprise, their new-found militance, which scored some dramatic successes in exposing corruption and injustice, resulted in some public hostility. As William Rivers (1971: 23) observed, "It is ironic that just when the mass media have won important victories over their historic adversary, government, they are deep in trouble with their historic ally, the public." The "new muckrakers" and other journalists shared the spirit of the wider wave of crusaders against environmental pollution and other issues, who, like the Progressives, were turning to the "hero of justice" as a model of individualism in an organized society. However, some people were irritated by the crusading journalists' seeming arrogance and self-righteousness, and after a time many supporters lost interest.

Much of the protest and exposure had the scent of a moral war being waged by the New Class against other sectors of the population. There was some truth in Daniel Moynihan's (1971) charge that "adversary journalism" was an attack by an educated elite on persons perceived as inferiors, as there was some truth in William Tucker's (1980) charge that the environmental movement was a conservative strategy of the New Class that worked to the disadvantage of other groups. Similarly, the Progressives faulted other groups for failing to support their reform candidates in municipal races, but many workers and others correctly perceived that the reformers' favorite programs worked to their own disadvantage.

By the late sixties, various developments were altering the reform efforts. The earlier coteries of elitist liberals suddenly found that large numbers of middle-class people were taking up the call for change in the "new politics" and "consumer" movements. However, the new activists often had different objectives and tactics than the earlier reformers. In some cases, reform efforts conceived by elitists, who saw themselves as standing above the middle class, were overshadowed or transformed as a wider sector of the middle class redirected reform in line with its own spirit. One result was a proliferation of citizen action groups, while another was the inevitable clashes and standoffs.

The expanded wave of reformers of the late sixties and early seventies—the restricted use of the term New Class employed by some writers—may be likened to the Progressives, provided it is understood that such historical analogies indicate only partial similarities. In the widespread Progressive drive that surfaced after the turn of the century, Richard Hofstadter (1955: 131–173) showed, large sectors of the middle class assimilated and fused some of the spirit of the earlier populist movement with that of earlier elitist liberals and "mugwumps." Similarly, in the late sixties and seventies, some of the spirit of independent liberals visible since at least the forties was infused with a populist, democratizing, and moralistic thrust by wider sectors of the middle class.

Meanwhile, sizable numbers in the movement were turning away from American society, including some who were rejecting individualism in favor of various "communitarian" ideologies (Lodge, 1975). Numerous former liberals, embittered by the society that had turned a deaf ear upon their critique of its institutions and their plans for its future, turned to Freudo-Marxism and other forms of "adversary culture" criticism, retreated into a defense of their professional activities, or turned "neo-conservative" as liberalism was assimilated but transformed by the new activists.

The former liberals were sometimes embittered because they had overestimated their support in the turmoil of the "cultural revolution" in the wider society. As Jean-Francois Revel (1971) and Ralf Dahrendorf (1975) argued, wide sectors of the middle classes in the industrialized nations were engaged in a process of cultural reconstruction and reorientation often expressed in doctrines of new freedom and liberation. But as Revel realized, and as Orrin Klapp (1969: 57–70 passim) argued, what liberals sometimes mistook for an interest in political issues and an enthusiasm for institutional change was actually a search for new identities and life-styles in the altered rounds of life of what was widely called the Post-Industrial Society.

The restless psychic voyage by large numbers of Americans has resulted in the breakup of ties to departing cultural worlds, with a widespread individualization of behavior that has sometimes taken the form of the aimless "quest for thrills" noted by Park (1952: 59–60, 68 passim) when the "cake of custom" is broken. The cultural revolution included attacks on economic individualism, sometimes in the name of communal or public values, but more often, as Nathan Glazer (1979: 131–132) noted, in the name of alternative models of individualism. As David DeLeon (1978: 117–133) noted, the American tradition of radical individualism had laid dormant amidst the rise of increasing bureaucratic controls in American life, but surfaced poignantly again.

The identities, ideologies, and life-styles that appeared or gained widened followings in the cultural revolution were many and varied. The Protestant ethic and the old individualism of self-restraint lost ground to a hedonist ethic and the individualism of self-expression. Professional role models were widely taken up, as was the style of an "authentic self" seeking to liberate itself from an oppressive social structure—a pose assumed by numerous professionals in rebellion against institutions. The pose revealed the "contradiction between culture and social structure" noted by Daniel Bell (1973: 475–480), as large sectors of the new middle class ensconced in the constricted work roles of modern bureaucracies sought increased independence and autonomy.

One consequence of the cultural turmoil has been the widespread erosion of the authority of institutions and of the legitimacy of the American way of life, as such authors as Robert Bellah (1975) and Robert Nisbet (1975) have pointed out. In the resulting cultural vac-

uum, numerous cults, ideologies, and secular religions have flourished, leading to a fragmentation of the cultural and political scene.
Television has been an arena for the clash and confrontation of various
factions, some of which are represented by permanent media watch
groups. Moreover, the breakdown of any apparent consensus on a
framework of legitimacy has been met by rapid change in network
program lineups and varied experimentation with program types as
the industry has sought to connect with the uncertain tastes of the
audience. Surviving the breakdown in frameworks of legitimacy, however, are the consumer life-styles the industry promotes among the
"mass class" that arose with postwar prosperity.

Over the past century, America has been transformed into an
increasingly complex and interconnected marketplace of commerce,
politics, bureaucracy, professions, and so forth. With the failure of
the recent reform efforts to turn the society to some alternative values, an intensification of individualistic ambition and competitiveness
prevails. Conspicuous among the new individualists, in television as
elsewhere, are the professionals. In her studies of television producers, Muriel Cantor (1974: 103–118) found the spirit of professional
militance and independence widespread, and the struggles between
managers and professionals parallel those in other organizations.

Ben Stein (1979) used interviews to show that many television
writers and producers share an ideology defining themselves as a class
struggling against the class of businessmen, corporate managers, and
bearers of inherited wealth standing above them. But Stein noted the
paradox of persons who generally earn upwards of $100,000 a year,
and in many ways behave like businessmen, who nevertheless define
themselves as a class fighting their enslavement by the business class.

However, the spirit of the producers has found its way into much
of television programming, which reflects the rootless, mobile, tran-
sient life-styles of the new middle class, from whose ranks the producers come. The aimless drift and rootless quality of television
programming mirror the erosion of settled realms of local life and,
as Aubrey Singer (1966) noted, the cultural vacuum of the age. In
the spirit of Dewey's public philosophy, some of the recent reform
efforts sought to retrieve the moral certainty and communal involvement of local communities in the "big world" of modern organizations. However, as Park recognized, the "big world" is not a community
or a public. It lacks the shared cultural resources to retrieve either
the moral certainty or the communal involvement of settled local
worlds.

As De Tocqueville saw, the newspapers mushrooming in the Age of Jackson were supplying thin and evanescent social bonds, but those were the only bonds possible in vague social worlds that had cut themselves off from any deep fund of shared cultural resources. Similarly, Park (1955: 71–104) saw that the take-up of newspaper reading was associated with people's entry into wider worlds of experience, but as those worlds became wider the bonds possible within them became thinner. In the recent past, television has been the most conspicuous agency and symbol of the continued widening process. Television is an organ of the "big world." It can provide only flimsy bonds for the vast status worlds and the shallow consumer communities it serves.

REFERENCES

Arendt, Hannah (1961) "Society and culture," pp. 43–52 in N. Jacobs (ed.) Culture for the Millions? Princeton, NJ: Van Nostrand.
Bailyn, Bernard et al. (1977) The Great Republic. Boston: Little, Brown.
Barnouw, Erik (1978) The Sponsor. New York: Oxford University Press.
Bell, Daniel (1973) The Coming of Post-Industrial Society. New York: Basic Books.
_____ (1980) The Winding Passage. Cambridge, MA: Abt Books.
_____ (1978) "Mediating growth tensions." Society 15 (January-February): 34–38.
Bellah, Robert N. (1975) The Broken Covenant. New York: Seabury Press.
Bensman, Joseph, and Arthur J. Vidich (1971) The New American Society. Chicago: Quadrangle.
Cantor, Muriel G. (1974) "Producing television for children," pp. 103–118 in G. Tuchman (ed.) The TV Establishment. Englewood Cliffs, NJ: Prentice-Hall.
Carey, James W. and Norman Sims (1976) "The telegraph and the news report." Presented at the Association for Education in Journalism convention.
Chenoweth, Lawrence (1974) The American Dream of Success. North Scituate, MA: Duxbury.
Chevalier, Michael (1961) Society, Manners, and Politics in the United States. Garden City, NY: Doubleday. (Originally published in 1839.)
Dahrendorf, Ralf (1975) The New Liberty. Stanford, CA: Stanford University Press.
DeLeon, David (1978) The American as Anarchist. Baltimore: Johns Hopkins University Press.
De Tocqueville, Alexis (1969) Democracy in America. Garden City, NY: Doubleday. (Originally published in 1835.)
Edelman, Murray (1964) The Symbolic Uses of Politics. Urbana: University of Illinois Press.
_____ (1971) Politics as Symbolic Action. Chicago: Markham.
_____ (1977) Political Language. New York: Academic Press.
Featherstone, Joseph (1979) "John Dewey and David Riesman: from the lost individual to the lonely crowd," pp. 3–49 in H. J. Gans et al. (eds.) On the Making of Americans. Philadelphia: University of Pennsylvania Press.

Glazer, Nathan (1979) "Individualism and equality in the United States," pp. 127-142 in H. J. Gans et al. (eds.) On the Making of Americans. Philadelphia: University of Pennsylvania Press.

Gouldner, Alvin W. (1979) The Future of Intellectuals and the Rise of the New Class. New York: Seabury.

Grant, Gerald (1979) "Journalism and social science: continuities and discontinuities," pp. 291–313 in H. J. Gans et al. (eds.) On the Making of Americans. Philadelphia: University of Pennsylvania Press.

Greene, Theodore P. (1970) America's Heroes. New York: Oxford University Press.

Greenfield, Jeff (1978) "TV is not the world." Columbia Journalism Review 17 (May-June): 29–34.

Gusfield, Joseph R. (1979) "The sociological reality of America: an essay on mass culture," pp. 41-62 in H. J. Gans et al. (eds.) On the Making of Americans. Philadelphia: University of Pennsylvania Press.

Hofstadter, Richard (1955) The Age of Reform. New York: Random House.

Horton, Donald and R. Richard Wohl (1956) "Mass communication and para-social interaction." Psychiatry 19 (August): 215–229.

Johnson, Nicholas (1970) How to Talk Back to Your Television Set. Boston: Little, Brown.

Kennedy, David M. (1975) "Overview: the progressive era." The Historian 37 (May): 453–468.

Key, Wilson Bryan (1973) Subliminal Seduction. Englewood Cliffs, NJ: Prentice-Hall.
—— (1976) Media Sexploitation. Englewood Cliffs, NJ: Prentice-Hall.

Kirkpatrick, Jeane J. (1979) "Politics and the new class." Society 16 (January-February): 42–48.

Klapp, Orrin E. (1962) Heroes, Villains, and Fools, Englewood Cliffs, NJ: Prentice-Hall.
—— (1964) Symbolic Leaders. Chicago: Aldine.
—— (1969) Collective Search for Identity. New York: Holt, Rinehart & Winston.

Kristol, Irving (1978) Two Cheers for Capitalism. New York: Basic Books.

Lodge, George C. (1975) The New American Ideology. New York: Knopf.

Lynes, Russell (1950) Snobs. New York: Harper.

Marwick, Arthur (1980) Class. New York: Oxford University Press.

Mills, C. Wright (1956) White Collar. New York: Oxford University Press.

Moynihan, Daniel P. (1971) "The presidency and the press." Commentary 51 (March).

National Advisory Commission on Civil Disorders (1968) Report. New York: E. P. Dutton.

Nisbet, Robert A. (1966) The Sociological Tradition. New York: Basic Books.
—— (1975) Twilight of Authority. New York: Oxford University Press.

Novak, Michael (1974a) Choosing Our King. New York: Macmillan.
—— (1974b) "Why the working man hates the media." More 4 (October): 5–8.
—— (1975) "Television shapes the soul," pp. 9–21 in D. Cater et al., Television as a Social Force. New York: Praeger.

O'Neill, William L. (1975) The Progressive Years. New York: Dodd, Mead.

Park, Robert E. (1952) Human Communities. New York: Free Press.
—— (1955) Society. New York: Free Press.

Phillips, Gifford (1966) The Arts in a Democratic Society. Occasional Paper, Center for the Study of Democratic Institutions, Santa Barbara, CA.

Phillips, Kevin P., (1975) Mediacracy. Garden City, NY: Doubleday.

Potter, David M. (1965) "American individualism in the twentieth century," pp. 92–112 in G. Mills (ed.) Innocence and Power. Austin: University of Texas Press.

Quandt, Jean B. (1970) From the Small Town to the Great Community. New Brunswick, NJ: Rutgers University Press.

Revel, Jean-Francois (1971) Without Marx and Jesus. Garden City, NY: Doubleday.

Rivers, William L. (1971) "Monitoring media: 'who shall guard the guards?'" Progressive 35 (September): 23–28.

Schmitt, Peter J. (1969) Back to Nature. New York: Oxford University Press.

Schneyer, Theodore J., and Frank Lloyd (1976) The Public-Interest Media Reform Movement. Occasional Paper, Series on Communications, Aspen Institute for Humanistic Studies, Washington.

Schudson, Michael (1978) Discovering the News. New York: Basic Books.

Shibutani, Tamotsu (1955) "Reference groups as perspectives." American Journal of Sociology 60 (May): 562–569.

———— (1966) Improvised News. Indianapolis: Bobbs-Merrill.

Singer, Aubrey (1966) "Television: window on culture or reflection in the glass?" American Scholar 35 (Spring): 303–309.

Smith, Anthony (1978) "The long road to objectivity and back again," pp. 153–171 in G. Boyce et al. (eds.) Newspaper History. London: Constable.

Stein, Ben (1979) The View from Sunset Boulevard. New York: Basic Books.

Toennies, Ferdinand (1971) On Sociology. Chicago, University of Chicago Press.

Toffler, Alvin (1964) The Culture Consumers. New York: St. Martin's.

Tucker, William (1980) "Environmentalism: the newest Toryism." Policy Review, No. 14 (Fall): 141–152.

White, Theodore H. (1969–1970) "America's two cultures." Columbia Journalism Review 8 (Winter): 8–13.

Wiebe, Robert H. (1967) The Search for Order, 1877–1920. New York: Hill and Wang.

———— (1973) "The progressive years, 1900–1917," pp. 425–442 in W. H. Cartwright and R. L. Watson, Jr. (eds.) The Reinterpretation of American History and Culture. Washington: National Council of the Social Studies.

Chapter 2

TELEVISION AS A CULTURAL FORUM
Implications for Research

Horace M. Newcomb and Paul M. Hirsch

A CULTURAL BASIS for the analysis and criticism of television is, for us, the bridge between a concern for television as a communications medium, central to contemporary society, and television as aesthetic object, the expressive medium that, through its story telling functions, unites and examines a culture. The shortcomings of each of these approaches taken alone should be obvious.

The first is based primarily on a concern for understanding specific messages that may have specific effects and grounds its analysis in "communication" narrowly defined. Complexities of image, style, resonance, narrativity, history, metaphor, and so on are reduced in favor of that content that can be more precisely—some say more objectively—described. The content categories are not allowed to emerge from the text, as is the case in naturalistic observation and in textual analysis. Rather they are predefined in order to be measured more easily. The incidence of certain content categories may be cited as significant, or their "effects" more clearly correlated with some behavior. This concern for measuring is, of course, the result of conceiving television in one way rather than another, as "communication" rather than as "art."

The narrowest versions of this form of analysis need not concern us here. It is to the best versions that we must look, to those that do admit to a range of aesthetic expression and something of a variety of reception. Even when we examine these closely, however, we see that they often assume a monolithic "meaning" in television content.

AUTHORS' NOTE: We would like to express our appreciation to the John and Mary R. Markle Foundation for support in the preparation of this chapter and our ongoing study of the role of television as a cultural forum in American society. This chapter was originally published in *Quarterly Review of Film Studies*, 1983, Vol. 8(2). © Redgrave Publishing Company, South Salem, NY.

The concern is for "dominant" messages embedded in the pleasant disguise of fictional entertainment, and the concern of the researcher is often that the control of these messages is, more than anything else, a complex sort of political control. The critique that emerges, then, is consciously or unconsciously a critique of the society that is transmitting and maintaining the dominant ideology with the assistance, again conscious or unconscious, of those who control communications technologies and businesses. (Ironically, this perspective does not depend on political perspective or persuasion. It is held by groups on the "right" who see American values being subverted, as well as by those on the "left" who see American values being imposed.)

Such a position assumes that the audience shares or "gets" the same messages and their meanings as the researcher finds. At times, like the literary critic, the researcher assumes this on the basis of superior insight, technique, or sensibility. In a more "scientific" manner the researcher may seek to establish a correlation between the discovered messages and the understanding of the audience. Rarely, however, does the message analyst allow for the possibility that the audience, while sharing this one meaning, may create many others that have not been examined, asked about, or controlled for.

The television "critic" on the other hand, often basing his work on the analysis of literature or film, succeeds in calling attention to the distinctive qualities of the medium, to the special nature of television fiction. But this approach all too often ignores important questions of production and reception. Intent on correcting what it takes to be a skewed interest in such matters, it often avoids the "business" of television and its "technology." These critics, much like their counterparts in the social sciences, usually assume that viewers should understand programs in the way the critic does, or that the audience is incapable of properly evaluating the entertaining work and should accept the critic's superior judgment.

The differences between the two views of what television is and does rest, in part, on the now familiar distinction between transportation and ritual views of communication processes. The social scientific, or communication theory, model outlined above (and we do not claim that it is an exhaustive description) rests most thoroughly on the transportation view. As articulated by James Carey, this model holds that communication is a "process of transmitting messages at a distance for the purpose of control. The archetypal case of communication then is persuasion, attitude change, behavior modification, socialization through the transmission of information, influence, or conditioning" (Carey, 1975a).

The more "literary" or "aesthetically based" approach leans toward, but hardly comes to terms with, ritual models of communication. As put by Carey, the ritual view sees communication "not directed toward the extension of messages in space but the maintenance of society in time; not the act of imparting information but the representation of shared beliefs" (Carey, 1975a).

Carey also cuts through the middle of these definitions with a more succinct one of his own: "Communication is a symbolic process whereby reality is produced, maintained, repaired, and transformed" (Carey, 1975b). It is in the attempt to amplify this basic observation that we present a cultural basis for the analysis of television. We hardly suggest that such an approach is entirely new, or that others are unaware of or do not share many of our assumptions. On the contrary, we find a growing awareness in many disciplines of the nature of symbolic thought, communication, and action, and we see attempts to understand television emerging rapidly from this body of shared concerns.[1]

TELEVISION AS LIMINAL REALM

Our own model of television is grounded in an examination of the cultural role of entertainment and parallels this with a close analysis of television program content in all its various textual levels and forms. We focus on the collective, cultural view of the social construction and negotiation of reality, on the creation of what Carey refers to as "public thought" (Carey, 1975a). It is not difficult to see television as central to this process of public thinking. As Hirsch (1982) has pointed out, it is now our national medium, replacing those media—film, radio, picture magazines, newspapers—that once served a similar function. Those who create for such media are, in the words of anthropologist Marshall Sahlins, "hucksters of the symbol" (Sahlins, 1976). They are cultural bricoleurs, seeking and creating new meaning in the combination of cultural elements with embedded significance. They respond to real events, changes in social structure and organization, and to shifts in attitude and value. They also respond to technological shift, the coming of cable or the use of videotape recorders. We think it is clear that the television producer should be added to Sahlins's list of "hucksters." They work in precisely the manner he describes, as do television writers and, to a lesser extent, directors and actors. So too do programmers and network executives who must make decisions about the programs they purchase, develop, and air. At each step of this complicated process they function as cultural interpreters.

Similar notions have often been outlined by scholars of popular culture focusing on the formal characteristics of popular entertainment (see Cawelti, 1976; Thorburn, 1982). To those insights cultural theory adds the possibility of matching formal analysis with cultural and social practice. The best theoretical explanation for this link is suggested to us in the continuing work of anthropologist Victor Turner. This work focuses on cultural ritual and reminds us that ritual must be seen as process rather than as product, a notion not often applied to the study of television, yet crucial to an adequate understanding of the medium.

Specifically, we make use of one aspect of Turner's analysis, his view of the liminal stage of the ritual process. This is the "in-between" stage, when one is neither totally in nor out of society. It is a stage of license, when rules may be broken or bent, when roles may be reversed, when categories may be overturned. Its essence, suggests Turner,

> is to be found in its release from normal constraints, making possible the deconstruction of the "uninteresting" constructions of common sense, the "meaningfulness of ordinary life," . . . into cultural units which may then be reconstructed in novel ways, some of them bizarre to the point of monstrosity. . . . Liminality is the domain of the "interesting" or of "uncommon sense" (Turner, 1977: 68).

Turner does not limit this observation to traditional societies engaged in the *practice* of ritual. He also applies his views to postindustrial, complex societies. In doing so he finds the liminal domain in the arts—all of them.[2] "The dismemberment of ritual has . . . provided the opportunity of theatre in the high culture and carnival at the folk level. A multiplicity of desacralized performative genres has assumed, prismatically, the task of plural cultural reflexivity" (Turner, 1977). In short, contemporary cultures examine themselves through their arts, much as traditional societies do via the experience of ritual. Ritual and the arts offer a metalanguage, a way of understanding who and what we are, how values and attitudes are adjusted, how meaning shifts.

In contributing to this process, particularly in American society, where its role is central, television fulfills what Fiske and Hartley (1978) refer to as the "bardic function" of contemporary societies. In its role as central cultural medium it presents a multiplicity of meanings rather than a monolithic dominant point of view. It often focuses on our most prevalent concerns, our deepest dilemmas. Our most traditional views, those that are repressive and reactionary, as well as those that are subversive and emancipatory, are upheld, examined, maintained, and transformed. The emphasis is on process rather than product, on discussion rather than indoctrination, on contradiction and confusion rather than coherence. It is with this view that we turn to an analysis of the texts of television that demonstrates and supports the conception of television as a cultural forum.

THE COMPLEXITY OF IDEOLOGICAL COMMENTARY IN TELEVISION

This new perspective requires that we revise some of our notions regarding television analysis, criticism, and research. The function of the creator as bricoleur, taken from Sahlins, is again indicated and clarified. The focus on "uncommon sense," on the freedom afforded by the idea of television as a liminal realm helps us to understand the reliance on and interest in forms, plots, and character types that are not at all familiar in our lived experience. The skewed demography of the world of television is not quite so bizarre and repressive once we admit that it is the realm in which we allow our monsters to come out and play, our dreams to be firmed into pictures, our fantasies transformed into plot structures. Cowboys, detectives, bionic men, and great green Hulks; fatherly physicians, glamorous female detectives, and tightly knit families living out the pain of the Great Depression; all these become part of the dramatic logic of public thought.

Shows such as *Fantasy Island* and *Love Boat,* difficult to account for within traditional critical systems except as examples of trivia and romance, are easily understood. Islands and boats are among the most fitting liminal metaphors, as Homer, Bacon, Shakespeare, and Melville, among others, have recognized. So, too, are the worlds of the western and the detective story. With this view we can see the "bizarre" world of situation comedy as a means of deconstructing the world of "common sense" in which all, or most, of us live and work. It also enables us to explain such strange phenomena as game shows and late night talk fests. In short, almost any version of the television text functions as a forum in which important cultural topics may be considered. We illustrate this not with a contemporary program where problems almost always appear on the surface of the show, but with an episode of *Father Knows Best* from the early 1960s. We begin by noting that *Father Knows Best* is often cited as an innocuous series, constructed around unstinting paeans to American middle-class virtues and blissfully ignorant of social conflict. In short, precisely the sort of television program that reproduces dominant ideology by lulling its audience into a dream world where the status quo is the only status.

In this episode Betty Anderson, the older daughter in the family, breaks a great many rules by deciding that she will be an engineer. Over great protest she is given an internship with a surveying crew as part of a high school "career education" program. But the head of the surveying crew, a young college student, drives her away with taunts and insensitivity. She walks off the job on the first day. Later in the week the young man comes to the Anderson home where Jim Anderson chides him with fatherly anger. The young man apologizes and Betty, overhearing him from the other room, runs upstairs, changes clothes, and comes down. The show ends with their flirtation under way.

Traditional ideological criticism, conducted from the communications or the textual analysis perspective, would remark on the way in which social conflict is ultimately subordinated in this dramatic structure to the personal, the emotional. Commentary would focus on the way in which the questioning of the role structure is shifted away from the world of work to the domestic arena. The emphasis would be on the conclusion of the episode in which Betty's real problem of identity and sex role, and society's problem of sex role discrimination, is bound by a more traditional conflict and thereby defused, contained, and redirected. Such a reading is possible, indeed accurate.

We would point out, however, that our emotional sympathy is with Betty throughout this episode. Nowhere does the text instruct the viewer that her concerns are unnatural, no matter how unnaturally they may be framed by other members of the cast. Every argument that can be made for a strong feminist perspective is condensed into the brief, half-hour presentation. The concept of the cultural forum, then, offers a different interpretation. We suggest that in popular culture generally, in television specifically, the raising of questions is as important as the answering of them. That is, it is equally important that an audience be introduced to the problems surrounding sex role discrimination as it is to conclude the episode in a traditional manner. Indeed, it would be startling to think that mainstream texts in mass society would overtly challenge dominant ideas. But this hardly prevents the oppositional ideas from appearing. Put another way, we argue that television does not present firm ideological conclusions—despite its *formal* conclusions—so much as it *comments on* ideological problems. The conflicts we see in television drama, embedded in familiar and nonthreatening frames, are conflicts ongoing in American social experience and cultural history. In a few cases we might see strong perspectives that argue for the absolute correctness of one point of view or another. But for the most part the rhetoric of television drama is a rhetoric of discussion. Shows such as *All in the Family,* or *The Defenders,* or *Gunsmoke,* which raise the forum/ discussion to an intense and obvious level, often make best use of the medium and become highly successful. We see statements *about* the issues and it should be clear that ideological positions can be balanced within the forum by others from a different perspective.

We recognize, of course, that this variety works for the most part within the limits of American monopoly capitalism and within the range of American pluralism. It is an effective pluralistic forum only insofar as American political pluralism is or can be.[3] We also note, however, that one of the primary functions of the popular culture forum, the television forum, is to monitor the limits and the effectiveness of this pluralism, perhaps the only "public" forum in which this role is performed. As content shifts and attracts the attention of groups and individuals, criticism and reform can be initiated. We will have more to say on this topic shortly.

Our intention here is hardly to argue for the richness of *Father Knows Best* as a television text or as social commentary. Indeed, in our view, any emphasis on individual episodes, series, or even genres, misses the central point of the forum concept. While each of these units can and does present its audiences with incredibly mixed ideas, it is television as a whole system that presents a mass audience with the range and variety of ideas and ideologies inherent in American culture. In order to fully understand the role of television in that culture, we must examine a variety of analytical foci and, finally, see them as parts of a greater whole.

We can, for instance, concentrate on a single episode of television content, as we have done in our example. In our view most television shows offer something of this range of complexity. Not everyone of them treats social problems of such immediacy, but submerged in any episode are assumptions about who and what we are. Conflicting viewpoints of social issues are, in fact, the elements that structure most television programs.

At the series level this complexity is heightened. In spite of notions to the contrary, most television shows do change over time. Cavell (1982) has recently suggested that this serial nature of television is perhaps its defining characteristic. By contrast we see that feature only as a primary aspect of the rhetoric of television, one that shifts meaning and shades ideology as series develop. Even a series such as *The Brady Bunch* dealt with ever more complex issues merely because the children, on whom the show focused, grew older. In other cases, shows such as *The Waltons* shifted in content and meaning because they represented shifts in historical time. As that series moved out of the period of the Great Depression, through World War II, and into the postwar period, its tone and emphasis shifted too. In some cases, of course, this sort of change is structured into the show from the beginning, even when the appearance is that of static, un-developing nature. In *All in the Family* the possibility of change and Archie's resistance to it form the central dramatic problem and offer the central opportunity for dramatic richness, a richness that has developed over many years until the character we now see bears little resemblance to the one we met in the beginning. This is also true of *MASH*, although there the structured conflicts have more to do with framing than with character development. In *MASH* we are caught in an antiwar rhetoric that cannot end a war. A truly radical alter-native, a desertion or an insurrection, would end the series. But it would also end the "discussion" of this issue. We remain trapped, like American culture in its historical reality, with a dream and rhet-oric of peace and a bitter experience that denies those aims.

The model of the forum extends beyond the use of the series with attention to genre. One tendency of genre studies has been to focus on similarities within forms, to indicate the ways in which all westerns, situation comedies, detective shows, and so on are alike. Clearly, however, it is in the economic interests of producers to build on audience familiarity with generic patterns and instill novelty into those generically based presentations. Truly innovative forms that use the generic base as a foundation are likely to be among the more suc-cessful shows. This also means that the shows, despite generic sim-ilarity, will carry individual rhetorical slants. As a result, while shows like *MASH, The Mary Tyler Moore Show,* and *All in the Family* may all treat similar issues, those issues will have different meanings because of the variations in character, tone, history, style, and so on, this despite a general "liberal" tone. Other shows, minus that tone, will clash in varying degrees. The notion that they are all, in some sense, "situation comedies" does not adequately explain the treatment of ideas within them.

This hardly diminishes the strength of generic variation as yet another version of difference within the forum. The rhetoric of the soap opera *pattern* is different from that of the situation comedy and that from the detective show. Thus, when similar topics are treated within different generic frames another level of "discussion" is at work.

It is for this reason that we find it important to examine strips of television programming, "flow" as Williams (1975) refers to it. Within these flow strips we may find opposing ideas abutting one another. We may find opposing treatments of the same ideas. And we will certainly find a viewing behavior that is more akin to actual experience than that found when concentrating on the individual show, the series, or the genre. The forum model, then, has led us into a new exploration of the definition of the television text. We are now examining the "viewing strip" as a potential text and are discovering that in the range of options offered by any given evening's televiewing, the forum is indeed a more accurate model of what goes on *within* television than any other that we know of. By taping entire weeks of television content, and tracing various potential strips in the body of that week, we can construct a huge range of potential "texts" that may have been seen by individual viewers.

Each level of text—the strip as text, the television week, the television day—is compounded yet again by the history of the medium. Our hypothesis is that we might track the history of America's social discussions of the past three decades by examining the multiple rhetorics of television during that period. Given the problematic state of television archiving, a careful study of that hypothesis presents an enormous difficulty. It is, nevertheless, an exciting prospect.

INTERPRETIVE VARIANCE

Clearly, our emphasis is on the treatment of issues, on rhetoric. We recognize the validity of analytical structures that emphasize television's skewed demographic patterns, its particular social aberrations, or other "unrealistic distortions" of the world of experience. But we also recognize that in order to make sense of those structures and patterns researchers return again and again to the "meaning" of that television world, to the processes and problems of interpretation. In our view this practice is hardly limited to those of us who study television. It is also open to audiences who view it each evening and to professionals who create for the medium.

The goal of every producer is to create the difference that makes a difference, to maintain an audience with sufficient reference to the known and recognized, but to move ahead into something that distinguishes his show for the program buyer, the scheduler, and most importantly, for the mass audience. As recent work by Newcomb and Alley (1983) shows, the goal of many producers, the most successful and powerful ones, is also to include personal ideas in their work, to use it as all artists use their medium, as a means of personal expression. Given these goals it is possible to examine the work of individual producers as other units of analysis and to compare the work of different producers as expressions within the forum. We need only think of the work of Quinn Martin and Jack Webb, or to contrast their work with that of Norman Lear or Gary Marshall, to recognize the individuality at work within television making. Choices by producers to work in certain generic forms, to express certain political, moral, and ethical attitudes, to explore certain sociocultural topics, all affect the nature of the ultimate "flow text" of television seen by viewers and assure a range of variation within that text.

The existence of this variation is borne out by varying responses among those who view television. A degree of this variance occurs among professional television critics who like and dislike shows for different reasons. But because television critics, certainly in American journalistic situations, are more alike than different in many ways, a more important indicator of the range of responses is that found among "ordinary" viewers, or the disagreements implied by audience acceptance and enthusiasm for program material soundly disavowed by professional critics. Work by Himmleweit (1980) in England and Neuman (1980) in America indicates that individual viewers do function as "critics," do make important distinctions and are able, under certain circumstances to articulate the bases for their judgments. While this work is just beginning, it is still possible to suggest from anecdotal evidence that people agree and disagree with television for a variety of reasons. They find in television texts representations of and challenges to their own ideas, and must somehow come to terms with what is there.

If disagreements cut too deeply into the value structure of the individual, if television threatens the sense of cultural security, the individual may take steps to engage the medium at the level of personal action. Most often this occurs in the form of letters to the network or to local stations, and again, the pattern is not new to television. It has occured with every other mass medium in modern industrial society.

Nor is it merely the formation of groups or the expression of personal points of view that indicates the working of a forum. It is the *range* of response, the directly contradictory readings of the medium, that cue us to its multiple meanings. Groups may object to the same programs, for example, for entirely opposing reasons. In *Charlie's Angels* feminists may find yet another example of sexist repression, while fundamentalist religious groups may find examples of moral decay expressed in the sexual freedom, the personal appearance, or the "unfeminine" behavior of the protagonists. Other viewers doubtless find the expression of meaningful liberation of women. At this level the point is hardly that one group is "right" and another "wrong," much less that one is "right" while the other is "left." Individuals and groups are, for many reasons, involved in making their own meanings from the television text.

This variation in interpretive strategies can be related to suggestions made by Stuart Hall (1980) in his influential essay, "Encoding and Decoding in the Television Discourse." There he suggests three basic modes of interpretation corresponding to the interpreter's political stance within the social structure. The interpretation may be "dominant," accepting the prevailing ideological structure. It may be "oppositional," rejecting the basic aspects of the structure. Or it may be "negotiated," creating a sort of personal synthesis. As later work by some of Hall's colleagues (Morley and Brunsdon, 1978; Morley, 1980) suggests, however, it quickly becomes necessary to expand the range of possible interpretations. Following these suggestions to a radical extreme it might be possible to argue that every individual interpretation of television content could, in some way, be "different." Clearly, however, communication is dependent on a greater degree of shared meanings, and expressions of popular entertainment are perhaps even more dependent on the shared level than many other forms of discourse. Our concern then is for the ways in which interpretation is negotiated in society. Special interest groups that focus, at times, on television provide us with readily available resources for the study of interpretive practices.

We see these groups as representative of metaphoric "fault lines" in American society. Television is the terrain in which the faults are expressed and worked out. In studying the groups, their rhetoric, the issues on which they focus, their tactics, their forms of organization, we hope to demonstrate that the idea of the "forum" is more than a metaphor in its own right. In forming special interest groups, or in using such groups to speak about television, citizens actually enter the forum. Television shoves them toward action, toward expression of ideas and values. At this level the model of "television as a cultural forum" enables us to examine "the sociology of interpretation."

Here much attention needs to be given to the historical aspects of this form of activity. How has the definition of issues changed over time? How has that change correlated with change in the television texts? These are important questions that, while difficult to study, are crucial to a full understanding of the role of television in culture. It is primarily through this sort of study that we will be able to define much more precisely the limits of the forum, for groups form monitoring devices that alert us to shortcomings not only in the world of television representation, but to the world of political experience as well. We know, for example, that because of heightened concern on the part of special interest groups, and responses from the creative and institutional communities of television industries, the "fictional" population of black citizens now roughly equals that of the real population. Regardless of whether such a match is "good" or "necessary," regardless of the depiction of blacks on television, this indicates that the forum extends beyond the screen. The issue of violence, another deserving close study, is more mixed, varying from year to year. The influence of groups, of individuals, of studies, of the terrible consequences of murder and assassination, however, cannot be denied. Television does not exist in a realm of its own, cut off from the influence of citizens. Our aim is to discover, as precisely as possible, the ways in which the varied worlds interact.

Throughout this kind of analysis, then, it is necessary to cite a range of varied responses to the texts of television. Using the viewing "strip" as the appropriate text of television, and recognizing that it is filled with varied topics and approaches to those topics, we begin to think of the television viewer as a bricoleur who matches the creator in the making of meanings. Bringing values and attitudes, a universe of personal experiences and concerns, to the texts, the viewer selects, examines, acknowledges, and makes texts of his or her own.[4] If we conceive of special interest groups as representatives of *patterns* of cultural attitude and response we have a potent source of study.

On the production end of this process, in addition to the work of individual producers, we must examine the role of network executives who must purchase and program television content. They, too, are cultural interpreters, intent on "reading" the culture through its relation to the "market." Executives who head and staff the internal censor agencies of each network, the offices of Broadcast Standards or Standards and Practices, are in a similar position. Perhaps as much as any individual or group they present us with a source of rich material for analysis. They are actively engaged in gauging cultural values. Their own research, the assumptions and the findings, needs to be reanalyzed for cultural implications, as does the work of the programmers. In determining who is doing what, with whom, at what times, they are interpreting social behavior in America and assigning it meaning. They are using television as a cultural litmus that can be applied in defining such problematic concepts as "childhood," "family," "maturity," and "appropriate." With the Standards and Practices offices they interpret *and* define the permissable and the "normal." But their interpretations of behavior open to us as many questions as answers, and an appropriate overview, a new model of television is necessary in order to best understand their work and ours.

THE CULTURAL FORUM MODEL

This new model of "television as a cultural forum" fits the experience of television more accurately than others we have seen applied. Our assumption is that it opens a range of new questions and calls for reanalysis of older findings from both the textual-critical approach and the mass communications research perspective. Ultimately, the new model is a simple one. It recognizes the range of interpretation of television content that is now admitted even by those analysts most concerned with television's presentation and maintenance of dominant ideological messages and meanings. But it differs from those perspectives because it does not see this as surprising or unusual. For the most part, that is what central story telling systems do in all societies. We are far more concerned with the ways in which television contributes to change than with mapping the obvious ways in which it maintains dominant viewpoints. Most research on television, most textual analysis, has assumed that it is thin, repetitive, similar, nearly

identical in textual formation, easily defined, desc..
plained. The variety of response on the part of audienc..
received, as a result of this view, as extraordinary, an as..
"discovery."

We begin with the observation, based on careful textual analy.. .,
that television is dense, rich, and complex rather than impoverished.
Any selection, any cut, any set of questions that is extracted from
that text must somehow account for that density, must account for
what is *not* studied or measured, for the opposing meanings, for the
answering images and symbols. Audiences appear to make meaning
by selecting that which touches experience and personal history. The
range of responses then should be taken as commonplace rather than
as unexpected. But research and critical analysis cannot afford so
personal a view. Rather, they must somehow define and describe the
inventory that makes possible the multiple meanings extracted by
audiences, creators, and network decision makers.

Our model is based on the assumption and observation that only
so rich a text could attract a mass audience in a complex culture. The
forum offers a perspective that is as complex, as contradictory and
confused, as much in process as American culture is in experience.
Its texture matches that of our daily experiences. If we can understand
it better, then perhaps we will better understand the world we live
in, the actions that we must take in order to live there.

NOTES

1. See Silverstone (1981) on structural narrative analysis, Fiske and Hartley (1978)
on the semiotic and cultural bases for the analysis of television, Thorburn (forthcoming)
on the aesthetics of television, Himmleweit et al. (1980) and Neuman (1980) on the
role of the audience as critic, Gitlin (1979) and Kellner (1979) on hegemony and new
applications of critical theory, Lull (1979, 1980) and Meyer et al. (1980) on audience
ethnography and symbolic interactionism, and, most important, the ongoing work of
the Centre for Contemporary Cultural Studies at Birmingham University, England, as
recently published in Hall (1980) on the interaction of culture and textual analysis from a
thoughtful political perspective.

2. In various works Turner uses both the terms "liminal" and "liminoid" to refer
to works of imagination and entertainment in contemporary culture. The latter term
is used to clearly mark the distinction between events that have distinct behavioral
consequences and those that do not. As Turner suggests, the consequences of entertainment in contemporary culture are hardly as profound as those of the liminal stage
of ritual in traditional culture. We are aware of this basic distinction, but use the former
term in order to avoid a fuller explanation of the neologism. See Turner (1974, 1979).

3. We are indebted to Professor Mary Douglas for encouraging this observation. At the presentation of these ideas at the New York Institute for the Humanities seminar in The Mass Production of Mythology, she checked our enthusiasm for a pluralistic model of television by stating accurately and succinctly, "there are pluralisms and pluralisms." This comment led us to consider more thoroughly the means by which the forum and responses to it function as a tool with which to monitor the quality of pluralism in American social life, including its entertainments. The observation added a much needed component to our planned historical analysis.

4. We are indebted to Louis Black and Eric Michaels of the Radio-TV-Film department of the University of Texas-Austin for calling this aspect of televiewing to Newcomb's attention. It creates a much desired balance to Sahlins's view of the creator as bricoleur and indicates yet another manner in which the forum model enhances our ability to account for more aspects of the television experience. See especially Michaels (1982).

REFERENCES

Carey, James (1975a) "A cultural approach to communications." _Communication_ 2 (1).

Carey, James (1975b) "Culture and communications." _Communication Research_ 2 (1).

Cavell, Stanley (1982) "The fact of television." _Daedalus_ 111 (4).

Cawelti, John (1976) Adventure, Mystery, and Romance. Chicago: University of Chicago Press.

Fiske, John and John Hartley (1978) Reading Television. London: Methuen.

Gitlin, Todd (1979) "Prime time ideology: the hegemonic process in television entertainment." Social Problems 26 (3).

Hall, Stuart (1980) "Encoding and decoding in the television discourse," in Culture, Media, Language. London: Hutchinson.

Himmleweit, Hilda et al. (1980) "The audience as critic: an approach to the study of entertainment" in P. Tannenbaum (ed.) The Entertainment Functions of Television. Hillsdale, NJ: Lawrence Erlbaum.

Hirsch, Paul (1982) "The role of popular culture and television in contemporary society," in H. M. Newcomb (ed.) Television: The Critical View. New York: Oxford University Press.

Kellner, Douglas (1979) "TV, ideology, and emancipatory popular culture." Socialist Review 45 (May-June).

Lull, James T. (1979) "Family communication patterns and the social uses of television." Communication Research 7 (3).

——— (1980) "The social uses of television." Human Communication Research 7 (3).

Meyer, Tim, Paul Traudt, and James Anderson (1980) "Non-traditional mass communication research methods: observational case studies of media use in natural settings," in D. Nimmo (ed.) Communication Yearbook 4. New Brunswick, NJ: Transaction Books.

Michaels, Eric (1982) "TV tribes." Ph.D. dissertation, University of Texas at Austin.

Morley, David (1980) "Subjects, readers, texts," in S. Hall. Culture, Media, Language. London: Hutchinson.

Morley, David and Charlotte Brunsdon (1978) Everyday Television: "Nationwide". London: British Film Institute.

Newcomb, Horace (1982) Television: The Critical View. New York: Oxford University Press.

———— and Robert Alley (1983) The Television Producer as Artist in American Commercial Television. New York: Oxford University Press.

Neuman, W. Russell (1980) "Television and American culture: the mass medium and the pluralist audience." (unpublished)

Sahlins, Marshall (1976) Culture and Practical Reason. Chicago: University of Chicago Press.

Silverstone, Roger (1981) The Message of Television: Myth and Narrative in Contemporary Culture. London: Heinemann Educational Books.

Thorburn, David (forthcoming) The Story Machine. New York: Oxford University Press.

Thorburn, David (1982) "Television melodrama," in H. M. Newcomb. Television: The Critical View. New York: Oxford University Press.

Turner, Victor (1974) "Liminal to liminoid, in play, flow, and ritual: an essay in comparative symbology." Rice University Studies 60 (3).

Turner, Victor (1977) "Process, system and symbol: a new anthropological synthesis." *Daedalus* 106 (2).

Turner, Victor (1979) "Afterword," in B. Babcock (ed.) The Reversible World. Ithaca, NY: Cornell University Press.

Williams, Raymond (1975) Television, Technology, and Cultural Form. New York: Schocken.

Chapter 3

AN ALTERNATIVE APPROACH
TO TELEVISION RESEARCH
Developments in British Cultural Studies
at Birmingham

Thomas Streeter

THIS CHAPTER has two purposes: to introduce the British cultural studies tradition to American students of the media, and to discuss in detail some of the television research that has come out of the Birmingham Centre for Contemporary Cultural Studies in the last decade.[1] The television research associated with the Birmingham Centre represents an important example of the new approaches in media research currently attracting the interest of media scholars worldwide; understanding British cultural studies is important to understanding the Centre's work. The Birmingham Centre's television research, however, is just one variant of the broad and varied work that has emerged from the cultural studies tradition. An understanding of cultural studies, therefore, is useful both as a background to the Centre's work and as an intellectual tradition of value to media studies in general.

It is typical in the field of communication to introduce a new approach by first explicating its theory and then showing some examples of how the theory is applied in research. In describing the Birmingham Centre for Contemporary Cultural Studies' approach to television, this would be not only difficult but misleading. While the Centre's approach is admirably sensitive to its own and others' un-

AUTHOR'S NOTE: I would like to thank Larry Grossberg and David Swanson for their help in the preparation of this chapter.

derlying theoretical assumptions, the process of intellectual investigation is not understood in a way that allows for the easy separation, empirical. In cultural studies, the process of making explicit the assumptions and presuppositions of a body of thought is not, as it often is in this country, simply something to be used to critique social scientific research paradigms; "theoretical criticism" is considered a fundamental intellectual activity applicable to all aspects of life, including things typically thought of as belonging to the empirical realm, such as the everyday experiences and activities associated with television. The theoretical and the empirical are thus ultimately inseparable, a fact reflected in the character of the Birmingham Centre's research.

In much of contemporary American research, the goal of theory, at least implicitly, is a fixed system of understanding that will provide a better, more objective understanding of the empirical world. The Centre's use of theory, on the other hand, is not so much a matter of a particular set of assumptions, hypotheses, and so on as it is an intellectual practice of questioning what seems to be obvious in both one's own and others' thought, a practice to be applied and reapplied continuously.

Concurrent with the Centre's use of theory is an alternate conception of the role and nature of research. Rather than conceiving of itself as founded on the search for objective knowledge, cultural studies sees itself as engaged with and part of a series of cultural and historical developments and processes. Cultural studies views itself as embedded in society, not outside society looking in. Social and historical developments are self-consciously as important to the developments and progress of cultural studies as are theoretical issues and empirical discoveries; ultimately, the former are inseparable from the latter just as the theoretical is inseparable from the empirical.

In discussing the program of television research that emerged from the Birmingham Centre, therefore, I will try to trace the historical, cultural, and intellectual directions in which the research has been developing, rather than treat it as a fixed approach or research paradigm. I will begin with a brief discussion of the historical roots of cultural studies and its concerns, describe the particular variant of cultural studies that developed at the Birmingham Centre during the decade of the 1970s, describe some key examples of its research, and conclude with a discussion of the general merits of a cultural approach to television as well as some of its as yet unresolved problems.[2]

CULTURAL STUDIES IN BRITAIN

Like most approaches to the mass media, British cultural studies can trace its roots back to concerns with the rise of new forms of communication that accompanied the development of modern industrial society. Cultural studies, however, differs from the largely quantitative, social scientific tradition dominant in the United States—often called "mainstream research"—in a number of fundamental ways. While mainstream research has understood individuals primarily in terms of the measurable differences between them, cultural studies has focused on the nature of everyday experience, the sense the individual makes of the world. Where mainstream research has seen mass society, cultural studies has seen cultures, subcultures, classes, and institutions. And while mainstream research has perceived itself as objective and scientific, and focused on questions of propaganda, manipulation, and persuasion, cultural studies has perceived its role as one of socially responsible activism, and has focused on questions of social change.

Raymond Williams and Richard Hoggart, two of the seminal figures in cultural studies, came from backgrounds in literary criticism and thus approached the modern mass media with an eye toward their "imaginative working," or their "meaningfulness" (Hoggart, 1963: 259). Both men, however, had the experience of growing up within the working class in Britain, and then moving into the more respected world of the successful academic, an experience that made them acutely aware of the realities of class in British society. Moreover, their personal experiences also made them sensitive to, on the one hand, the elitism of traditional literary criticism, which generally dismissed the bulk of popular literature and the social life that went with it as vulgar and unworthy of consideration, and, on the other hand, the reductiveness of traditional sociological approaches to class structure and the mass media. Both men made it clear in their work that any adequate understanding of the modern world could not afford to ignore either the full complexity of everyday subjective experience, or the material realities of class divisions. Following the leads of Hoggart and Williams, therefore, cultural studies has approached the study of modern society and its forms of communication with two primary concerns: (1) avoiding the mechanistic determinism of much sociology (including many forms of Marxism) by focusing on the full complexity and importance of subjective experience, and (2) avoiding the elitism of more literary approaches by seeing experience in its context of the material realities of class and social structure.

It should be noted that the dual concerns of cultural studies do *not* constitute a simple synthesis of what Lazarsfeld called "administrative" and "critical" research, nor an attempt to bridge the gap between humanistic and scientific approaches. Cultural studies, on the contrary, denies that there is any essential difference between humanistic and scientific modes of thought, not that the two realms should somehow be combined (see Slack and Allor, 1983, for an elaboration of this argument). It is with this in mind, therefore, that Stuart Hall has described cultural studies as a concerned approach to questions of modern society in opposition to the "false antithesis" of literary criticism versus "scientific" sociology. (Hall, 1980a: 21).

THE DEVELOPMENT OF THE BIRMINGHAM CENTRE

A principal site in the development of cultural studies has been the Centre for Contemporary Cultural Studies at the University of Birmingham, founded in 1964 under the leadership of Richard Hoggart. In searching for an alternative to traditional quantitative sociology, the Centre developed an early interest in symbolic interactionism and ethnographic approaches. The work of Mead, Blumer, Becker, and other interactionists used a qualitative methodology to investigate "the ways in which social actors define for themselves the conditions in which they live" and thus put everyday experience and social life at the center of attention, while also allowing for exploration of the "differences in 'lived' values and meanings which differentiated subcultures from the dominant culture" (Hall, 1980a: 24). Because it offers access to the meaningfulness of social life without the reductiveness of sociology or the text-bound elitism of literary criticism, the ethnographic approach has remained important to the Centre's work.

However, interactionism proved unable to address the full range of the Centre's concerns. While it proved useful for the study of perceived meaning, it was unable to deal adequately with the study of systematic "misrecognition." Also, interactionism offered no easy route to the study of relations *between* cultures and subcultures; it tended to obscure the material conditions—the larger structures of society as a whole such as the relations between classes—that lay behind the patterns of interaction and perception. It was in part for this reason that work at the Centre, under the leadership of Stuart Hall, turned to Western Marxism.

The work of the Frankfurt School, Lukacs, the later Sartre, and other Western Marxists consciously opposes itself to the economic determinism of "vulgar" Marxism. While the latter tends to reduce all of culture to a superstructural reflection of the economic base, Western Marxism has been highly concerned with the relation of culture to social life. The terms of its discussion have largely centered around an understanding of ideology, not simply as false consciousness, but as a complete system of thought or mode of understanding. On a general level, the importance of a complex understanding of ideology to cultural studies has been that it incorporates and reshapes the issue of misrecognition by making it, not a matter of failed perception or of intentional deception, but a logical product of a particular system of thought. In this light, everyday "common sense" need not be taken as the sole basis for social reality. What is made to appear obvious, the unquestioned background assumptions of everyday life, can also be subject to critical analysis. The experience of common sense, of what seems transparent and obvious, need not be studied only within the limited interactionist focus, but can also be systematically analyzed within the larger context of the society as the product of ideologies born in larger class and economic structures.

A final important influence on cultural studies at the Centre is that of the European structuralist movement exemplified in Levi-Strauss, Barthes, and Althusser. Structuralism places an emphasis on understanding social life in terms of patterns, arrangements, and relations; it focuses on structure rather than on content. Language is viewed as a system of signs whose significance is determined solely by the internal arrangement of the system, and this in turn becomes a model for the whole of human activity. Symbolic activity takes on a privileged role in social life, and leads to an interest in the construction of "myths" through codes and systems of signification as a fundamental social process.

A number of characteristics made the structuralist movement attractive to cultural studies. Structuralism was antipositivist and placed imaginative activity at the heart of human existence. While it brought culture to the level of the everyday, it offered the hope of a rigorous, systematic access to the structure of everyday experience that did not rely on "common sense" but instead focused on the structure of the myths of contemporary society that constituted ideology. Further, through the introduction of notions such as the "necessary complexity" and "overdetermination" of structures, and the "relative autonomy" of relations, it offered the hope of a rigorous study of social life without the seemingly inevitable mechanistic reductiveness of both many kinds of Marxism and most sociology. In sum, structuralism offered the possibility of the study of "constraint alongside expression and agency," and thus systematically integrated the dual concerns of cultural studies (Hall, 1980a: 31).

Within the cultural program, then, these various schools of thought were integrated in a way that can be summarized as follows: ethnographic methods, with their focus on the conscious definitions used in everyday interaction, became situated in the larger framework of myths and ideologies, which focused on the unconscious relations revealed in what is not said, or what is left unquestioned. While subjective experience is still seen at the heart of social activity, it is not viewed as simple or unproblematic. The consciousness that functions at the center of everyday life is a key moment in the larger framework of myths and ideologies upon which the obviousness of common sense is constructed. A useful understanding of social life, therefore, requires both attention to the conscious definitions used in interaction and the critical analysis of unconscious processes of structuration that underlie those definitions. Ideology needs to be understood in terms of its role in the creation of the "natural" or the "obvious."

MEDIA RESEARCH AT BIRMINGHAM

"In the analysis of culture," writes Stuart Hall, "the interconnection between societal structures and processes and formal or symbolic structures is absolutely pivotal" (Hall, 1973: 1). For this reason, media research has been a central concern of cultural studies from the outset. In contrast with most approaches to the mass media, however, cultural studies has viewed the larger observable aspects of the media not as simple "facts" but as the surface-level products of complex cultural practices and social structures. The concepts that form the stock in trade of mainstream research in the United States—effects, uses, gratifications, and so on—are not thought of simply as raw data or self-explanatory facts, but as socially structured complexes. "Effects, uses, 'gratifications,'" writes Hall, "are themselves framed by structures of understanding, as well as social and economic structures which shape its 'realization' at the reception end of the chain, and which permit the meanings signified in language to be transposed into conduct or consciousness" (Hall, 1973: 4). In viewing the facts of media production and use, therefore, it becomes necessary to understand the framework of social practices, assumptions, and "competencies" brought to bear on the construction and perception of media messages.

Hall has characterized the Birmingham Centre's approach to the media as differing from mainstream research in four essential ways. First, instead of seeking the direct influence of media on audiences, cultural studies focused on the ideological role of the media in society. Second, the Centre moved away from understanding "media texts as 'transparent' bearers of meaning—as the 'message' in some undifferentiated way—and gave much greater attention than had been the case in traditional forms of content analysis to their linguistic and ideological structuration." Third, the Centre has avoided an understanding of audiences as passive and undifferentiated, and has instead focused on an active audience and the process of "reading" or decoding media messages, especially the ways in which decodings vary according to different structures of understanding associated with different cultural and ideological contexts. Fourth, the Centre has been concerned with the role of the media in maintaining the current structure of society through "the circulation and securing of *dominant* ideological definitions and representations" (Hall, 1980b: 117-118).

ENCODING/DECODING

Stuart Hall articulated an influential conceptual framework for the analysis of television in an article called "Encoding and Decoding in the Television Discourse" (Hall, 1973). Television messages, Hall observes, can only be made intelligible by way of culturally shared codes and competencies; this is true at every step along the way, from the producer's studios to the audience's living rooms. A news event, for example, can never be transmitted directly, but must be first structured and encoded within the framework of professional and social practices surrounding television news programs, and then must be decoded within various complex cultural and social contexts. "To put it paradoxically," Hall writes, "the event must become a 'story' before it can become a *communicative event*" (Hall, 1973: 2). It follows, therefore, that a principal focus for research should be the formal subrules of televisual language that make the communicative event of television possible.

Unlike many other structuralist and semiotic analyses, however, research at the Centre has generally refused to disassociate the formal rules and codes of television from the social and cultural conditions that create the possibility of the use of the rules. What Hall calls the "maps of meaning" that are brought to bear in the creation and perception of television programs rest within larger maps of social reality possessed by producers and viewers of television, and these larger maps in turn are consciously and unconsciously engaged with the whole range of social meanings and practices and the material relations of power that undergird them (Hall, 1973: 13).

It is on this level that the notion of ideology comes into focus. Ideology, understood in Althusser's sense as "the representation of the imaginary relationships of individuals to their real conditions," is viewed as a system for "coding" social reality (Heck, 1980: 123). It is via ideological codes that television messages are understood and have their effect.

Consequently, television research comes to have two interlinked aspects: one, the study of television messages themselves, and the other, the study of the culturally determined maps of meaning that go into their production and perception. The approach to messages is informed by the structuralist interest in the systematic relations within the text as a whole, as opposed to the isolated "meanings" or isolated elements of message "content." A violent event in a television Western, for example, gains meaning only in relation to the other elements of the story and in terms of the rules and conventions that govern their combination. What the audience receives is not violence, but messages about violence that have significance only in terms of the audience's decoding of the structured relations embodied in the televisual text.

These structured relations, furthermore, are always complex. A central tenet of semiotic theory is that the relations between signifiers and signifieds is arbitrary. This means that, in principle, any given sign or symbol can have an infinite number of possible meanings, a quality sometimes called "polysemy." The fact of polysemy does not mean, however, that the audience is free to choose among an infinity of equally weighted meanings. If there were not some degree of shared interpretations, nothing would assure that we would ever interpret any given communicative event in the same way. We would never be able to penetrate the mist of infinite possible interpretations to communicate. The key question is thus, how, out of the infinite number of possible meanings, do we select a limited number? What limits the potentially infinite proliferation of meanings?

A central goal of television research, therefore, is understanding how television creates a set of what Hall calls "preferred" meanings, that is, how television prefers a set of interpretations stable enough to be coherent across the enormous numbers of people who participate in a television broadcast. Borrowing from linguistics and discourse analysis, Hall speaks of these, not as "a set of prearranged codes, but of *performative rules*—rules of competence and use, or logics-in-use," which are grounded in social and cultural relations and which seek to give preference to one or another set of meanings (Hall, 1973: 14). The processes of encoding and decoding, therefore, are seen as a matter of engaging the rules of competence and use that are generated in, and are an integral part of, everyday life and interaction.

Obviously, not all social actors engaged in the production and reception of television possess the same competencies, nor are they engaged with television in the same way. The producers of television, for example, are driven by a complex set of institutional, political, and economic concerns and a set of rules about "professional" television that are quite different from the performative rules brought to bear by, say, the housewife who turns on the news after dinner, and hers in turn are different from those of the shop steward who watches the same news program with a concern for the relation of news events to his role as an active trade union member.

Along with the interest in how television creates a set of "preferred" meanings, therefore, research is faced with the task of analyzing the nature of *varied* encodings and decodings and their relations to the culture and social roles of the various participants. This latter task reinterprets the phenomena that mainstream research has called distortion, misunderstanding, and selective perception as a matter of varied or "aberrant" decodings. When someone seems to misunderstand a television program, in other words, they are likely just to be decoding it in a different, nondominant way. The mapping of systematic variations in decoding has thus become a major interest for television research in cultural studies.

EXAMPLES OF TELEVISION RESEARCH AT THE CENTRE

Because cultural studies is not interested in any particular isolated "effect" of television, but is concerned with the entire process of television as a cultural institution, the kinds of research done under its name are necessarily diverse and eclectic. Furthermore, because the process of research is thought of, not as the testing of theoretical hypotheses by their application to empirical data, but as the critical engagement with cultural processes and social facts, as a process of "empirical dialogue," culturalist television research makes deliberate use of a great deal of rich, multileveled detail, focusing not on a single aspect or analytical approach but on the relations between levels and details. The nature of the research thus prohibits any reduction of it to a series of major findings, theoretical principles, and so on. A full appreciation of the Centre's work can only come from the work itself. For these reasons, any survey of television research at the Centre can only hope to sketch some representative examples and themes in order to illustrate the major trends that characterize the approach.

TEXTUAL ANALYSIS

Television research in cultural studies can be divided into two kinds, that which focuses on media texts, and that which focuses on media audiences. (This division is for the purposes of analysis only; the two types often have been combined in the same project.) The general pattern in the analysis of media texts has been a focus on the particular version of "common sense" constructed in the background assumptions of a televisual message, what a particular program or genre assumes to be "natural" or taken for granted.

In one example of textual analysis, Connell investigated news coverage of the Labour government's attempts over a period of years to persuade British trade unions to voluntarily follow a policy of wage restraint (Connell, 1980: 139–156). Television news coverage of disputed viewpoints on the issue was extensive and thus at first glance seemed to refute common arguments that news coverage was biased or distorted in a direct way. Connell did find, however, that routine broadcast and journalistic practices served to construct a set of premises about the nature of the controversy that favored the government's position. This was accomplished by conceiving of the controversy through the frame of the question of "how well the government was doing." Opponents of the government position were depicted in terms of the strategies and likelihood of success of their attempts to undermine the government's efforts. Coverage rarely, if ever, allowed for discussion of the basis for their position, and thus the widely publicized premise of wages-led inflation—the premise behind wage restraint policy—took on the status of "common sense" and cast the government in the role of the most reasonable party in the debate. The media, therefore, helped "set the agenda" of political activity, not by simply giving more coverage or priority to certain events, but by constructing a background of "rational understanding" and "the consensus" that framed the course of events.

A second approach to textual analysis is represented in Hall, Connell, and Curti's detailed study of a broadcast of *Panorama,* a famous BBC current affairs program (Hall, et al., 1976). The study investigates the program on several different levels, from the con-temporary political situation to the specific journalistic and broadcast criteria that the BBC officially applied to the program. The heart of the study, however, is an analysis of the program itself, with particular attention paid to the presentation of a roundtable debate between several political figures on the political state of Britain. Besides the standard rules for debate, the discussion is seen to proceed by means of a series of performative rules, all of which rest on and affirm the presupposition of neutral, objective media as central to a centrally ruled, parliamentary democracy. These rules are shown to form the basis for the broadcaster's encoding practices. The presence of the practices is strikingly illustrated in the politician's reactions when the broadcaster/moderator refers to a Labour official's policy with the word "dogma." This violation of the rules, like an ungrammatical sentence, throws the debate off course for all the participants, and considerable cooperative effort amongst all the supposed adversaries in the debate is required to restore order. Both the use of the rules and the response to their violation thus are seen to reaffirm the basic premises of the dominant parliamentary system, with its belief in structured debate through neutral objective media.

One of the most extensive textual analyses produced by the Centre is Brundson and Morley's book on the BBC public affairs program *Nationwide* (Brundson and Morley, 1978). Like the other examples of television research, this study investigates the particular kind of "common sense" constructed in the background assumptions of the program, and interprets this in its ideological context.[3] *Nationwide* frames itself deliberately within a kind of "down home" wisdom, thought of as common sense and practical, an approach of "getting to the heart of the matter." In their very detailed analysis, Brundson and Morley demonstrate that this particular kind of common sense rests on a concept of "the people" as something outside the structures of politics and government and opposed to faceless bureaucracies. This view presumes politics to be irrelevant to everyday life. The structure and content of the program, and the language and behavior of the TV journalists, are premised on the identity of the (logically distinct) concepts of (1) the pragmatic and direct, and (2) the norm. Further, this approach works to generate an assumption of a national unity of the British people in the image of the common man. Like *PM Magazine,* the program is broadcast in different versions for the different regions of Britain, where each version consists of a mix of events from the audience's own region and national events. Through a technologically complex set of interconnections based in London, reporters from different regions are seen simultaneously on the screen talking to each other and with the national news team as if they were side by side. Regional differences are presented as quaint and quirky differences in accent, life-style and so on. Regional disputes of a more substantive nature, such as those involving the Scotch and Welsh nationalist movements, are avoided. Consequently, in its choice of stories, language, and overall structure, the *Nationwide* program presents a vision of Britain as a national unity, varied, but not in conflict. The program was created in response to criticisms of the BBC's nationally dominated programming, but its "regionalism" is thus revealed as a kind of nationalism.

Brundson and Morley's study, informed by Hall's interest in the process of decoding, pays close attention to the way *Nationwide* "prefers" particular decodings not only through its use of background assumptions but also in the way it creates an "image" of the audience itself that is coherent with the ideological frame of the program. *Nationwide,* scheduled to fit into the early evening activities of a typical employed British family, focuses on individuals, not in their public and institutional roles, but in their relations to their families and their "private" nonworking lives. The reporters, known by their first names, constantly refer to "us" and "we" (meaning them and the audience), and speak and act as if they were guests in the audience's homes. They frequently make the illogical implication that the viewers are involved in the selection and construction of news stories, and they otherwise engage in "constantly concealing the one-way nature of the television system in our society" (Brundson and Morley, 1978:20). Interpreted in light of the structuralist interest in the structuration of the social subject (i.e., the social construction of self-identity), these textual implications about the nature of the audience are crucial. The program prefers certain decodings not simply by transmitting certain messages to its audience, but by creating for the audience an image of itself as pragmatic, down-to-earth, and in unity with the people of Britain, even if not with its political system. The audience member is identified, not by his or her social role, but by his or her private habits, leisure activities, and other qualities of the "domestic sphere." Issues of conflict over work, status, regional politics, and the fact of the dominance of the British nation-state over a heterogenous population—areas that could disturb the vision of national harmony—are obscured and not included in the television discourse, and, by implication, in the audience's self-identity.

AUDIENCE RESEARCH

While a televisual discourse can "prefer" certain interpretations of the audience's image of itself, and thus to some extent "create" its own audience, Morley points out that "the relation of an audience to the ideological operations of television remains in principle an empirical question" (Morley, 1980: 162). Consequently, besides exposing background assumptions associated with television and their potential ideological effects, the Centre has also been concerned with exploring the extent and nature of these effects on real audiences, that is, with empirical research of television audiences, their sociocultural contexts, and their various decoding practices. In his article, "Reconceptualizing the Media Audience: Towards an Ethnography of Audiences," Morley laid out the basic foundations of culturalist empirical research of television audiences (Morley, 1974). While expressing sympathy for uses and gratifications research insofar as it argues against the "passive audience" and thus recognizes the polysemic nature of messages, Morely criticizes it for placing too much emphasis on individual differences in interpretation and for not exploring the social character of different interpretations. "Of course," Morley writes, "there will always be individual, 'private' readings; but we need to see the way in which these readings are patterned into cultural structures and clusters" (Morley, 1974: 1). Moreover, potential relations between differences in interpretation and socioeconomic structures of society should not be ignored.

A further difference between Morley's cultural approach and that of uses and gratifications is that culturalism seeks not only to understand the social patterns behind differences in interpretation but also sees interpretations themselves as more than the products of unrelated, self-explanatory "uses." Interpretations occur within socially constructed meaning systems, or "maps of meaning," which in turn rest in larger ideological frameworks. The goal, therefore, is an understanding, not only of the role of social factors in determining differences in interpretation, but also of the relation of these differences to the construction of different "social worlds" and in determining varied access to meaning systems. Towards this end, Morley suggests an approach that parallels Basil Bernstein's investigation of restricted and elaborated codes in language use, with an eye towards mapping the "distribution of cultural competencies throughout society" (Morley, 1974: 2).

An early example of audience research in cultural studies that coheres with Morley's principles is Dorothy Hobson's study of housewives and the mass media (Hobson, 1980). Hobson used the ethnographic method of the focused interview to investigate the role of television and radio in the lives of working class housewives. She found, among other things, that housewives tended to believe that television news was both boring and important, while the kinds of programs that they enjoyed watching were of lesser significance. Because they believed what they liked to be of lesser significance, it seemed "natural" for them that their own needs and wishes were justifiably subordinated to those of their husbands' program choices. Their own structures of understanding, products of their ideological environments, were therefore found to reflect and reinforce their passive domestic roles in the home. Their viewing preferences served to steer them away from matters of political power and control, while their system of value served to justify and affirm their own subordinate rank. Their own particular modes of viewing or decoding television programming, therefore, while not the same as those of their husbands, were integrated within the same ideological framework.

Towards the goal of understanding the variety of ways in which television messages can be decoded, Hall, following Parkin, suggested a typology of four general kinds of potential decoding practices involved in television, especially news broadcasts (Hall, 1973: 16). The first is the "dominant" or "hegemonic" code that for the most part is "given by political elites" and stands for an interpretation of an event in the form that the dominant powers intend it to be interpreted. A dominant decoding is the closest one can come to a transparent transmission model of communication; the encoding and decoding of the message are relatively equal and symmetrical. The second type is the professional code, a sort of metacode engaged by media professionals in selecting news events, formats, staging, and technical quality. The professional code is largely encompassed in what is called "professional judgment" and is characterized by a continual striving towards what is believed to be "neutrality." The third type is the "negotiated code," which accords a privileged position to dominant definitions but allows for a negotiated application in some cases, particularly those that relate to the decoder's own position. An example of a negotiated decoding would be a British factory worker who accepts the government's premise that inflation is wages-led and thus the general belief that strikes are bad for the economy, but interprets his own need for higher wages and desire to go on strike as a justified exception to the rule. The negotiated code, consequently, is shot through with contradictions. The fourth type of decoding is the "oppositional code," which interprets messages within a framework wholly different from and in opposition to the dominant one. An oppositional decoding might be that of the Marxist shop steward, who reinterprets every mention of the "national interest" on the news to mean "class interest."

In the most extensive example of culturalist audience research to date, *The Nationwide Audience,* Morley attempts to use Hall's categories empirically (Morley, 1980a). Data for the study were obtained from 29 taped, focused interviews with groups of five to ten people who had just seen videotapes of either the *Nationwide* program in the preceding study, or a special *Nationwide* program dealing with the national budget. The groups were of varied social, cultural, ethnic, and economic backgrounds, but all were involved in educational courses of one sort or another, "a situation where the groups already had some existence as a social entity" (Morley, 1980a: 36). The videotape showings and interviews were arranged to fit into the respective courses "in the context of their established institutional setting" (p. 36).

Because of the lack of sophistication of the available analytical methods, Morley considers his own analysis preliminary and describes the data itself at great length. The analysis he does provide draws on a variety of concerns and methods. In keeping with the culturalist pattern, he focuses on the structures of discourse and frameworks of interpretation amd meaning rather than on, say, responses to particular questions or opinions on particular issues. He also tries to ascertain the extent to which groups could be classified according to Hall's four coding categories, and the relation of these to sociodemographic factors, cultural frameworks, and the relevance of discussion topics to participants' own lives.

The results of Morley's study are complex and by his own admission incompletely analyzed, so that a thorough discussion of them in this context would be impossible. Instead, I will try to highlight some of Morley's more interesting conclusions and observations. On a crude level, Morley did find that groups of schoolboys, apprentices, and management trainees exhibited generally dominant decodings, that teacher training college students fell on the dominant end of the "negotiated" spectrum, and photography and university students fell closer to the oppositional end of the spectrum. Several different groups of black students did not seem to decode the program at all. "The concerns of *Nationwide,*" Morley writes, "are not the concerns of their world" (1980a: 134). Various kinds of active trade union members produced a mixture of oppositional and negotiated decodings. The interviews revealed differences within categories as well; bank managers, for example, exhibited "traditional Conservative" decodings, while apprentices voiced what Morely calls "populist-conservative/ cynical" decodings, based on a sort of damn-all-politicians attitude (p. 137). Decodings did not always correlate with class; in fact, for one of the programs viewed, most of the more oppositional decodings were among groups from more middle-class, educated backgrounds. For the special program on the national budget, decodings tended to fall out more along class lines (p. 138).

Morley makes a number of interesting observations about the formal characteristics of the interpretations. Unexpectedly, the awareness of "preferring" mechanisms in the programs bore little or no relation to whether or not the interpretations preferred were accepted or rejected; consciousness of the constructed nature of the program did not entail the rejection of what was constructed (Morley, 1980a: 140). Critical comments, however, took different foci in different groups, revealing different understandings or systems of meaning surrounding the act of interpretation. Bank managers, for example, directed considerable criticism towards the formal qualities of the program (e.g., the program's populist mode of address) and had little to say about its ideological implications. Shop stewards, on the other hand, displayed an exactly opposite set of concerns (p. 144). The nature of the groups' respective meaning systems were thus suggested by the ways in which kinds of qualities were thought important while others were either thought trivial or accepted as obvious.

PROBLEMS WITH MORLEY'S RESEARCH

Besides the obvious need for more audience research in different social and cultural contexts, Morley's project, and the more general project of cultural studies, have several problems that have yet to be resolved. Given the current interest in television research projects that combine textual analysis with audience studies, it is worth discussing in detail some of the difficulties encountered by Morley's attempt. Some of these have been elaborated in a critical postscript to *The Nationwide Audience* (Morley, 1981). Morley points out that, while the broad textual analysis of *Nationwide* devoted considerable attention to the ideological implications of the program as a whole, the audience interviews centered only on reactions to specific elements and issues in the program; the deeper level of analysis was consequently lost. Since one of the most significant "effects" of television is considered to be the circulation of dominant ideological definitions on this deeper level, this is a serious lack in the project.

Morley was surprised to find that consciousness of the constructed nature of news stories bore little correlation to acceptance or rejection of the interpretations constructed. This weakens the belief that information that was coherent with the audience's own maps of meaning would be perceived as natural, common sensical, and thus unbiased. While this belief, common to much work in cultural studies, need not be dismissed, it is obviously not as simple a matter as some have assumed. While the ideological effect of "creating the obvious" is probably important, it may not be the primary effect it has been expected to be. Other aspects, such as Morley's observation that different audience groups focused on different characteristics of the program in their criticisms, need to be investigated.

Morley has also indicated a number of difficulties with the encoding/decoding model and his use of it. For one, the interpretation of dominant decodings as relatively transparent (and the correlative definitions of negotiated and oppositional decodings as relatively non-transparent) can imply an understanding of language as the intentional transmission of atomized meanings from one person's head to another. The goal in cultural studies, however, has been to understand language, not as a mechanism for sending messages, but as "the medium in which consciousness takes shape" (Morley, 1981: 4). In a related problem, the notion of "preferred" decodings, central to Morley's analysis, makes sense only when applied to news "facts" (e.g., "inflation is wages-led"). The same notion applied to, say, fiction would lead to a reduction of the text to a mere vehicle of a substantive proposition (i.e., this story means x), again, a tendency cultural studies has been trying to avoid (Morley, 1981: 6). The notion of "preferring mechanisms," it can be seen, still contains the risk of an implicitly referential view of language and communication. Morley's work sometimes implies that the preferred meaning is the intended one, that which is "really meant," and deviations from the preferred meanings are thus simply distortions of the intended meaning. Morley's conceptual framework, therefore, risks collapsing back into a mechanistic model simply qualified by a limited notion of polysemy.

The latent referential tendencies in the encoding/decoding model, I believe, are reflected in some conceptual ambiguities with the decoding categories themselves. If polysemy is truly a fundamental characteristic of communication, and not an occasional exception to the standard referential workings of language implied by a positivist model of language, then *all* communication is "shot through with contradiction," a property Hall ascribes only to the negotiated code.[4] While social and cultural forces clearly serve to generate relative stability in the process of negotiating decodings, this stability cannot be characterized by simple comparison with the referential ideal of preferred or dominant intended meanings. The significant issue for research, therefore, is how, given the *fundamentally* polysemic and contradictory nature of communication, social and cultural forces act to generate relative coherence and stability. To ascribe that stability to an unproblematic transmission of intended meanings "given by the dominant elite" is to bypass the crucial question. (For a detailed discussion of these and related issues, see Wren-Lewis, 1983).

A final problem with the encoding/decoding model centers around the ambiguity of the notion of an oppositional code. An oppositional code can be understood in two ways. In the first sense, an oppositional decoding is simply a coherent but different interpretation from within an opposed framework, where each dominant meaning gets supplanted by an oppositional meaning on a one-for-one basis (e.g., "national interest" equals "class interest"). This first sense of oppositional is more pronounced in much of Morley's and Hall's work, but it seems to deny what they would assert, that meaning is *continuously* generated in social and linguistic systems, not predetermined in a mechanical way by one's ideological frame. In the second sense, an oppositional decoding denies the validity of a simple one-for-one basis of meaning altogether, and instead reveals the artificial, constructed nature of the text as a whole by foregrounding what a "one-for-one" decoding leaves in the background with the assumption that the background is natural or common sense. This second sense of oppositional, scattered sparsely but regularly throughout their work (and perhaps related to the practices of various, more literary writers with whom Hall and Morley, with their more sociological slant, are engaged in dialogue), resembles what Hall and Morley take to be the politically oppositional quality of their *own* work. While both of these interpretations of the meaning of "oppositional" have interesting and complex implications, they are distinct from one another.

An incorporation of this distinction into cultural studies might help clarify both its analyses and its understanding of its own political and intellectual stance.

These problems are perhaps related to an ambiguity that underlies many of the ideas of cultural studies as they have been expressed at Birmingham. Cultural studies originally moved to the search for unconscious ideological effects because of a concern for lived relations of power. A purely interactionist focus tended to make meaning look like an innocent moment of intersubjective sharing, a moment devoid of the exercise of power and domination. The addition of critical and structuralist methodologies provided access to these potentially non-innocent aspects of communication. Unfortunately, however, the resulting model tended to relegate all effects of power to the unconscious level, and thus tended to reserve a privileged, innocent sense of meaning for the conscious level. The formula seems to have become: ideological, socially constructed meanings = unconscious meanings; obvious, "natural," taken-for-granted meanings = conscious meanings. This formula is the basis, for example, of the expectation—put into question by the results of Morley's research—that viewers would be unaware of the constructed nature of a television program if they agreed with its political position. The problem is that this formula surreptitiously retains a sense of a nonproblematic, innocent transmission of meaning on the conscious level. Of course the problem of the relations between the conscious and the unconscious is a thorny one, but, clearly, if meaning is inextricably embedded in relations of power, interest, and ideology, then this must be true for both unconscious *and* conscious meanings. The conscious level of experience must not be assumed to be unproblematic. To acknowledge the unconscious is also to problematize consciousness. The problem is encapsulated in Althusser's phrase: ideology "only appears as *'conscious'* on condition that it is *unconscious*" (Althusser, 1969). Cultural studies' oversimplification of the conscious level may be responsible, not only for the overemphasis on the "creation of the obvious" in cultural studies, but also for the latent referential tendencies and the unsatisfactorily limited notion of polysemy.

CONCLUSION

In most ways, television appears to be just an amalgam of cultural forms and social institutions that preexisted the medium itself. Television, however, has delivered the same programs to the largest audiences in history, often at the same moment. It is perhaps this sociological spectacle that has created a dual focus of attention in thought about television. On the one hand, attention has been directed at the same questions that have been asked about other cultural forms—questions about the televisual texts, their interpretation, production, and so on. But at the same time, the massive size and unique nature of television audiences has generated much interest in the audiences as objects of study in their own right. This duality, in turn, is perhaps responsible for the persistence of questions about the relations between the two poles of the texts and audiences—questions about the impact of the texts on audiences, of the feelings of the audiences towards the texts, and so on. In the past, attempts to answer these questions have often focused on one side of the duality at the expense of the extreme reduction of the other side; research that focuses on audiences often ends up simplifying great blocks of diverse and complex programming into crude categories such as "entertainment," or "information." Research that looks in great detail at particular programs, on the other hand, often refers to the vast audience and its heterogenous experiences in terms of vaguely applied sociological categories (e.g., "middle class") or, even worse, in terms of the classifications of market researchers (e.g., "daytime viewers"). A dissatisfaction with this state of affairs is one of the prime motivations for the current interest in research projects that try to do justice to *both* sides of the duality, without sacrificing one for the sake of the other. (Current examples of such projects include Newcomb and Hirsch's work in this volume, and Katz et al.'s international project on *Dallas*). Given this context, the work of Morley, Hall, Brundson, et al. has come at an opportune moment. Their efforts, particularly Morley's, represent a pathbreaking example of research that attempts to combine textual with audience analysis. Any serious student of television would benefit by exploring their work in detail.

But television research is just one aspect of the project of cultural studies, and Hall and Morley's work is just one version of culturalist television reseach. Of all the research that has been associated with the Birmingham Centre, Morley's probably comes closest to directly addressing and engaging the concerns of mainstream television reseachers. This should not be taken to mean, however, that his work can be understood as simply a research methodology or research approach, as just one more attempt to answer the question of "what does television do to us?" from within a traditional sociological framework. What Morley shares with mainstream researchers is the dual concern about audiences, programs, and the relations between them.

Any familiarity with the project of cultural studies as a whole, however, makes one realize that there are many other ways to study television, and many other ways to address the concerns typically embodied in television research. An important strain of British cultural studies, for example, can be found in the journals *Screen* and *Screen Education*. The contributors to these journals have developed an approach that, while addressing many of the same concerns as Morley's work, such as the relations between visual texts, audiences, and social and cultural structures, have relied heavily on various currents of French poststructuralism and film theory. Morley has been engaged in a dialogue with this group, and to a large degree his audience research, particularly that in *The Nationwide Audience,* should be viewed as a response to what he sees as a mechanistic view of the audience in the "Screen" group, rather than as an attempt to contribute to the tradition of audience and effects research of mainstream media research. Other important strains of cultural studies include the school that can be referred to as "discourse theory," which also addresses concerns similar to Morley's but with a stronger focus on language and the theoretical framework of certain thinkers such as Michel Foucault. Both of these strains, it should be noted, put a heavy emphasis on complex theoretical and philosophical problems, such as the question of textual, social, and cultural subjectivity, and the problem of the nature of causality and determination in social systems; these concerns, in turn, should be seen as part of the background from which research like Morley's emerges. (See Chambers et. al, 1977–1978; Coward, 1977, 1977–1978; Hall, 1980c; and Morley, 1980b.) And finally, there is the entire tradition of Marxist and non-Marxist studies of the political economy of the media, the study of various economic, institutional, and political forms of control in which media institutions take shape. While students of cultural studies have perhaps eyed this tradition warily, the questions it asks and the concerns it raises are generally thought of as a necessary, though not sufficient, ingredient to any understanding of modern cultural phenomena such as television.

This intellectual background to television research in cultural studies is not just of historical significance. It should have implications for any future research projects that are informed by the work coming out of Birmingham. Television research with the sociological goal of an objective impartial understanding is fundamentally different, irrespective of any superficial resemblances, from research that procedes, as does cultural studies, in the spirit of an engaged, concerned, "empirical dialogue." For example, the notion of causality is radically altered in the context of cultural studies. A study of, say, *Dallas,* that uses the classical notion of causality associated with "objective" scientific understanding might go to great lengths to try to isolate the single most salient factor that accounts for the worldwide popularity of the program. For cultural studies, however, with its emphasis on the necessary overdetermination of social forces, the goal would not be to isolate a single factor (a project that would be viewed as not only hopeless but pointless) but rather to ascertain the particular ways that multiple forces come together in the phenomenon of *Dallas.* This would necessitate the exploration of a multitude of phenomena ranging from international patterns of commercial distribution of television programs, to international and national political situations, to the experiences of various audience members, to the reasons why researchers are motivated to ask this question in the first place.

Hence, while the television research that has emerged from the Birmingham Centre represents a major alternative to traditional forms of research, the fundamental philosophical and political issues that characterize cultural studies as a whole should not be forgotten. In many ways, cultural studies represents a useful answer to the common calls for "active audience" research and for alternatives to research methods naively modeled on the physical sciences. Cultural studies' insistence on the importance of everyday experience, of our lived relations with the world, provides a rich framework for understanding the "active audience" in its fullest sense. The close attention to cultures, subcultures, class and institutional roles represents a sophisticated focus on the socialized nature of audiences. Cultural studies' approach to systems of meaning, its attempts to incorporate both conscious and unconscious processes of decoding and encoding, and its interest in the social nature and function of both systematic differences and similarities in maps of meaning offer a highly developed set of concepts for grappling with the central issues of perception and meaning.

But before one proceeds to compare, evaluate, and contrast cultural studies with other research, the concerns that spawned it should be kept in mind. The locus of attention in cultural studies television research is not, as it has been for the effects tradition, the relationship between the dual poles of television programs and television audiences. In fact, the very idea that research can proceed by positing for itself a single, overriding question is antithetical to the cultural studies approach. For cultural studies, to understand the significance of a news broadcast, a sitcom, or an episode of *Dallas,* one must interpret the text as inextricably enmeshed in the social, cultural, and historical conditions of the lives of its audience. The study of a television program, therefore, must inevitably lead one towards the study of those conditions. Research, moreover, must try to grasp those conditions in their full complexity, which requires a constant willingness to question not only the objects of research, but also the research itself.

NOTES

1. Associating this television research with the Birmingham Centre is slightly anachronistic. Two of the major figures involved, Stuart Hall and David Morley, are no longer working with the Centre, and the Centre is now pursuing a different set of concerns. Nonetheless, the television research in question did evolve out of the particular concerns and approaches that characterized the Birmingham Centre in the 1970s; it is for this reason that I refer to the media work of Morley, Hall, Brundson, and so on as "the work of the Birmingham Centre."

2. All references to "cultural studies," "the cultural approach," and so forth refer to the British tradition associated with Williams, Hall, Hoggart, and to some extent E. P. Thompson. This should not be confused with the related but distinct approach often called "culturalism." For a discussion and overview of both these schools of thought, see Lawrence Grossberg, "Cultural Studies Revisited and Revised," in *Communications in Transition,* ed. Mary Mander, Praeger 1984.

3. *Nationwide,* directed at a broader, more "popular" audience than *Panorama,* is in many ways similar to the U.S. program *PM Magazine,* although the former is still understood as a public affairs program, while the latter hesitates to call itself "news" at all.

4. I'd like to thank Martin Allor for pointing this out to me.

REFERENCES

Althusser, Louis (1969) "Marxism and humanism," in For Marx. New York: Pantheon.
Brundson, Charlotte and David Morley (1978) Everyday Television: Nationwide. BFI Monograph No. 10. London: British Film Institute.
Chambers, Iain, John Clarke, Ian Connell, Lidia Curti, Stuart Hall, and Tony Jefferson (1977-1978) "Marxism and culture." Screen 18 (4): 109-119.
Connell, Ian (1980) "Television news and the social contract," in S. Hall et al. (eds.) Culture, Media, Language. London: Hutchison.
Coward, Rosalind (1977) "Class, 'culture' and the social formation." Screen 18 (1): 75–106.
_____.(1977-1978) "Response." Screen 18 (4); 120-122.
Hall, Stuart (1973) "Encoding and decoding in the television discourse." Presented at the Council of Europe Colloquy on Training in the Critical Reading of Televisual Language, University of Leicester, September. (Reprinted in S. Hall et al., eds., Culture, Media, Language)

———— (1980a) "Cultural studies and the centre: some problematics and problems," in S. Hall et al. (eds.) Culture, Media, Language. London: Hutchinson.

———— (1980b) "Introduction to media studies at the centre," in S. Hall et al. (eds.) Culture, Media, Language. London: Hutchinson.

———— (1980c) "Recent developments in theories of language and ideology: a critical note," in S. Hall et al. (eds.) Culture, Media, Language. London: Hutchinson.

———— Ian Connell, and Lidia Curti (1976) "The 'unity' of current affairs television." Working Papers in Cultural Studies 9 (Spring).

Heck, Marina Camargo (1980) "The ideological dimension of media messages," in S. Hall et al. (eds.) Culture, Media, Language. London: Hutchinson.

Hobson, Dorothy (1980) "Housewives and the mass media," in S. Hall et al. (eds.) Culture, Media, Language. London: Hutchinson.

Hogart, Richard (1963) "Schools of English and contemporary society." Inaugural lecture, Centre for Contemporary Studies, University of Birmingham, 1963, reprinted in Speaking to Each Other, Vol. 2. New York: Oxford University Press, 1970.

Morley, David (1974) "Reconceptualizing the media audience: towards an ethnography of audiences." CCCS stenciled occasional paper.

———— (1980a) The Nationwide Audience: Structure and Decoding. BFI Monograph No. 11. London: British Film Institute.

———— (1980b) "Texts, readers, subjects," in S. Hall et al. (eds.) Culture, Media, Language. London: Hutchinson.

———— (1981) "The nationwide audience—a critical postscript." Screen Education 39 (Summer).

Slack, Jennifer Daryl and Martin Allor (1983) "The political and epistemological constituents of critical communications research." Journal of Communication 33 (3): 208–218.

Wren-Lewis, Justin (1983) "The encoding/decoding model: criticisms and redevelopments for research on decoding." Media, Culture and Society 5: 179–197.

Chapter 4

AN INTERPRETIVE APPROACH TO CULTURE PRODUCTION

Joli Jensen

INTEREST IN MEDIA production reflects a substantial shift in the focus of American communications inquiry. Until recently, the field has been dominated by concern with the effects of media messages or, to a lesser extent, with the nature of the messages themselves. In taking up production questions, the field has defined a set of processes that were seen as given and unproblematic in previous analyses.

The focus on production has had two interesting, and unintentional, results. First, it offers a reentry into the difficult issues of the mass culture debate. The concern of that now dated debate was with the nature and worth of cultural material; its fervor was spent on content categorization, but its charges still animate popular debate on mass communication, and it remains crucial to inquiry into contemporary life. Second, recent research on culture production foregrounds a consistent divide in communications research—the division between positivistic and interpretive modes of inquiry. These aspects are intertwined; my interest in them underlies this paper.

The advent of television sparked the mass culture debate, fueled research on media effects on audiences, and dominated analyses of content. A production focus, however, emerged in a more general context of a "sociology of the arts," with primary research originating in the study of culture producing industries, particularly the recording industry. The development of a self-defined "production of culture perspective" was intended to encompass all aspects of symbol production, including television. Recent research on television production reflects the biases and influence of a production of culture perspective; it also reveals the difficulties and weaknesses of such an approach.

The purpose of this paper is to locate and define an alternative to the dominant mode of study, which sees commercial culture production as an organizational process, with its "product," culture, defined by extracultural "constraints." The alternative I suggest is an interpretive approach, which takes as central the expressive nature of the material produced, and the symbolic negotiations that give it rise. In order to discuss this alternative, I reprise the mass culture debate and consider the usefulness of a production focus in addressing the issues it raised. I then summarize and critique the dominant production perspective, in general, and in relation to television research. Finally, I outline an interpretive approach to commercial culture production, suggesting that it more appropriately addresses the still vital issues surrounding the mass mediation of cultural forms.

THE MASS CULTURE DEBATE

The mass culture debate, as it has since been called, flourished in the fifties, and dissolved in the sixties (Carey and Kreiling, 1975). It was a debate over the nature, worth, and implications of mass mediated culture. It was conducted by a diverse assortment of intellectuals, brought together by a common subject, but bringing with them divergent political and aesthetic concerns. Their discussion, in retrospect, can be seen as having a dual focus—the categorization and description of levels of cultural material, and consideration of the effects of commercial culture on authentic expression and experience.

The debate dissolved, yet the issues that it raised remain important because they are issues that are crucial to consideration of the mass mediation of cultural material. The mass culture debate assumed that culture was a central aspect of human experience and that its nature and role in everyday life was of social, psychological, and political importance. The questions it raised about the value of various forms, the nature of their creation and consumption, their connections with social groups and mass production, and the implications of their transformation, remain questions that are both interesting and intractable.

Early in the debate, much energy was devoted toward the construction of various categories of cultural material, typifications based in aesthetic and sociological concerns. In spite of some differences in categorization, there were commonalities. Cultural material was divided historically into a higher, aristocratic level, and a lower, folk level. The forms that came in the middle were seen as based in a developing mass society, connected to the emergence of a democratized middle class. What was at issue was the nature, worth, and influence of such middle forms, since they are the ones that dominate mass communication. Macdonald (1953) sees mass mediation as spawning a tepid, oozing midcult. Shils (1971) sees mass mediation as allowing increased access to all three levels of culture, enhancing the possibility of a rich cultural life for all. Nye (1970) shares in this optimistic view, seeking popular art as an extension of folk art, predisposed to appeal to a wide audience. For Handlin (1959), the question is not whether mediated culture is worthy, but how it is related to the defined and popular culture it absorbs and transforms. His concern is with transformation rather than typology, bringing us to the second focus of the mass culture debate—the concern over the implications of commercial culture for authentic experience.

It is this focus that engages the emotions of the debaters, because it contains within it the hopes and fears of modern society. The transformation of traditional cultural forms, especially forms that have personal meaning, is a transformation that is difficult to consider dispassionately. A common thread among the writers is a deep concern that something precious, human, and vital has been or will be lost in the mass mediation of culture. Most of the concern is, logically enough, for what is deemed "elite" or "high" culture, even when the writers speak from a radical tradition. Their description of the effects of mass mediation on the nature and worth of cultural forms reveals a concern with loss and change, and can be used to illuminate the complex charge of "commercialization."

Arendt (1971) dismisses typologies like highbrow, middlebrow and lowbrow as "obviously snobbish and philistine terms." The only "nonsocial and authentic criterion for works of culture is, of course, their relative permanence and even their immortality" (p. 95). She argues that in the eighteenth and nineteenth centuries society commoditized culture, transforming it into a currency that bought status. Such transformation was a devaluation, but not a consumption—cultural objects "retained their worldly objectivity."

Mass society, in contrast, *consumes* culture in the guise of entertainment.

> The entertainment industry is confronted with gargantuan appetites, and since its wares disappear in consumption, it must constantly offer new commodities. In this predicament, those who produce for the mass media ransack the entire range of past and present culture in hopes of finding suitable material. This material, however, cannot be offered as is; it must be prepared and altered in order to become entertainment (p. 98).

Thus the essential, immortal nature of cultural objects is obliter-
ated when "life seizes upon them and consumes them for its pleasure,
for entertainment (p. 100). It is the disappearance of true culture in
mass society that Arendt fears:

> If we understand by culture what it originally meant (the Roman *cul-
> tura*—derived from *colere,* to take care of and preserve and cultivate),
> then we can say without any exaggeration that a society obsessed with
> consumption cannot at the same time be cultured or produce a cul-
> ture. . . . Culture can be safe only with those who love the world for
> its own sake, who know that without the beauty of man-made, worldly
> things which we call works of art, without the radiant glory in which
> potential imperishability is made manifest to the world and in the world,
> all human life would be futile and no greatness would endure (p. 100).

In Arendt's analysis, modern society, through its need for mass entertainment, uses up cultural objects, leaving us without material to
truly grasp and move us.[1]

The ability to be truly moved underlies Adorno's (1941) earlier
critique of popular music. He distinguishes it from serious music,
using the concept of "standardization." Popular music, he argues,
exists in a pregiven, preaccepted framework, that the listener auto-
matically supplies. The music "hears for the listener." It is composed
to make any effort in listening unnecessary, to minimize surprises,
to ensure favorable response. Standardization is a structural characteristic of popular music, linked to its industrial mediation. The
processes of promotion and distribution necessitate a standardized
process of creation that struggles to construct something both "stimulating" and "natural"—falling within an acceptable framework. Variety in popular music is a case of "pseudo-individuation," that "endows
cultural mass production with the halo of free choice . . . on the basis
of standardization itself" (p. 25). The listener does not recognize that
the music has been predigested for him, because he has the illusion
of choosing among a variety of forms.

For Adorno, the issue is not the transformation and obliteration
of cultural objects, but the function of standardization (grounded in
mass production) in the maintenance of effort to accept that which
is forced on the listener. To him, taste preferences are misguided
energy, directed at the material rather than at the forces that allow
a limited, standardized range. Mass mediated culture, in this case
popular music, is material that cannot, because of its mode of pro-

duction, genuinely extend and deepen experience. In fact, it blinds us to the real causes of our own discomfort.

Van den Haag (1968) extends this aspect of Adorno's analysis in less political terms. It is his contention that "by distracting from the human predicament and blocking individuation and experience, popular culture impoverishes life without leading to contentment" (p. 11). Whereas art deepens the perception of reality, popular culture "veils it, diverts from it, and becomes an obstacle to experiencing it" (p. 6). The mass media must, by their very nature, offer "homogenized fare to meet an average of tastes" (p. 5), and the offerings of the media are trivialized because they are continuously, indiscriminately, and casually absorbed:

> Even the most profound of experiences, articulated too often on the same level, is reduced to a cliché. The impact of each of the offerings of the mass media is thus weakened by the next one. But the impact of the stream of all mass media offerings is cumulative and strong. It lessens people's capacities to experience life itself (p. 6).

Thus, mass mediation both trivializes profound experiences expressed in art, and lessens the likelihood that the individual will recognize and cherish the experience art offers. Popular culture offers a spurious substitute to real gratification, hindering or blocking the individual from discovering and experiencing a meaningful life.

For Mills, the danger of mass mediation is that it facilitates "a sort of psychological illiteracy" (1956: 311), organizing our external reality into stereotypes, entering into our experience of ourselves, confining us to a limited range of opinion, and encroaching on face-to-face discussion. In his analysis, "our standards of reality tend to be set by these media rather than by our own fragmentary experience." Accordingly, even direct contact with reality is organized by stereotypes. "It takes long and skillful training to so uproot such stereotypes that an individual sees things freshly, in an unstereotyped manner" (p. 312). Stereotypes operate on our inner reality as well. The media provide us with models of conduct that tell us who we are, what we want to become, how to become it, and how to escape if we cannot become who we want to be. To Mills, the media invent and sustain a pseudo-world in which "the gaps between the identity and aspiration lead to technique and/or to escape" (p. 314).

Mills's critique of mass mediation includes both news and entertainment, and links psychological implications with political rather than explicitly cultural concerns. The more specific question of the commercialization of "authentic" culture and experience addressed by Arendt, Adorno, and Van den Haag, is directly confronted by Handlin.

Handlin (1959) suggests that the communication of culture through the mass media has had a disturbing effect on popular culture. He notes that popular culture lacks a history, so that it is difficult to ascertain the exact effects of mass mediation on it. But he argues that the popular culture of the late nineteenth century is different from contemporary fare in several ways. Popular culture, in his analysis, dealt directly with a concrete world that was intensely familiar to its audience. It involved a direct rapport between creators and consumers; they sprang from the same milieu, and maintained firm identification with it. Also, it was tied deeply to tradition and was capable of arousing in the audience sentiments of wonder and awe. People found in popular culture "a means of communication among themselves and the answers to certain significant questions that they were asking about the world around them" (p. 67).

The effect of mediation on this culture was threefold. It altered earlier forms of control, deprived the material of much of its relevance to lived experience, and opened a gulf between the artist and the audience. To Handlin, mass mediated culture has an aimless quality, due in part to the vastness of its audience, and the scale of its production organizations. The performer and writer in it is doomed to "sterility" because they can address themselves only to "the empty outlines of the residual American" (p. 68). All manner of fare is presented on an identical plateau of irrelevance. The audience accepts passively, without differentiation or choice, and so cannot establish meaningful, direct relationships with the material or its performers. Mass mediation weakens the rapport between creator and consumer, making their communication both hazy and fragmentary. The performer is bound up in the medium, not the milieu of the audience, and can thus no longer sense its mood and connect with it.

Ultimately, then, mass mediated culture cannot serve the same communicative functon as popular culture. Handlin suggests that much of the earlier popular culture was "simply swallowed up in the new forms," and that what survived "existed in obsolete enclaves, without the old vitality" (p. 70). Paradoxically, the effectiveness of cultural communication was diminished as its techniques improved.

What becomes clear, in these analyses of mass mediation within the mass culture debate, is that (1) cultural material is seen as capable of deepening and extending experience, and (2) mass mediation is seen as deleteriously affecting that capacity by transforming us and/ or the cultural material we share in. It consumes cultural objects that have real meaning (Arendt) or swallows up forms that allow real communication (Handlin) or blocks us from real experience (Van den Haag) or from recognizing that we are not experiencing the real (Adorno). It infiltrates our knowledge of ourselves and each other (Mills) and drowns us in the trivial and mundane (Macdonald). The only writers who treat mass mediation with equanimity are Shils and Nye, who see such mediation as extending, rather than transforming, cultural material and experience.

The typologies on which these analyses are based are inherently elitist, and reveal the difficulty of discussing culture in nonjudgmental terms. Absolute aesthetic criteria of subtlety, depth, and complexity are used to distinguish among cultural forms, as are sociological distinctions of status and class. The two are unintentionally intertwined, and even attempts at nonevaluative hierarchies eventually founder on implicit evaluations.[2] The charges of elitism combined, possibly, with the rapid dating of examples, helped usher the mass culture debate from the intellectual scene.

Yet the debate incorporated a still vital issue—the relationships among culture, experience, and mass communication. Its terrain of typologies and obsolete examples has been left behind, but the issues linger, implicit in academic and popular discussions.

A production perspective can illuminate the still vital issues of the mass culture debate. Its crucial assumption—that mass mediation alters and transforms symbolic material—can be illuminated by direct examination of commercial culture production.

How is culture constructed and/or transformed in mass mediation? Is it commercialized, trivialized, homogenized, falsified? If so, how? Why? How permeable is the process? How inevitable? A production perspective, focusing on the ways in which mass mediated culture is created, could address these concerns.

Yet the dominant mode of production inquiry prevents such considerations. As will be shown, the dominant mode of inquiry is grounded in a transmission model of communication, one which sees culture as a product that is created, disseminated, and consumed (Carey, 1975). The focus of inquiry is on determining the "forces" that "shape" the product along the route. Cultural material is conceptualized as a dependent variable, reflecting the influence of extracultural production factors. Such conceptualization, I argue, artifically severs expressive material from its natural relationship to its creation and consumption. It also prevents connection to the mass culture debate, because it prevents consideration of culture as symbolic material that expresses and extends experience.

THE PRODUCTION OF
CULTURE PERSPECTIVE

When Peterson (1976a, 1976b) first proposed a "reorientation of the sociology of culture around the problem of production," he suggested that it could serve as an alternative to the continuing debate over the relationship between culture and social structure that had polarized scholars into self-perpetuating idealist versus materialist camps. Rather than entering the debate, he suggests that we should take the alternative tack of studying the processes by which elements of culture are fabricated.

In this article, Peterson defines production as the "processes of creation, manufacture, marketing, distribution, exhibiting, inculcation, evaluation and consumption" (p. 10). The advantages of focusing on the "production milieu," as he calls it, are that (1) research is circumscribed and can become cumulative, (2) concepts from industrial, organizational, and occupational sociology, social psychology, and economics can be used, and (3) parallels among art, science, and religion will become more apparent.

Peterson suggests two modes of analysis—diachronic and synchronic. Synchronic study would focus on the production process from creation to consumption, while diachronic study would explain changes in culture over time. Finally, he suggests that the production perspective might crystallize a new "genetic" perspective on the society-culture relationship, where culture is the code by which social structures reproduce themselves. This, he suggests, might reinvigorate a general sociology exhausted by the debate between materialists and idealists.

His prolegomenon locates the production perspective in a metaphoric "genetic" theory of the society-culture relationship. It is to study the "production milieu" in terms of processes, using methods developed in established social sciences. It studies both the process of production from creation to consumption and the changes in cultural production and material over time.

The production of culture perspective, in relation to popular culture in general, was redefined six years later by Clinton Sanders (1982). It has become a "model" as well as a perspective, a model of how organizational constraints affect production activities. It is Sanders's view that two foci of investigation have emerged since Peterson's article—cooperative social interaction and the structural features that constrain the social process. His definition, then, explicitly includes what he calls "coordinated social behavior," as well as the structural and organizational features of the milieu in which they operate.

What is important about Sanders's analysis is that he clearly focuses on the role of people as "consciously and creatively involved" in culture production. He suggests that interactional as well as structural and organizational factors are to be examined in culture production. In making his case in this manner, he highlights a central problem of the production of culture perspective: the definition of the "production milieu."

To Sanders, the production milieu includes the "shared conventional understandings that make collective action possible" (p. 71) as well as structural and organizational features of the production environment. He goes so far as to say that organization is the *result* of coordinated social behavior, not the determiner of it. This is an explicitly theoretical statement that runs counter to the work that dominates production study in America. The context of production, in work by Peterson and others, is a milieu defined by organizational and technological constraints, not shared conventional understandings.

Both Peterson and Hirsch offer a variety of definitions of what those constraints are, and how they operate. In "Processing Fads and Fashions" (1972), Hirsch develops a filtration model of culture industries, where an overabundance of cultural material is gradually limited using three "coping strategies"—contact men at organizational boundaries, overproduction and differential promotion of product, and co-optation of gatekeepers at the level of the media. The production environment, in this case, is viewed as a system, as a "single, concrete and stable network of identifiable and interacting components" (p. 642).

In another article (1976), Hirsch considers the production milieu in terms of a "task environment" of suppliers, customers, competitors and regulatory agencies. Here he clearly views the production milieu as a situation, constrained by external structural and social forces, rather than as a shared understanding that makes possible collective action. He argues elsewhere that the task environment must be operationalized by the independent sociological researcher because, "while W. I. Thomas' famous dictum concerning the definition of reality is an admirable method of determining respondents' *perceptions,* it is at best a risky venture to equate participant's views with independent sociological judgment and analysis" (Hirsch, 1975).

Peterson, too, has offered a variety of definitions of the context of production. It is a system of collaborative production influenced by such factors as organization structure, technology, law, market, reward systems, and the like (Ryan and Peterson, 1982). It is a complex apparatus that is interposed between culture creators and consumers (Peterson, 1978). It is the "social, legal and economic milieu in which symbolic products are produced," in terms of the constraints of law, technology, the market, organizational structure, and occupational careers (1982). For Peterson, then, the context of production apparently both contains, and is constrained by "factors" like role definition, organizational structure, industry relationships, and technology change.

In production research, industry structure, market turbulence, product image, new technologies, licensing changes, and organizational roles, among other things, have been linked to changes in the nature of commercial culture. Are they all equally important? Is each autonomous, or do they determine each other? What is their connection to the rest of the world? And how do they manage to make culture? By leaving the definition of the production milieu to the interests and talents of the investigator, the production of culture perspective has encouraged voluminous work of limited use in addressing what shapes and limits cultural material, or in addressing relationships between cultural forms and experience. Culture, as symbolic material, has no particularity or predispositions; it is a product reflecting only the structure and process of its production.

This treatment of culture as "that which is shaped" characterizes recent work on television production. Ettema (1982) examined the creation of three children's television pilots and explained them as each being "a solution to a puzzle formulated within the organization." Turow (1982) defines several television series as being "innovative," then supports several hypotheses on the organizational contexts that promote innovation. Pekurny (1982) examines "coping mechanisms" such as ratings, producer track records, and formulas, and their influence in determining television programming. In these cases the material itself, the nature and character of that which is constructed, is tangential to the analysis. This treatment of culture is characteristic of positivistic social science, because, as Kreiling points out, "symbols are not real or consequential to most sociologists, who try to explain their manifest forms and intrinsic meanings into some 'real' world of forces behind them" (1978).

Related to this treatment of culture as a product of "more real" production forces is the consideration of content in a transmission context. Producers of television programming, in Elliot's seminal work (1972), are seen as part of a "relay system" between society as source and society as audience. Mass communication is criticized for leaving the audience "largely on its own to respond to the materials put before it" (p. 164). In other words, content is created somewhere, travels to an audience, who "reacts" to it on its own.

To summarize, the production of culture perspective, congruent with mainstream American sociological thought, treats cultural material as a reflection of more real organizational and social processes. Television programming, as cultural material, is interesting to the researcher in terms of its ability to demonstrate the actions of the forces being studied. Beyond this, the perspective treats culture production as part of a linear process of information transferral, using an industrial, mechanistic metaphor of culture fabrication.

An alternative to this view of culture production depends on a significant reconceptualization of the nature of cultural material, and its role in collective life. Culture is *not* defined as a container of messages processed along a line from sender to receiver, but as the means through which people construct meaningful worlds in which to live. This "ritual" view (Carey, 1975) is linked to a larger recasting of the nature and relationship of culture, communication, and experience. The interpretive approach to culture production is grounded in this recasting and is to be understood in relation to it.

CULTURE, INTERPRETATION, AND COMMUNICATION

To say that culture matters, that it is the means through which people construct meaningful worlds in which to live, is to place it at the center of human life. It is to suggest that it is through culture that we establish our identity, our connections with each other, and our understanding of what it means to live in the world. Cultural material maps a world of social relations (Carey and Kreiling, 1975); it is in it and through it that we find ourselves, and each other.

Cultural material is symbolic material that both expresses and constitutes experience. The world we live and act in is given shape, form, and meaning through our symbolic constructions; in turn, these symbolic constructions offer us worlds in which to dwell, when the lights go down, the coin falls in the jukebox, the page is turned. To divide the human world into "real life" and "symbolic accounts" is to sunder artificially a rich and necessary interaction between lived experience and constructed accounts. As humans, we construct accounts in the process of experiencing, and experience in the process of constructing accounts.

Thus, cultural material is not diversion or escape. It confirms, explains, extends, and contains our lives. Moreover, culture is not a reflection of more real psychological or social forces; its role is constitutive, not reflective. We live our feelings and our relationships in and through culture, not in some other realm of which culture is a report. And finally, culture is not a veil of false consciousness that can and should be lifted to reveal "real" experience—we know and experience through symbolic constructions. Forms of culture can be more or less deeply implicated in lived experience, but experience cannot be separated from symbolic expression.

Culture, in this analysis, is the interpretive process made manifest. It is material that is constructed to make sense of the world, and to study it is to study the ways in which we together construct a world that makes sense. The "interpretive turn" is an intellectual approach to inquiry in which "both the object of investigation—the web of language, symbol and institutions that constitutes signification—and the tools by which investigation is carried out share inescapably the same pervasive context that is the human world" (Rabinow and Sullivan, 1979).

From an interpretive perspective, the human world is a circle of meaning that we can never truly surpass. It contains interpretations and practices that are not reducible to anything else. We live within this circle of meaning as self-interpreting and self-defining beings, suspended in webs of signification we ourselves have created.

To study the human world is to attempt to understand a cultural world of shared meanings, practices, and symbols. We, as investigators, live within this world, and so, in inquiry, there is "no privileged position, no absolute perspective, no final recounting" (Carey, 1982). There are, instead, interpretations of interpretations that illuminate a common world of meaning.

This is different from a positivist perspective, which seeks to find a truth *behind* symbols, practices, and customs. The positivist seeks a detached standpoint from which to gather brute data, to be combined into context-free categories. Rabinow and Sullivan argue that the reductionist ideal (to develop stable, self-evident, context-free categories) is evident in structuralism as the reduction of meaning to operationally defined rules. To the structuralist, logical structures and rules of inference exist prior to, and independent of, everyday understandings. This perspective runs counter to the interpretive turn, which studies varieties of cultural meaning, rather than seeking that which supposedly lies behind them.

What constitutes reality, and adequate knowledge of it, has divided inquiry into camps that have been variously labeled science versus the humanities, objectivity versus subjectivity, rationalism versus romanticism, analysis versus interpretation, and administrative versus critical research. Carey (1982) discusses the divide as originating in Vico's response to Descartes, and appearing in media studies as administrative versus critical research. He redefines the distinction within communication research as being between objectivism and expressivism—in a debate over whether reality is neutral, contingent fact, or an expressive product of human action. He locates this divide in the American context in an exchange between Walter Lippmann and John Dewey, and ultimately, in two metaphors of knowledge: vision and speech. He argues that it is in speaking, in conversation, that language acts to express the world—it constitutes a world, rather than merely representing it. Language does not refer to an external, picturable reality, rather it creates a shared reality in conversation.

Communication, then, is a constructive, not a reportorial act. From a ritual view, it is the process through which we symbolically construct meaningful worlds in which to live. It is more than words or beliefs, it is "at once a structure of human action—activity, process, practice—an ensemble of expressive forms, and a structured and structuring set of social relations" (Carey, 1982). An interpretive perspective, then, defines the human world as cultural, to be investigated by the same tools that construct it. Communication is the central human process, a process that actively constitutes the world.

From this perspective, it is impossible to study culture as a product of noninterpretive forces. The character and nature of cultural material are determined by the assumptions, biases, and beliefs of the producers about their work, the business, the audience, the times, the genre. Cultural material is not "processed" like soap by organizational, technical, and economic "factors," it is constructed in and through interpretations. To study its genesis, one must study what holds true in the world of its production, a world centered on expressive material, and encompassing both the producers and audience for which they create. In the following section, I discuss the concept of a cultural world, in relation to the study of commercial production.

CULTURE PRODUCTION IN A CULTURAL WORLD

To conceive of a culture production in terms of a "world" centered on expressive material in which people share is to do two things.

First, it restores the particularity of expressive material, without resorting to absolute criteria, because it defines the nature of symbolic material from within the interpretive world of the participants. That cultural forms vary and are distinguishable from each other is seen as linked to the values, beliefs, and practices each form embodies, rather than as a result of their inherent perception, subtlety, or complexity. That different cultural forms are associated with different social groups is considered in terms of habits and styles of life and thought, expressed and invoked through the material, not exteriorly defined by income, education, or class. Thus, the hierarchical underpinnings of the mass culture debate's typifications are recast as definitional characteristics from within the world of the participants. That such definitions "matter" is clear from the ways forms define themselves against each other; that such definitions are "real" follows from the interpretive approach to inquiry.

The second characteristic of the conceptualization of a cultural form in terms of a cultural world is that it restores creation, content, and consumption to their natural relationship. In practice, symbolic material is created in connection with its consumption. To consider content separately from its processes of creation and consumption is to sunder it from its expressive relationship to the lives and people it speaks for and to. To consider consumption as a separate and distinct process is to transform culture into a "force" that enters people's lives from the outside; culture is functionalized as being "consumed" by people seeking psychological or social gratification. To separate creation from its relationship to content and consumption is to construct a mechanical analysis that flattens the particularity of the world a cultural form expresses and invokes.

This definition of a cultural world, embodying a natural relationship between expressive material and its practices does not, of course, deny the existence or "reality" of institutions, technologies, and social structure, or their role in the "setting of limits and the exertions of pressures within which variable social practices are profoundly affected but not necessarily controlled" (Williams, 1975). To conceive of a cultural world, with expressive material at its center, is not to deny the existence or influence of the material world. It is only to suggest that the realities of the material world are known, grasped, revised, and reworked through interpretive processes, evidenced and enshrined in cultural material. To study a cultural world is to gain access to the means through which we make and remake worlds, worlds that both express, and are shaped by, patterns of collective action defined as political, social, economic, and institutional.

The concept of a cultural world, based on an interpretive approach to inquiry, considers symbolic material in relation to the practices of the people creating and sharing in the material. An interpretive perspective allows culture to express the meanings of its own production, meanings that are constructed by people within a cultural world.

This interpretive perspective has not been explicitly articulated in contemporary media research. Studies on aspects of culture industries have been done in ways that appear, on the surface, to address culture production from an interpretive perspective. Yet they continue, in various ways, to sunder content from practices of production and consumption.

Sanders (1982) locates a split between studies that focus on structure and organization, and studies that focus on interaction and shared conventional understandings. Production conventions coordinate social behavior. Howard Becker is perhaps the clearest example of someone who takes the notion of production conventions seriously. He sees them as underlying patterns of cooperation. "Conventions make possible the easy and efficient coordination of activity among artists and support personnel" (1982).

Concern with conventions is not the same as concern with constructed meanings. Conventions are treated, by Becker and others, as structures that affect the process of production. They are invoked, and left unexamined, and unconnected to symbolic material. The study of conventions has been a mechanistic one, an attempt to describe how commercial production works, with conventions invoked as an aspect underlying production. But what are the conventions? How are they negotiated? How do they articulate, and how are they articulated by, cultural material? To be taken seriously within an interpretive framework, artistic conventions must be seen as values that define and express a world, not merely invoked as expeditors of collective behavior.

Becker himself has moved from a position that takes constructed meaning as central, to one that locates it as part of a more general organizational process. In an article drawn from his master's thesis (Becker, 1951), he describes the conceptions jazz musicians have of themselves, their work, and the audience. Through evocative quotes (from participant observation work), he illuminates a rich interpretive world. But in his recent book *Art Worlds,* organizations, not beliefs, are described. He constructs a general description of collective behavior, but no "art world" of meaning and practice is illuminated (Becker, 1982).

Cawelti (1978) sees conventions as one of four major elements in a "pattern of process" called artistic matrices. His argument is an attempt to renegotiate the mass culture debate by defining four model matrices (communal, mythical, professional, and reflexive) as the result of different cultural processes. This analysis divides creation and reception into various components with relative autonomy. Conventions are but one component; the creator, the medium, and the audience are the other three. The process of culture production is broken down into parts, and questions of meaning negotiation are relegated to one separate-but-equal part of the formulaic process of matrix definition.

In terms of television production, Elliot and Chaney (1969) attempt to integrate the sociology of art with organization theory and develop a theoretical framework that involves the producer's definitions within social contexts. They grapple with the connections between production and content, seeing as definitional what is deemed appropriate by the producers. This is negotiated; the program is a result of such negotiation. Their analysis is hampered by a transmission view of communication, but underlying their analysis is a serious attempt to view production as a meaningful symbolic process, rather than a merely organizational one.

Tuchman (1978) and Epstein (1973) both examine news production. Epstein wants to examine the process by which news is gathered, synthesized, and presented—he is interested in the process of selecting and organizing information. His analysis is essentially a filtration model, where information is packaged and transported along a route from real world through organization to audience. Tuchman takes a deeper look at what is being reported, arguing for viewing news as a construction of reality set within a web of facticity. Altheide (1976) and Gitlin (1980) also see news as a symbolic construction of reality. Their analyses are self-consciously interpretive, seeing newsworkers as invoking and applying norms in a reflexive definitional process that is news reporting. Their analyses resemble what I define as an interpretive approach to production, but deal with news, not commercial culture production.

Newcomb and Alley (1982), in an article that is framed within a ritual approach to communication, consider production from the point of view of producers who "personalize" their work. Their study, while rich, is a close examination of personal beliefs, not a study of the shared assumptions that define a cultural world. Qualitative analysis of individual interpretations is the basis for understanding a cultural world, but such analysis must seek that which is taken for granted, so basic as to be unspoken, not that which is idiosyncratic or personal. It must also connect that which is expressed in the material with what is believed by its producers and the audiences who find meaning in it. Theirs is a beginning and addresses the issue of production permeability, but does not directly address questions of the nature and predispositions of mass mediation.

This brief description of studies with interpretive characteristics illustrates the nature and difficulty of an interpretive approach to television production. In the final section, I summarize my discussion, in order to delineate the nature of an interpretive approach to commercial culture production.

SUMMARY

I have argued, in this paper, for the development of an interpretive approach to commercial culture production. It is my contention that the dominant style of production inquiry is grounded in positivistic social science and in a transmission view of communication. I criticize this approach as denying the very thing that makes production inquiry both interesting and useful—the expressive nature of the material itself. I suggest that it is through taking symbolic expression seriously that we can illuminate the actual nature of culture production and address the real issues of the mass culture debate. Those issues were taken up at the beginning of this paper; they will be considered again, after a brief detour to delineate more clearly what is involved in an interpretive approach to production.

I have described a conception of a cultural world, one centered on expressive material, and including those who construct and share in it. Such a conception restores connections between content, production, and consumption. Each aspect is by its nature implicated in the others. My suggestion is that, in studying production, we take the expressive nature of the material as seriously in inquiry as it is taken in actual practice. The symbolic material at the center of a cultural world is an arena of negotiation; it is in and through it that ideas, values, and beliefs are worked. An interpretive approach to production would involve a close and careful reading of what is being negotiated, how that negotiation develops and changes over time, what is taken as given, what is up for grabs. It would include analyses of what eventually becomes public, from what is suggested, and how that is determined, by people's beliefs about the business, the materials, the audience, the times. Such beliefs, of course, are articulated in practices. An interpretive analysis would demonstrate the existence and connection of production practices and beliefs.

Such analysis requires qualitative methods designed to sensitively articulate the assumptions and expressions of others. The goal is to determine and express "what holds true" in the cultural world being examined, since that is what determines the nature and character of symbolic expression. In other words, we as investigators seek to "gain access to the conceptual world in which our subjects live so that we, in some extended sense of the term, converse with them" (Geertz, 1973).

What can this mode of inquiry offer to the mass culture debate? First, it offers a clear alternative to the division of cultural material along hierarchical dimensions. While it is intuitively obvious that cultural material varies, it is difficult to construct a typology that is not, somehow, based in an evaluative scheme. What this approach offers is a way to consider cultural forms and genres in terms of beliefs and practices, rather than in terms of intrinsic worth. Music, film, radio and television, books and magazines are based in different constellations of habits and values. Genres within these forms are also centered in specific beliefs and practices—country music is not rock, soap operas are not crime dramas, musicals are not skin flicks, the *New Yorker* is not *People* magazine. Their commonalities and differences become clear when the constellations of beliefs embodied in practice are explicated. Considering them as high, low, or mass culture, as in the mass culture debate, or as products of culture-producing industries, as in the production of culture perspective, denies the very characteristics that give them their expressive particularity.

This need not, however, lead us into a sanguine relativism. The mass culture debate is based in a concern with the influence of mediation on authentic expression. Underlying it is a belief that there is a worthwhile and natural relationship between experience and expression, and that commercial culture production disrupts or deforms that relation. The charges of standardization, homogenization, trivialization, and destruction are based in a belief that modernization is "a transformation of the meanings by which men live, a revolution of the structures of consciousness" (Berger, 1973: 2). Mass mediation of culture is deeply implicated in modern life, and its influence cannot be sunnily denied by a relativistic study of the particularities of cultural worlds.

But such study is the appropriate beginning. Close and careful analyses of what holds true in the interpretive world of commercial production will not, and cannot, tell us whether the culture at its center is trivializing and deforming our experience. But it gives us a beginning toward that knowledge, because it takes seriously the connections between experience and expression, and reveals the taken-for-granted assumptions in which we share. It allows us to address the charges of the mass culture debate from a position of complicity, not judgment. From the understandings we gain of how and why commercial culture is what it is, we can better ask questions of what it can become. That understanding, in relation to the mass culture debate, requires an acknowledgement of the relationship between experience and symbolic expressions of it. This paper argues, ultimately, for that acknowledgement in production inquiry.

NOTES

1. Arendt's metaphor of "consumption" seems strong, but applies to phenomena like the *Mona Lisa,* which in the original now resembles a giant postcard, and Hamlet's soliloquy, which has been parodied to the point that it cannot be heard afresh.
2. Herbert Gans's *Popular Culture and High Culture* attempts to construct a non-evaluative collection of "taste cultures," but he ultimately evaluates them in relation to the level of education required to partake of them (Schocken Books, 1975, p. 130).

REFERENCES

Adorno, T. W. (1941) "On popular music." Studies in Philosophy and Social Sciences 9: 17–48.
Altheide, D. L. (1976) Creating Reality: How TV News Distorts Events. Beverly Hills, CA: Sage.
Arendt, Hannah (1971) "Society and culture," in B. Rosenberg and D. M. White (eds.) Mass Culture Revisited. New York: Van Nostrand Reinhold.
Becker, Howard S. (1951) "The professional dance musician and his audience." American Journal of Sociology 57 (September): 137–144.
———— (1982 Art Worlds. Berkeley: University of California Press.
Berger, Peter (1973) The Homeless Mind. New York: Vintage.
Blumer, Jay G. and Elihu Katz [eds.] (1975) The Uses of Mass Communication: Current Perspectives on Gratifications Research. Beverly Hills, CA: Sage.
Carey, James W. (1975) "A cultural approach to communications." Communication 2 (1): 1-22.
———— (1982) "The mass media: the critical view," in M. Burgoon (ed.) Communication Yearbook 5. New Brunswick, NJ: Transaction Books.
———— and Albert L. Kreiling (1975) "Popular culture and uses and gratifications:

notes toward an accommodation," in J. G. Blumer and E. Katz (eds.) The Uses of Mass Communication: Current Perspectives on Gratifications Research. Beverly Hills, CA: Sage.

Cawelti, John G. (1978) "The concept of artistic matrices." Communication Research 5 (3).

DiMaggio, Paul and Paul M. Hirsch (1976) "Production organizations in the arts," in R. A. Peterson (ed.) The Production of Culture. Beverly Hills, CA: Sage.

Elliot, Philip (1972) The Making of a Television Series: A Case Study in the Sociology of Culture. Beverly Hills, CA: Sage.

―――― and David Chaney (1969) "A sociological framework for the study of television production." Sociological Review 17.

Epstein, Edward J. (1973) News from Nowhere: Television and the News. New York: Vintage.

Ettema, James S. (1982) "The organizational context of creativity: a case study from public television," in J. S. Ettema and D. C. Whitney (eds.) Individuals in Mass Media Organizations: Creativity and Constraint. Beverly Hills, CA: Sage.

―――― and D. Charles Whitney [eds.] (1982) Individuals in Mass Media Organizations: Creativity and Constraint. Beverly Hills, CA: Sage.

Geertz, Clifford (1973) "A thick description: toward an interpretive theory of culture," in The Interpretation of Cultures. New York: Basic Books.

Gitlin, Todd (1980) The Whole World Is Watching: Mass Media in the Making and Unmaking of the New Left. Berkeley: University of California Press.

Handlin, Oscar (1959) "Comments on mass and popular culture," in N. Jacobs, Culture of the Millions? Princeton, NJ: D. Van Nostrand.

Hirsch, Paul (1972) "Processing fads and fashions: an organization-set analysis of cultural industry systems." American Journal of Sociology 77: 639–659.

―――― (1975) "Organizational analysis and industrial sociology." American Sociologist 10 (February): 3–12.

Kreiling, Albert (1978) "Toward a cultural studies approach for the sociology of popular culture." Communication Research 5 (3): 240–263.

Macdonald, Dwight (1953) "A theory of mass culture." Diogenes 3 (Summer): 1–17.

Mills, C. Wright (1956) The Power Elite. Oxford: Oxford University Press.

Newcomb, Horace and Robert Alley (1982) "The producer as artist: commercial television," in J. S. Ettema and D. C. Whitney (eds.) Individuals in Mass Media Organizations: Creativity and Constraint. Beverly Hills, CA: Sage.

Nye, Russell (1970) "The popular arts and the popular audience," in The Unembarrassed Muse. New York: Dial Press.

Pekurny, Robert (1982) "Coping with television production," in J. S. Ettema and D. C. Whitney (eds.) Individuals in Mass Media Organizations: Creativity and Constraint. Beverly Hills, CA: Sage.

Peterson, Richard A. [ed.] (1976a) The Production of Culture. Beverly Hills, CA: Sage.

―――― (1976b) "The production of culture: a prolegomenon," The Production of Culture. Beverly Hills, CA: Sage.

―――― (1978) "The production of cultural change: the case of contemporary country music." Social Research 45 (2).

―――― (1982) "Five constraints on the production of culture: law, technology, market, organizational structure and occupational careers." Journal of Popular Culture 6 (2): 143–153.

Rabinow, Paul and William M. Sullivan (1979) "The interpretive turn: emergence of an approach," in Interpretive Social Science: A Reader. Berkeley: University of California Press.

Rosenberg, Bernard and David M. White [eds.] (1971) Mass Culture Revisited. New York: Van Nostrand Reinhold.

Ryan, John and Richard A. Peterson (1982) "The product image: the fate of creativity in country music songwriting," in J. S. Ettema and D. C. Whitney (eds.) Individuals in Mass Media Organizations: Creativity and Constraint. Beverly Hills, CA: Sage.

Sanders, Clinton (1982) "Structural and interactional features of popular culture production: an introduction to the production of culture perspective." Journal of Popular Culture 16 (2): 66–74.

Shils, Edward (1971) "Mass society and its culture," in B. Rosenberg and D. M. White (eds.) Mass Culture Revisited. New York: Van Nostrand Reinhold.

Tuchman, Gaye (1978) Making News: A Study in the Construction of Reality. New York: Free Press.

Turow, Joseph (1982) "Unconventional programs on commercial television: an organizational perspective," in J. S. Ettema and D. C. Whitney (eds.) Individuals in Mass Media Organizations: Creativity and Constraint. Beverly Hills, CA: Sage.

Van den Haag, Ernest (1968) "Of happiness and despair we have no measure," in A. Casty (ed.) Mass Media and Mass Man. New York: Holt, Rinehart & Winston.

Williams, Raymond (1975) Television: Technology and Cultural Form. New York: Schocken.

Chapter 5

ENCOURAGING SIGNS
Television and the Power of Dirt, Speech, and Scandalous Categories

John Hartley

Men make their own history, but they do not make it just as they please; they do not make it under circumstances chosen by themselves, but under circumstances directly encountered, given and transmitted from the past. The tradition of all the dead generations weighs like a nightmare on the brain of the living. And just when they seem engaged in revolutionizing themselves and things, in creating something that has never yet existed, precisely in such periods of revolutionary crisis they anxiously conjure up the spirits of the past to their service and borrow from them names, battle-cries and costumes in order to present the new scene of world history in this time honoured disguise and this borrowed language.

Karl Marx, *18th Brumaire of Louis Bonaparte*

This chapter takes up the theme of borrowed languages; both those of television itself and those that have become established within analytical discourses in the study of television. I want to argue that some of the most familiar analytical categories we use to study television are in need of rethinking, and that television itself will emerge from this process shorn of its time honoured disguise. Instead, television will be seen for what it is—a new scene of world history that supplants what has traditionally been understood as the power of speech. Despite our habit of anxiously conjuring up the spirits of the past to exorcise its power, I shall argue that for modern, industrialized societies, television *is* the power of speech. To begin with, then, I want to make a problem out of the received notions of textual analysis,

AUTHOR'S NOTE: This chapter was originally presented orally, and signs of that previous form will appear occasionally as palimpsests under its written surface.

especially where texts and readers have been conceptualized as an abstract binary opposition, with meaning somehow batted back and forth between the two.

TEXTS

The practice of "reading" television texts has demonstrated fairly clearly that individual segments, programs, series, and so forth are far from unitary in their meaning. In fact television provides a convincing instance of the structuralist axiom of "no intrinsic meaning." Television texts are polysemic, and they resist attempts even to identify their smallest signifying units since there are so many different kinds on the screen at once: visual, verbal, aural, discursive, narrative, and so on. But even though television texts are saturated with meaningfulness, there is no textual warrant for any particular meaning to be privileged as "true." The best that the analyst can do is to show how texts thmselves try to limit and close their own meaningfulness with ideological "preferred readings" and so forth. But the problem of the text goes further than this. Television is recalcitrant when it comes to identifying where the text should stop. Quite apart from the problem of rationalizing what must in the end be an arbitrary act, namely the choice of this rather than that as the "text" to analyze, television cannot be reduced, even for the sake of analysis, to "what's on telly." The forms of television representation are not specific to television; its discourses are produced, regulated, and reproduced just as much off-screen as they are on it: its institutionalization of *these* rather than *those* signifying practices cannot be explained by looking at the practices by themselves; and even its own programs are made meaningful "outside" television itself, in newspapers, magazines, conversions, learned papers, and the like. In short, television texts do not supply us with a warrant for considering them either as unitary or as structurally bounded into an inside and an outside. If television has a distinctive feature, it is that it is a "dirty" category.

READERS

The notion of the reader is similarly a problem. Traditionally conceptualized (for the sake of analysis) as either one individual reader or a mass of individual readers, the category "reader" has become established as both unitary and abstract. But, as anyone who studies television must know, there are differences in the way the same bit of television can be watched by the "same" individual reader. Such differences may depend on mood, company, or place, but there is also the question of which discursive resource, or combination of resources, the person brings to bear on the program. Today I may be "reading television" as critic, but tonight I'll be "watching television" as "audience." And sometimes (always) these two ways of watching will slide into each other or even contradict each other. Following from this, it is hard to sustain the notion of a unitary individual who is in possession of a unitary subjectivity in view of television. Without (necessarily) claiming that everyone here is schizophrenic, it is possible to use television as a way of showing how no individuals have unitary subjectivity in their possession, but rather there are clusters of significant identifications that may combine, split, contradict, or confirm each other in provisional orientations that will for the time being serve the purposes of a social "I." These identifications form an extensive, changing, and informal paradigm that is carried in various discourses. What sense "I" might make of television depends, therefore, on the discursive resources available. But although "I" might identify with them, not all of them fit each other— some will necessarily marginalize or deny others, and some are more obvious, wellworn and time honoured than others. Both paradigmatically (the discursive identifications) and syntagmatically (their combinations/contradictions), "I" is a "dirty" category too.

DIRT[1]

It seems to me that the dirtiness both of television texts and of individual readers is a matter worth looking into further. The notion that both of these categories are *by definition* dirty is not a new one. In respect of television, Hans Magnus Enzensberger has put it forcefully:

> The electronic media do away with cleanliness; they are by their nature "dirty." That is part of their productive power. . . . The desire for a cleanly defined "line" and for the suppression of "deviations" is anachronistic and now serves only one's own need for security. (1972: 105).

As for individuals, this is how Edmund Leach puts it:

> Individuals do not live in society as isolated individuals with clear-cut boundaries; they exist as individuals interconnected in a network by

relations of power and domination. Power, in this sense, resides in the interfaces between individuals, in ambiguous boundaries. The logical paradox is that (i) I can only be completely sure of what I am if I cleanse myself of all boundary dirt, but (ii) a completely clean 'I' with no boundary dirt would have no interface relations with the outside world or with other individuals. Such an 'I' would be free from the domination of others but would in turn be wholly impotent. The interface is the opposition:

$$\text{clean/dirty} = \text{impotence/potency}$$

and hence that *power is located in dirt*. (1976: 62).

The idea that power is located in dirt, which itself can be defined as ambiguous boundaries, strikes me as useful in respect to television. It suggests that the interface between texts and readers is capable of producing both meanings and "relations of power and domination" precisely because it is not a clean opposition but always and necessarily ambiguous. What I shall be looking for, then, is not texts and readers as opposed entities, but the way boundaries between them are erected, transgressed, and policed.

THE POWER OF TELEVISION

But first I would like to introduce just one more dirty category into the discussion, and that is the power of speech. The power of speech, as commonly understood, is a natural attribute of the human species, and is therefore distributed evenly among all members of the species. Not only is the power (or competence) equally distributed, but speech itself is understood as natural, direct communication, as natural language. Small wonder that speech is taken as the model for linguistic and other kinds of analysis, such as semiotics, that are interested in meaning. However, the work of Derrida has shown that the privileging of speech is by no means an innocent act—on the contrary, as Jonathan Culler has explained:

> Privileging speech in this way by treating writing as a parasitic and imperfect representation of it is a way of repressing or setting aside certain features of language, or certain aspects of its functioning. If distance, absence, misunderstanding, insincerity are features of writing, then by distinguishing writing from speech one can construct a model of communication which takes as the norm an ideal associated with speech—where the listener is thought to be able in principle to grasp precisely what the speaker has in mind. . . . Writing, supposedly

an external accessory in the service of speech, threatens to taint the purity of the system it serves (1979: 167).

If writing—the medium of Literature, Philosophy, and Science—can be reckoned "parasitic," "imperfect," and "tainting" because of its distance, absence, misunderstanding, and insincerity, then what are we to say of television? The medium of trivia and sensationalism, of sex, violence, and bad language, of corruption and moral decline is commonly seen as the ultimate supplement. It threatens the purity of both speech *and* writing. It does not even have the artistic pretensions of cinema to redeem it. Nonetheless, it was Hollywood that first provided the model of impurity and the discourse of contagion for later use against television. Here is the Spens Report of 1938:

> Certainly it would be an advantage if all our children could learn the same English speech, though we agree with [*The Newbolt Report*] in recommending the preservation of true dialect, as distinct from affected or debased forms which have no roots in history. Teachers are everywhere tackling this problem, though they are not to be envied their struggle against the natural conservatism of childhood allied to the popularization of the infectious accents of Hollywood. The pervasive influence of the hoarding, the cinema, and a large section of the public press are, in this respect as in others, subtly corrupting the taste and habits of the rising generation.

Television has been policed by this discourse continuously since its earliest prehistory. It is still beyond the pale. Here is one commonplace example of the common sense barricade between literacy (hooray!) and television (boo!). It is from a Sunday issue of *The London Times:*

> The great TV and literacy debate which has been rumbling on for 30 years or so shows no sign of reaching a conclusion yet. The impression—always strong among adults—that a race of square-eyed and weirdly dressed non-readers, non-writers and non-counters is in the making isn't the sort of thing that statistical proof or disproof does much to shake or confirm. It isn't exactly a sign of literary attainment or public spirit when half the adult population is counted as "readers" of the tabloids; and it's not necessarily a sign that television encourages children to read when publishers produce so many spin-offs from children's programmes (April 10, 1983).

In the teeth of its own concern with the ambiguity of television's boundaries with its media neighbors (the piece is a review of "spin-off" books), the article seems to need the security of a cleanly-defined line between itself and television. Television isn't much good for anything from this point of view, except to encourage children to stop using it in favor of "literary attainment," and naturally it's not even very good at that. But the main thing is to reduce contact with the contagion to the shortest possible time. The review as a whole is called "Ways to Wean Children Off TV." Clearly the "power of speech" is a dirty category. But here the dirt is identified, equally clearly, as "belonging" not to speech itself but to television, the other electronic media, and the popular press. The power that is located in this dirt is of course of the negative kind—it infects and corrupts the rising generation, turning them into a race of weird monsters with funny eyes and dubious habits. What is it that makes television into such a potent (dangerous) extension of language? Can you imagine a headline that read "Ways to Wean Children Off Reading." or even "Ways to Wean Children Off Speech?"

Another way of asking these questions without having to weigh the relative merits of the different concepts of motherhood that are implied in the weaning metaphor is to return to the notion of the power of speech and to concentrate for a moment not so much on the speech as on the power. For Saussurians, the power of speech is not only separated from the taint of writing, it is also protected from the grubby world of speaking: the *power* of speech is *langue,* an abstract system that lies beyond the individual and social will. Only *parole,* the abstract binary opposition of *langue,* is allowed contact with the social relations that, as Saussure concedes, are the sole precondition for the creation of *langue* in the first place (Saussure, 1974). It seems that the protection of *langue* from the social/individual will has more to do with the power of binaries than with the logic of the case. For Chomskians, the power of speech is an attribute of the species—innate competence. Here too it is regarded as almost unthinkable to suggest that such a power can be interfered with socially. But when it comes to the networks of power and domination that characterize social relations, individual natural capacities are neither here nor there. The notion of linguistic competence does not raise the question of who has power over it, just as the notion of a natural capacity to eat or to make tools does not explain who goes hungry or who owns the means of production. It appears, then, that both the concept of *langue* and that of competence have the effect of defining power out of the terms of study. But, as Stuart Hall has very briskly put it:

Of course, a native language is not equally distributed amongst all native speakers, regardless of class, socio-economic position, gender, education and culture: nor is competence to perform in language randomly distributed. The Linguistic performance *and competence* is socially distributed, not only by class but also by gender. Key institutions—in this respect, the family-education couple—play a highly significant role in the social distribution of cultural 'capital', in which language plays a pivotal role (1982: 79).

Perhaps here we have a clue as to why television is commonly regarded as a dirty, dangerous medium that "our" children must be weaned off. In the first place, it has none of the abstract purity of *langue,* nor the natural pure individualism of competence—it is all too evidently a *social* relation of sense-making from which power cannot be excluded. And second, maybe even consequently, television is *threatening:*

In this sense the electronic media are entirely different from the older media like the book or the easel-painting, the exclusive class character of which is obvious. . . . Potentially the new media do away with all educational privileges and thereby with the cultural monopoly of the bourgeois intelligentsia. This is one of the reasons for the intelligentsia's resentment against the new industry. As for the 'spirit' which they are endeavouring to defend against 'depersonalization' and 'mass culture', the sooner they abandon it the better. The new media are oriented towards action, not contemplation; towards the present, not tradition. Their attitude to time is completely opposed to that of bourgeois culture which aspires to possession, that is to extension in time, best of all, to eternity. The media produce no objects that can be hoarded and auctioned. They do away completely with 'intellectual property' and liquidate the 'heritage', that is to say, the class-specific handing on of non-material capital (Enzensberger, 1972: 108–9).

It is perhaps just as well that Enzensberger prefaces these refreshingly optimistic remarks with the word "potentially," since television as presently instituted does not conform to its potential. But it is important to consider what that potential or "productive capacity" might be, in order to demonstrate the extent to which its development is not determined by "innate" capacities as such, but on the way these are organized socially and institutionalized. In fact, television supplies us with a model for understanding how the social power of communication—the power of speech—is neither abstract nor innate, but a power relation. Further, television demonstrates that the *production* of senses, knowledges, and meanings is thoroughly socialized, mark-- ing a decisive break with the kinds of cultures associated with the "older media."

BORROWED LANGUAGES

The implications of this argument for the analysis of television itself will, I hope, become clearer later on. For the moment, I want to take up Enzensberger's point about the analyst. He points to the cultural (class) monopoly of the intelligentsia, and their/our "resent- ment against the new industry." Such resentment may, of course, be expressed openly and with vigor ("Ways to wean children off TV"), but it may also have something to do with apparently neutral and respectable intellectual activities, like "reading texts." For "texts" as commonly understood are nothing short of institutionalized meaning; they are fixed, owned, and have clearly identifiable boundaries (usu- ally in the form of covers). They can be "possessed" in different ways by clearly identifiable authors and readers—they are a very good way of ensuring "extension in time, best of all . . . eternity." They can even be hoarded and auctioned. And as Roland Barthes has argued, this concept of text produces characteristically authoritarian social relations:

> The notion of the text is historically linked to a whole world of insti- tutions: the law, the Church, literature, education. The text is a moral object: it is the written in so far as the written participates in the social contract. It subjects us, and demands that we observe and respect it, but in return it marks language with an inestimable attribute which it does not possess in its essence: security (1981: 32).

Television analysts, especially those of us who are institutionalized within education, are notoriously susceptible to the appeal of security, whether of text or tenure. But television is, equally, resistant to classification into texts, and its ambiguity extends even to the "dirty" boundary that surrounds its institutionalized study (there is no aca- demic "discipline" called Television). Small wonder that we are driven to borrowing the costume of the text in order to dress this scandalous subject in respectability. However, the consequence is that we tend to analyse the costume, to use television to demonstrate an inestim- able attribute that it does not possess in its essence: security of texture. In short, we need to find "Ways to Wean Critics Off Texts."

But of course the notion of the text is a thoroughly naturalized term in analysis. And as Stuart Hall has put it,

> Changing the terms of an argument is exceedingly difficult, since the dominant definition of the problem acquires, by repetition, and by the weight and credibility of those who propose or subscribe it, the warrant of 'common sense' (1982: 81).

Hall invokes Volosinov's concept of "sign as the arena of class struggle" to suggest that "the same term could be disarticulated from its place within one discourse and articulated in a different position" (1973: 80). Hence, it is not necessary to *abandon* the notion of the text in respect of television. But the ideological inflections of the term need to be recognized, and where necessary changed (though that may prove "exceedingly difficult"). What is needed is not to reduce television to texts, but to disarticulate the notion of the text from the discourse of possession, and rearticulate it in the position(s) of television.

ACCESSING

Before I attempt that, however, I would like to bring the other term of the text:reader binary back into play.

First of all, rearticulating the notion of the text calls into question the separability of text and reader. Recent work on subject positioning by *Screen* theorists, for example, suggests that subjectivity itself is an effect or product of textual relations. Readers, in this model, are *written on* by texts. Of course television is not written, it is *produced,* which is a suggestive metaphor for its reader-relations, but I would like to propose that the relations between television and its viewers might be thought of in terms of *accessing*. Viewers "access" television discourses and representations both in and beyond the act of watching television ("accessing" goes on after the television set is switched off). And vice versa: television accesses its viewers' (culture's) discourses and identifications in the act of production.

I have argued elsewhere (Hartley 1982; O'Sullivan, et al., 1983) that accessing on television has some peculiar features. It is not a case of information retrieval. When you are quoted or interviewed or appear on television (accessed), you may "have your say" but you do not "speak for yourself." Your contribution is semiotically "stolen," that is, appropriated by the overall television discourse. It is made to mean something different from whatever you may have intended by its status as a "quote." You are rearticulated into an actor in the drama, and what you say is like fictional dialogue—it is subservient to what else is being said, to who is saying it, and to what the drama is about. Further, accessing lends the credibility and legitimacy (realism) of your authenticity and authority to television.

If television can be thought of as a means of accessing a multiplicity of discourses and representations, so can the viewer. Everything I have just said about the way television accesses applies equally to the individual viewer. We are all a means of accessing a multiplicity of discourses and identifications. Not only is what we say and the way we make sense of the world largely "quoted," but also the resources from which we "steal" these discourses and identifications cannot control the way we use them in combination. However, although I take the relation between television texts and "readers" to be similar in that it is a process of mutual accessing, I am not arguing that it is uniform or evenhanded. It is still a hegemonic power-relation in the way it is currently organized socially. In brief, some viewers have more discursive resources than others, and television has more than all.

EVEN TYPES OF SUBJECTIVITY

I shall return to the power inequalities later. At this point I would like to take up the idea of individuality (subjectivity); not as a self-contained and clearly identifiable entity, but as a "dirty" structure of accessed identifications. In order to be more definite about what I am referring to, I will suggest seven of what I take to be the more important identifications that are available or encouraged. They are what I am tempted to call seven types of ambiguity: namely *self, gender, age-group, family, class, nation, ethnicity*. The list is both abstract and analytical (I do not have a *textual* warrant for it), and in the concrete instance of television it is not even a list, since the seven categories get very mixed up, and some are encouraged more than others (family more than class), while others do not coexist very peacefully (some notions of nation with some types of ethnicity). These identifications are neither self-evident nor essential, in either television or individuals. What I hope to do is to show how television produces them. In the context of this paper that means I shall pay attention to the way ambiguous boundaries are erected and transgressed within and between the identifications.

I am looking, then, for *textual* processes and representations that may encourage *reader* identifications. It is implicit in my argument that none of the seven types is represented in isolation. Further, the *way* each one is taken up ideologically (produced) is similar in structure to the way each of the others is treated. They can be seen, structurally, as homologous transformations of each other. Thus, each type of identification (together with others I've not included in my list) serves to define and limit the others. And there are what I will call condensations of them, where, for instance, particular senses of all seven are collapsed into one star-sign, the signifier for which may be a person, like Prince Charles or the Princess of Wales, or it may be an emblematic object or practice, like a car, a landscape, or a sports event. Television produces its own star-signs, from news-presenters to more obviously fictional characters, and these too are available as condensers for our seven types of subjectivity.

EX-NOMINATION

In this paper I am going to have to concentrate on just one identification to serve as a representative for the others. The one I have chosen is that of age-group. In the spirit of the paper, however, what I am looking for are the marginal, ambiguous "edges" of the category, and the way these offer what looks like a settled, positive, natural "inside" for "us" to access as our own selves. In this respect I have found Barthes's notion of *ex-nomination* very useful. Barthes (1973) suggests that "capitalism" is quite easily *named* in economic discourses. It is uncontroversial to say that ours is a capitalist economy. In political discourses, however, capitalism is less easily named—there is no Capitalist Party as such. In cultural discourses, capitalism "disappears"—it is completely ex-nominated. As Barthes puts it, the bourgeoisie is the social class that does not want to be named (see also Fisk and Hartley 1978).

This notion can be applied to all of our seven types of social identification, to show how within each one there are ex-nominations going on. The way to spot such absences, of course, is to look for those nominations or namings that are in play. In the instance of gender, women are frequently nominated as women. They are represented first in terms of gender—defined by their looks, procreative ability, "feminity," and so on. Men, on the other hand, appear to be "beyond gender"—they just get on with whatever they are doing and are defined in terms of their job, character, actions, and so forth. Men are *ex-nominated* as men. Similarly, in the instance of class, there are plenty of representations of "working classness," which is nominated as such, whereas "middle-classness" is rarely presented as a significant signifier on its own. More often it is taken for granted, while the focus of the story lies elsewhere (see *Dallas* from television, or, interestingly in view of its title, *Ordinary People* from cinema). In the instance of ethnicity/nation, in Britain blacks and non-English nationals are often signified as "belonging" to their respective race or nation (this includes nationals of the non-English parts of Britain: Wales, Scotland, and Northern Ireland). For English whites these attributes are apparently devoid of significance—they are exnominated. Finally, "the family" is a thoroughly exnominated category, despite evidence that the classic family is now very rare (see Ellis, 1982), unless you belong to a "broken" one, a "single-parent" one, and the like.

YOUTH: A SCANDALOUS CATEGORY

As for the identifications within the category age group, these too have a naturalized, ex-nominated center—the category of *adult*—with other more ambiguous, marginalized identifications on its boundaries. Like television, I am going to concentrate on one of the nominated, ambiguous boundaries, namely youth.

Youth is a very "dirty" category indeed. First of all I will explain in general terms why this is so, and then have a look at some examples to see how it is represented. Youth is a *scandalous category* because it offends against binary logic. Binary systems are two-term universes, and binary logic requires the two terms to be not just equivalent-but-opposite, but also mutually exclusive. For instance, there are plenty of such binaries in play in analytical discourses—signifier:signified; subject:object; text:reader; producer:consumer; speech:writing. Binaries are also capable of being applied to both the physical and social world. The surface of the earth can be understood in terms of the binary land:sea, and the people on it in terms of the binary child:adult. All very neat and clean. But if we look closer at, for instance, the binary land:sea, we find things are not quite so simple. There is a margin between the two that is ambiguous. Sometimes it is land, sometimes sea. It is neither one thing nor the other, and both one and the other. I refer, of course, to the beach—the very same ambiguous category that people flock to in order to escape all sorts of otherwise strict *social* boundaries. The ambiguous beach is the place where you can do all sorts of scandalous things, from taking your clothes off in public to being more or less continuously preoccupied with pleasure, sex, and self, without getting arrested. And of course you flock there in the ambiguous nontime of Sundays and other holidays, especially (in Britain) on bank holidays.

Youth is just this kind of scandalous category. It is neither child nor adult. To see why youth is so very dirty, then, all that is necessary is to list some of the most general, naturalized, and common-sense attributes that separate chlid (as a category) from adult, and to notice how completely youth transgresses them all. For instance,

child:adult
family of origin:family of destination
not working:working
single:married
asexual:gendered sexuality
irresponsible:responsible
and so on:and so on

With youth, all such oppositions are transgressed; youth has the attributes of *neither* child nor adult, and *both* child and adult. Just to show that the scandalousness comes from the categorical ambiguity of youth and not from what it does, I have located several examples of media stories in which age group is significant. I have taken these from popular newspapers; I hope these "fixed" texts will illustrate at least part of what goes on in the more complex "moving" text of television, especially in view of television's own ambiguous boundaries with its media neighbors.

The first, headlined "Tiny Terror," tells of a 3-year-old child who "leaves a trail of havoc" at home. What would you think of someone who brutalized a goldfish, terrorized a cat (three times), assaulted his father, set fire to his aunt, vandalized a car, disrupted a social club, and pinched people's bottoms with a pair of pliers? Normally, this is just the kind of behavior we are encouraged to think of as scandalous and to associate with the excesses of youth. But not in this case. For as the (London) *Sun* (May 11, 1979) tells us, "little imp Colin" is a *child* of 3. Leafing through the same newspaper, we come across someone who, at 21 years, is closer to the category of youth in age. Further, this person is sitting at a school desk wearing virtually no clothes. Again, however, the action is not represented as scandalous. Quite the reverse, for of course this is a pin-up, and thus firmly within the realms of gendered sexuality. The woman/girl may be (must be) youthful, but the representation is addressed to *adult* men.

Despite the reputation of youth, then, it is not violence or overt sexuality as such that constitutes the problem. The problem is that youth transgresses the naturalized limits of both childhood and adulthood. In anthropological terms it is a *rite of passage,* a crossing of boundaries, and that means it becomes the subject of taboo and is subjected to ritual and repression. The next example is from the (London) *Sunday Mirror* (May 17, 1981). It describes, in detail, the youth gangs (cults) referred to as "skinheads." The whole story is a ritual condensation of boundary transgressions and scandalous categories. It is set in that special place and time—the seaside on a bank holiday. The story is presented irrationally, as "disturbing," "frightening," and as about "victims," "fear," and "thugs." The transgressors themselves are represented as "Britain's young tribes," "sworn enemies," and "like animals," and in the pictures, as Nazi-sympathizers whose appearance is precisely tribal, even their faces look like masks, and their clothes and haircuts are all paraded to confirm our worst fears. The story itself comprises a succession of transgressions: of speech (they swear); of the peace (they fight); of patriotism (they parody the national flag); of politics (they are racists and admire Hitler); of sexuality (they stir up your murky psychological depths); of gender (the women swear and fight); of marriage (they insult a happy young couple); of the home (they live alone with a naked light bulb, greasy plates, and a crinkled picture of Hitler); and of sobriety (at least one of them gets drunk while being plied with pints of lager by the reporter).

Mixed up in the unfolding of all these transgressions are almost all of the seven types of subjectivity I have mentioned. Of course, the story is not encouraging its readers to identify with the skinheads. But it is not just a matter of excluding them as "foreign," or as unlike us, since that would not implicate the reader in the various identifications. I think there is an (ex-nominated) we:they binary in play in the story's mode of address, but once again the object of attention, youth, is significant precisely because it transgresses it. The skinheads certainly are not "us," but they are not foreigners either (which is why they are "frightening"). The reporter can talk and even joke with them, and he gets invited to bedsit and pub. He purports to understand and even like them: "playing with the body is one of the great preoccupations of the young. They can be bright, chirpy, quickwitted." He pities them and advises us to do the same: "for their lives are very, very empty." He fancies the girls too: "Many skinhead girls, with their close-cropped hair, sparse make-up and skin tight around the cheekbones, can look totally breathtaking—making you wonder what murky psychological depths in you they are stirring up." None of these concessions would be possible if the skinheads really were alien "tribes" of "animals."

In fact one of the appealing aspects of this story is the uneasiness of its movements between the skinheads and "all of us": "All of us may lose our tempers, lash out when provoked, or fight in self-defense. But skinhead violence is different." As the story thinks through the transgressions of the skinheads, then, it establishes boundaries between "we" and "they" identifications. It establishes a narrative point of view that takes for granted—ex-nominates—the "we" identifications it requires its readers to access in order to make sense of the story in its own terms. Thus, the skinhead girls mark the limit of sexuality for women, and it is not without significance that the story is written from a male point of view while speaking for "all of us." This point of view carefully distinguishes between those girls who look "totally breathtaking" and those who, "with their loud-mouthed effing and blinding and their constant egging on of the blokes to fresh violence, seemed to me totally unwomanly." In another instance, what the skinheads do with the national emblem is distinguished from "all I understand our national flag to stand for." And so on.

EXCESSES OF MEANINGFULNESS

It seems to me that this is a highly risky strategy if the story's scandalized tone is taken at face value. Carefully separating the transgressors from "us" is of course one good way to encourage fantasy identifications, but quite apart from that there is another risk too. The strategy generates far more meaningfulness than it can control. Ambiguous categories are by definition more meaningful than the two (or more) categories they transgress, since they partake of the attributes of both. On television, the more complex modes of representation generate an even greater excess of meaningfulness, since television signifies by color, motion, sound, and time as well as by pictures, words, and composition. All these are variously affected by their internal juxtapositions and their external relations with discourses and social relations off-screen. Thus, beyond a *social* risk (of encouraging love rather than hate, attraction rather than repulsion), there is a *semiotic* risk that is even more fundamental. For excess of meanings and overlapping opposites are among the defining characteristics of madness, or at least of non-sense. It is hardly surprising, then, to find television itself characterized by a will to limit its own excess, to settle its significations into established, taken-for-granted, common senses, which viewers can be disciplined to identify and to identify *with*. Disciplining is done partly by television's convention-alized codes of composition, lighting, movement, narrative, genre, and the like, and partly by "external" limits such as those professional, legal, and other exclusion devices that limit who and what gets on the air.

However, I would argue that television can never succeed in its will to limit its own excesses of meaningfulness. For in order to think through abstract problems associated with various kinds of categorical ambiguity, television must necessarily scandalize the overlapping boundaries. In order to limit meanings, then, it must first produce excess. It does this in both fictional and factual programs (so much so that the separation of fact from fiction is another abstract binary that has a "dirtier" boundary than is commonly admitted).

In fictional programs, characters rarely act as mere persons. Usu-ally they signify some mighty opposite like man:woman; individ-ual:institution; good:evil; active:passive; efficient:inefficient; normal:deviant; nature:culture; rural:urban; heart:head; and the like (a recent example of a text that unfolds its narrative by means of an unusually obvious series of such binaries is the film *ET:The Extra-Terrestrial*). So the barroom or bedroom brawl is a ritual condensation of the opposites being distinguished and thought through. Action sequences are "calculating machines" and their outcome is as "pure" as a mathematical QED. But meanwhile, of course, the action itself may be as "dirty" or excessive as the budget allows. In factual pro-grams—especially news—their *raison d'etre* is scandal, conflict, and the disruption of normally settled categories. Internally, such pro-grams make sense by producing abstract binaries (we:they, and so forth), which serve as the ex-nominated point of view from which the particular event or person can be recognized as ambiguous, marginal, scandalous, and hence newsworthy. In short, television's signifying practices are *necessarily* contradictory—they must produce more than they can police. Concomitantly, for the viewer, the discipline of the "preferred reading" must be disrupted continuously by the presence of the very ambiguities it is produced out of.

It seems, then, that the signifying practice of mainstream, broad-cast network television is not so much to exploit as to control tele-vision's semiotic potential. The ideological strategies it uses continuously to draw the line between categories are, I suggest, the "text" that should constitute the object of analysis. Both in general and in detail, television's efforts to make signification into sense, representations into reality, and to interpellate *this* rather than *that* reader-subject, raise important theoretical and political issues. And these include its strategies of inclusion and exclusion; the ex-nomination of dominant identifications and the marginalization of "emergent" ones; the attempt to clarify ambiguous categories while scandalizing their overlaps; using the "power" of ambiguity to collapse or condense different social identities into each other in order to represent them as naturally fused; and the transformation of different identifications, and different scandalous categories, into each other. Such analysis would, of course, be impossible if these ideological strategies actually *worked*—the analysis is founded on the active contradictions within television discourse.

VIDEOLOGY

Television's active contradictions can in fact be quite revealing, and the kind of analysis I am suggesting—which, I confess, I would like to call *Videological Analysis*—offers principles by which we can select from television's "dirty" texts and social relations those that reveal what television is up to, as opposed to those that reflect back to us our inherited or established presumptions about what a text should look like. Here are one or two brief examples. The main commercial television news (ITN *News at Ten*) for October 25, 1982, in Britain carried as its lead story an item about two kidnap/murders in Northern Ireland. Despite the obvious political implications of this, the story was not made sense of in terms of nation, nor of ethnicity, nor of class, but almost exclusively in terms of *family*. Verbally, the story foregrounded the numbers of children each of the two victims had and described details of their family situation, including how one was identified by a watch his family had given him for his birthday, and how many "orphans" the killings had produced. Visually, one of the men's daughters was filmed against a domestic background, a bishop was filmed inside one of the men's home, and the reporter did his closing piece to camera in the setting of a residential street. ITN's textual strategy, then, was to disarticulate the Troubles from any national/political discourse and to rearticulate them in the discourse of domesticity. In this context, the events are literally senseless, and this is how they are described in the story. Interestingly the source of this description—"a cycle of senseless depravity," and "vicious primitivism in its most depraved form"—was that of Authority in the shape of the Chief Constable. The local bishop was also quoted as expressing his "horror" at the "acts of violence." These accessed voices of Authority allowed ITN to accomplish the double move of exnomination and marginalization without appearing to "editorialize." The "acts of violence" themselves, together with their history, politics, agents, and so forth, are marginalized with the strongest possible rhetoric—depravity and primitivism, senseless and horrible. Meanwhile, the category of the family is ex-nominated—it is taken as self-evidently the "natural" point of view from which to observe the events. Without having to deny that such events are horrific, it can be said that these discursive strategies belong to ITN and to television rather than to the events, and that "we" are being "informed" more about the ideology of the family than about Northern Ireland's troubles.

Similarly, political and industrial news offers a point of view that is television's rather than "ours" (the viewers) or "theirs" (the participants in the event). Again, families are foregrounded, usually as victims, and usually in the guise of "consumers." The parties to industrial disputes are sorted out by both camera and narrative point of view into "we" and "they" positions. But just as youth is ambiguous in this respect—it is both "us" and "them"—so too are the initiators of negative action (strikers). They partake of the attributes of foreigners (the paradigm example of which are of course the Russians), which is what makes them scandalous. I have followed the semiotic fate of both strikers and political opposition elsewhere (Hartley, 1982).

HEGEMONY

It may by now be apparent that this paper too is ambiguous as to its boundaries. I am aware that the material I have introduced has been excessive and is not entirely under my control—certainly there is more to say about the examples I have used than I have said. Perhaps finally I should try to clean up some of the remaining dirt. The point about dirt, crudely, is that it encompasses notions of ambiguity, contradiction, power, and social relations all in one. This strikes me as a helpful condensation, since part of my purpose here has been to show that our analytical discourses tend sometimes to operate with categories that are too unitary, pure, abstract, and clearcut, especially in a field of study that holds as axiomatic that nothing is *intrinsically* anything, but that entities are defined negatively by what they are *not*. Working back through my argument then, I have tried to show that television is a prolific producer of meaningfulness, which it seeks to discipline, by prodigious feats of ideological labor, into familiar categories that it proffers to "us" as appropriate identifications for our subjectivity to access. But I have also tried to suggest that television's meaningfulness is, literally, out of control. For instance, despite rearticulating the Northern Ireland story into the discourse of domesticity, the news could neither ignore nor silence all of the event, some contradictory aspects of which were even able to erupt into and disrupt the "text." Even as the daughter-scene established a powerful chain of family-significations, the drone of an unseen military helicopter above provided an appropriate metaphor for all the absences the "videological" text itself sought to repress. It is at this point that my argument can be referred to the concept of hegemony. It is by now well established that television plays its part in the diffusion of consent for a power monopoly—not least in its own social relations of production and consumption. However, the concept of hegemony should not be collapsed into the old "pure" text:reader binary, where there is a clear-cut division between the hegemonic text and the subjected reader. Hegemony is a good deal dirtier than that—it is not just a matter of "them" telling "us" what, how, and when to think. Television is not just videology—it is also a resource. There are contradictions even in its most confident assertions of the supremacy of "natural" categories, and there are marginal places and times on television where "common" sense slides into "good" sense. Even as it is presently constituted, television's productive capacity cannot be policed at every point. And what it says depends on how you look at it.

Even so, how you look at it depends on what it says. And this brings me back to the beginning of this paper, where I suggested that what any one viewer can bring to bear on a television program is a combination of discursive resources. Such resources are determined by the same social relations as are represented on television, and by institutions such as education. They will, of course, include aspects of the hegemonic (hegemony is a social relation, and hence an attribute of the individual bearers of that relation), which is what makes hegemony "dirty"—it is an attribute of "us," not "them." But television plays a part in distributing and popularizing hegemonic discursive resources too—it *is* a discursive and representational resource. One way of demonstrating just how potent it can be is to take each of my seven types of subjectivity in turn, and try to access one of its marginal, nominated, scandalous identifications while watching mainstream television. How can you watch the news and, at the same time, feel yourself to be a nonunitary self, and/or a woman, and/or a youth, and/or outside "the" family, and/or working class, and/or Welsh, and/or black? You will soon, I think, discover that television is not addressing you at all, and that it does encourage certain social relations and discourage, deny, or marginalize others.

THE POWER OF SPEECH

One regular response to these discoveries is to develop an understandable but, I think, mistaken, hostility to television. However, that response would be to take television not for what it is but for what it sometimes aspires to be—a private conversation between two friends, excluding outsiders from their private world. But television is not like that. It is social, public, open. It is for this reason that I want to open up the apparently closed frontier between television and the power of speech itself. I think it is possible to argue that the power of speech should no longer be seen as the primary model for all signification and communication, but as a primitive technology that occupies in the economy of sense-making the sort of position that wood-burning does in the economy of energy. Speech may, historically, be one of the original forces of production, but it has been industrialized and transformed in line with other forces. Like them, it is barely recognizable in its modern form: the power of speech is now the electronic media in general and television in particular. Its source is no longer (if it ever was) the individual human subject, but society. It is characterized by socialized production and family/individual consumption; by a division of labor between and within producers and consumers; and by the exchange of a "subsistence wage" that is just sufficient for the sense-making economy to sustain and reproduce itself and its social relations—the "wages" of common sense. Speech is, of course, supposed to be exempt from all these impure influences, because of its general availability and individualized production, but I do not think it is (or ever has been). The example of television, in fact, leads to questions about speech—about who has appropriated, historically, the power to produce discourse (make speeches), and how speech as a force of production has been organized socially in relation to the prevailing mode and phases of production. It also suggests that in speech, as in television, there are marginalized, muted, and scandalized identities for subjects whose powerlessness entails that the only means they have to represent themselves to themselves represents them as marginal, muted, and scandalous.

The reason why I want to pursue this line of thought is not to discredit speech. On the contrary, the notion that speech is more like television than is commonly realized allows for some highly embarrassing questions to be asked. It would be truly scandalous to discover that whole sections of the population were systematically being denied access to the power of speech by a power bloc of professionals and their allies in commerce and government. But this is just the situation that obtains in television. Conversely, the model of television suggests that discourse is socially produced and disciplined in ways that our sentimental attachment to the individualism of speaking only masks. Speech too is a power relation, but we need to be reminded of that fact by the "poor relation" whose productive power is greater than that of speech but whose reputation has been "scandalized" by segments of the very power bloc that operates it. Could it be that this behavior itself signifies that television is beyond the control of its controllers, that its potential for socialized sense-making is being resisted because television is not a "boob-tube," "goggle box," or any other dangerous, silly, or contemptible thing, but a valuable weapon that is currently in the hands of those who despise but must use it in the struggle to maintain cultural supremacy?

ENCOURAGING SIGNS

It seems to me that because television's productive and social relations are industrialized it is clear that little can be done to alter those social relations in isolation from others. But equally it seems wrong to abandon the medium to its own kind of "free market" of meanings. And there are signs that determined efforts can produce changes, even in the face of state and commercial hostility. The signs I have in mind include two recent British television ventures: Channel Four (a new national network) and Sianel Pedwar Cymru (S4C—a new network for Wales that broadcasts in Welsh during peak hours). Despite commercial hostility (from advertising agencies, the ITV companies, and the like) Channel Four has been instituted with a parliamentary mandate to provide "experiment and innovation in form and content" across the range of its programs. It prioritizes "minority" programming, foreign language films, and so forth. Sianel Pedwar Cymru is the direct result of a decade of militant, direct-action campaigning by Welsh language activists in the teeth of sustained government hostility. In both cases there is plenty to worry about (see Blanchard & Morley, 1982), since neither venture is exempt from the prevailing climate of what television "should" be like, and in both cases there are power relations and struggles whose outcome is not always encouraging. But both of them have an institutional commitment to putting marginalized groups and ambiguous categories a little closer to the center of the screen. I take these to be encouraging signs.

NOTE

1. The concept of dirt in play in this paper is necessarily ambiguous, but may be seen as not unconnected with Mary Douglas's use of it in *Purity and Danger: An Analysis of the Concepts of Pollution and Taboo* (London: Routledge & Kegan Paul, 1966).

REFERENCES

Barthes, Roland (1973) Mythologies. London: Paladin
———(1981) "Theory of the text," in R. Young (ed.) Untying the Text: A Post-Structuralist Reader. London: RKP.
Blanchard, Simon and David Morley [eds.] (1982) What Is This Channel Four? London: Comedia Publishing Group.
Culler, Jonathan (1979) "Jacques Derrida," in J. Sturrock (ed.) Structuralism and Since. London: Oxford University Press.
Ellis, John (1982) Visible Fictions. London: RKP.
Enzensberger, Hans Magnus (1972) "Constituents of a theory of the media," in D. McQuail (ed.), Sociology of Mass Communication. Harmondsworth: Penguin.
Fiske, John and John Hartley (1978) Reading Television. London: Methuen.
Gurevitch, Michael, Tony Bennett, James Curran, and Janet Woollacott (1982) Culture, Society, and the Media. London, Methuen.
Hall, Stuart (1982) "The rediscovery of ideology: return of the repressed in media studies," in M. Gurevitch et al. (eds.) Culture, Society and the Media. London: Methuen.
Hartley, John (1982) Understanding News. London: Methuen.
Leach, Edmund (1976) Culture and Communication. Cambridge: Cambridge University Press.
Marx, Karl (1977) Karl Marx: Selected Writings (David McLellan, ed.). Oxford: Oxford University Press.
O'Sullivan, Tim, John Hartley, Danny Saunders, and John Fiske (1983) Key Concepts in Communication. London: Methuen.
de Saussure, Ferdinand (1974) Course in General Linguistics. London: Fontana.

Screen: For examples of the work of this journal, see Screen Reader 1, Cinema, Ideology, Politics and Screen Reader 2, Cinema and Semiotics, both available from SEFT, 29 Old Compton Street, London W1.

Spens Report (1938) Report of the Consultative Committee on Secondary Education, with special reference to Grammar Schools and Technical High Schools. London: HMSO.

Volosinov, Valentin (1973) Marxism and the Philosophy of Language. New York: Seminar Press.

widespread public pressures with their oft-proclaimed desire to respond to audience tastes? What consequences do certain kinds of challenges to programming materials by advocacy organizations have for the entertainment that television viewers share? With the exception of a number of solid though unrelated case studies, mass communication literature tends to be silent on these questions (see Cole & Oettinger, 1978; Cowan, 1978; and Montgomery, 1981). Notably absent is a conceptual framework by which network programmers' reactions to organized pressure on them (directly from advocacy organizations and through intermediaries such as government agencies and advertisers) can be examined, explained, and perhaps even predicted.

The purpose of this chapter is to present the beginning of such a framework, a "resource dependence" perspective from industrial sociology. To keep the subject manageable, the focus will be on public advocacy organizations that demand change directly from the networks and production firms or that try to influence television advertisers to push the networks toward change. A number of examples will be presented to support and extend the framework. They will be drawn from a few systematic investigations that are relevant as well as from more informal, though close, readings of television industry trade magazines.

The basic question I ask is this: To what extent, and how, does organized pressure on networks, production firms, and advertisers lead to changes in programming? The answers that the framework and examples suggest underscore a central distinction that television executives see between "public" demands and "audience" demands. Too, the answers suggest the difficulty of thrusting programming demands on the networks and guiding the consequences. And, they indicate that even when advocacy organizations do not intend to attack liberal capitalism in their demands, network protective stances sometimes treat them as if they have offended values at its core. The result in any event is the protection and reinforcement of the basic routines that undergird the dominant ideological scheme.

A RESOURCE DEPENDENCE FRAMEWORK

The resource dependence approach helps explain the way the commercial networks' relationships with production firms, advertisers, public advocacy organizations, and audiences affect production-related routines and the television content that results from them. It starts with the basic notion that all organizations are continually competing with other organizations for resources—money, people, supplies, permission, information. These resources are not distributed randomly through an organization's environment. Rather, they are concentrated in various areas of the environment and are often under the control of other organizations. (Unions sometimes regulate a company's access to trained personnel, for example.) As Howard Aldrich (1974) notes, the implications of this straightforward idea are quite broad:

> The resource dependence perspective . . . goes beyond the idea of simple exchange in arguing that one consequence of competition and sharing of scarce resources is the development of dependencies of some organizations on others. This proposition is the basis for Yuchtman and Seashore's definition of organizational effectiveness: the ability of an organization to exploit its environment in obtaining resources while at the same time maintaining an autonomous bargaining position. The implicit assumption made regarding managerial and administrative behavior is that major goals of organizational leaders are avoiding dependence on others and making others dependent on one's own organization. The general picture is one of decision makers attempting to manage their environments as well as their organizations (p. 4).

Executives worry most about managing their dealings with companies that affect their solvency most directly. Such companies become what Evan (1976) has called "normative reference organizations." That is, they become entities that executives see as generating requirements that they must respond to if their firm is to remain viable. Often, however, executives do not simply relinquish their independence of action to their normative reference organizations. Rather, they try to manage and shape the demands so that they fit the aims and needs of both parties to the relationship.

In order to work profitably with normative reference organizations and other environmental entities, executives develop routines—patterned behaviors—for themselves and specialized "boundary" personnel who deal with the environment (marketing personnel, salesmen, and the like). A prominent body of material on the sociology of work stresses that routines allow people to work much more efficiently than if they had to consider every task, every problem, anew (March and Simon, 1976; Tuchman, 1971). Of course, if they are to couch their work in routines, organization members must ensure that the requirements on them carry a certain level of predictability. The reason is basic. If you cannot predict what the organization or its environment requires of you, you cannot rely on routines for managing it.

The routines that executives develop reflect their evaluations of the importance of certain predictable influences on them. They recognize that in order to take resources from entities in the environment, they have to give resources in return. Routines that structure what and how much they give essentially structure how much autonomy the organization is willing to give up in order to get certain resources. That, in turn, is shaped by executives' consensus on the importance of those resources, the availability of the resources, the power of the entities to control them, the competition among firms for them, and alternative ways of getting the same or substitutable resources.

ADVERTISERS, AUDIENCES, AND PUBLICS

These considerations point to the kinds of routines that executives from television's production firms and commercial broadcast networks would develop in dealing with one another and in dealing with representatives from advertising firms and public advocacy organizations. Because of the triopoly they enjoy, the networks constitute powerful normative reference organizations for the production companies that supply them with entertainment fare. Technically, the networks only "license" their programs for exclusive first-run broadcasts. Practically speaking, though, the license fees are so crucial and the consequent network clout over the production firms is so great that the networks are able to manipulate a wide spectrum of production firms' routines, from scripting to casting to directing to editing. The result is that though sparks do often fly between Hollywood creators and network executives, environmental pressures for changes in programming typically fall on the networks and producers as a unit, with the networks generally in command.

For the networks, the key normative reference organizations are the major national advertisers. "Programs," notes Brown (1972), "come into being to deliver . . . an audience to advertisers." Sometimes, specific manufacturers or service companies stand out to network executives because of the huge amounts of money they spend on television time; in 1982, for example, Procter and Gamble invested $400 million in network television time (Advertising Age, 1983). Generally, however, network executives look to the needs of *classes* of advertisers—food firms, airlines, automobile makers, and the like—that pack a lot of financial clout. And even more important from a network standpoint are the interests of leading advertising agencies that service national advertisers. Ad agencies clarify, crystalize, even create, the marketing plans of their clients. They produce advertising material based on those plans, purchase media space or time for the material, and evaluate the success of the efforts with the aid of market research firms (which they sometimes own). In the process, they direct hundreds of millions of dollars toward the television networks. In 1982, for example, J. Walter Thompson (the third largest U.S. agency) allocated just over $750 million to network television in support of firms as diverse as H & R Block, Kellogg, Eastman Kodak, and the Ford Motor Company (Advertising Age, 1983).

Over time, the network-advertiser relationship has had an overarching influence on the routines that create television programming. A feel for that influence can perhaps be conveyed through a brief sketch of the relationship's implications for prime time. One need only begin with that basic viewership gauge, the Nielsen ratings. Broadcasters and advertisers have encouraged the development of Nielsen measurement categories (notably the number of households viewing as well as the sex and age of individual viewers) that directly reflect the specific marketing concerns of sponsors. The number of households the networks reach with their shows is very important to sponsors. Consequently, networks and ad agencies have made capturing blocks of households' viewing times, rather than winning a half-hour slot here and there, an important criterion for network success. Winning the year in a time block (whether it be morning, afternoon, evening, or latenight) means being able to charge substantially more for commercials in that block at the start of the next year.

For many national advertisers, however, the age and sex of viewers during those time blocks also hold strong importance. The most attractive target for the past decade and a half has been 18 to 49 year olds, since as a group they hold more discretionary spending money than do younger or older people. Prime time—the 8 p.m. to 11 p.m. block that is generally the most popular viewing period—presents the networks with the best opportunity to reach 18 to 49 year olds, since most of them are home from work during those hours. Consequently, each network's executives try to create a prime time schedule that will attract the largest possible number of households for the entire time period while they simultaneously try to grab the highest percentage of 18 to 49 year olds of the three networks.

Explaining how network executives try to do that explains to a considerable extent the shape and content of the prime time schedule. For example, with the aim of "winning the night," ABC, CBS, and NBC programmers set up their schedules to maximize "audience flow" from one show to the next. At 8 p.m. they choose programs designed to lure both children and their parents, since children are thought to control the set at that point in the evening. After 9 p.m. they schedule shows that are more "adult" in theme (since by that time many children have abdicated set control to parents), but that still fit into an overall tone or approach to the evening's schedule, to maintain that "flow." Because of advertiser interest in 18 to 49 year olds, the executives choose programs that they believe, or determine by research, will particularly attract that group along with others. "Counterprogramming" may occur if a competitor seems stubbornly successful at holding on to one segment of the desired audience. So, for example, when one network's football games on Monday night attracts a large percentage of 18 to 49-year-old males, another network may build its night around "women's" movies to lure 18- to-49-year-old females and advertisers interested in them.

Just as important as the material ABC, CBS, and NBC schedule during prime time, is the material the networks have learned not to place in that period as a response to the advertiser-network relationship. Programs aimed exclusively at youngsters are unacceptable, as are programs for people over 50. The reason is that the networks can attract much more advertising money at that time of day trying to lure 18- to 49 -year-old customers. Similarly, programs that are not upbeat in at least some basic way are frowned upon by network executives. The reason is that most advertisers feel that such programs do not provide the best environment for their commercials (see Barnouw, 1976).

Production firm executives have picked up these criteria, as well as the general advertiser-oriented network perspective. Consequently, over the years they have negotiated production guidelines with the networks—and translated those guidelines into routines— that make their shows acceptable for prime time. The guidelines extend to the very structure of the programs. So, for example, the plot must be created with natural breaks about every ten minutes so that commercials can be inserted. Too, the regular characters of a series should reflect (or attract) viewers whom the networks are hoping to draw for advertisers. A lot of action (cars bumping, people yelling, some physical violence) is desirable if the show is not a situation comedy. One reason is that many important advertising agency decision makers believe their research shows that action added to programs increases viewers' recall of commercials (Banks, 1978).

This thumbnail sketch can convey only some flavor of the way the network-advertiser relationship permeates the creation of programming. It can only hint at the way the production routines operate to create television content that legitimates dominant institutional values, including the economic establishment and its emphasis on private ownership. Space does not allow for a deeper exploration of this subject, which is elaborated elsewhere (compare Gitlin 1979b; Tuchman, 1974; and Turow, 1984). Here, however, it is important to draw out another point. It is that the demands advertisers place on the networks in exchange for resources foster a perception among network and production executives of the value of "audiences" as opposed to "publics," and of the relative legitimacy of attempts by audiences and publics to influence production routines.

Understanding the basis for this perception means first understanding that a network's "audience" is not real in any concrete sense of that word. As Turow (1982) has shown, there is an infinite number of ways to look at people who come into contact with mass media material; they can be described by any number of categories. From this standpoint, a network's audience is really a set of related categories, a construct built from the requirements and opportunities that network executives see in their dealings with advertising executives. These executives construct their audience—that is, they focus on particular categories (sex, age, income, and so forth) that they hope (or know) are being reached by their programming. Some members of the production firm (for example, writers, directors, actors) may very well hold personal audience "fantasies"—idiosyncratic conceptions of certain people or things—when they do their work (de Sola Pool and Shulman, 1964). Ultimately, though, the product they come up with has to attract the diverse, young adult, active, consumption-oriented audience that the networks hold in response to advertiser demands. Network executives try to make adjustments in the material they release to provide the most popular options within the initially established range of content choice. Thus, audience research, when conducted, does not provide a more accurate image of *the* true audience. Rather, audience research elaborates upon and makes explicit the categories of the target population that are of greatest interest to the networks, their station affiliates, and the advertisers.

This view of the television network's audience as a construct based on the requirements and opportunities of the network-advertiser relationship underscores the dilemma that public pressure groups find themselves in when they try to claim the attention of networks, production firms, and advertisers. For "audience response" is the activity of people in terms of the categories and concerns that networks and advertisers designate as important. "Organized public response," on the other hand, is the activity of people in terms of categories and concerns that they *themselves* define and that may not feed the network-advertiser relationship. So, for example, while television executives may find it profitable to focus on age, sex, income, and buying habits of viewers when they make programming decisions, public advocacy organizations may demand that the executives expend resources in considering how to adjust television programming not to age but to race, not to buying habits but to moral perspectives, not to income but to a minority group's desire to be visible in society's cultural mainstream. It is not hard to predict that network executives would see audience demands as fitting well with routines brought about by the advertiser-network relationship, while they would more likely see organized publics as threatening dangerous disruptions to those routines.

ROUTINES TO RESIST ORGANIZED PRESSURE

Clearly, then, we would expect that the further pressure group demands depart from network executives' perceptions of their broad obligations to advertisers and their "audience," the more network executives would hold an incentive to resist public advocacy demands. Considering how they might do that highlights some thorny problems that network executives face.

On the one hand, giving into an advocacy organization publicly, even on a selective basis, might open the floodgates for other, similar demands. On the other hand, simply dismissing the organization peremptorily could open a Pandora's box of difficulties. Most seriously, it could lead the organization so spurned to get the backing of sectors in the society that have strong resource-based leverage on the networks. Generally, that would mean the Federal government (which gives network affiliates permission to broadcast and regulates aspects of their financial activities) and the advertising industry (which holds direct monetary clout over the networks and their affiliates).

Network executives recognize that while advertisers as a whole benefit from (and demand) production routines that draw desirable audiences, advertising executives may place higher priority on protecting their companies' images and profits from large-scale boycotts.

Network executives also recognize that politicians, despite traditional support of the television industry, might well take positions against broadcasters in the face of rising popular anger over television material (see Rowland, 1983). Lawmakers' decision to do that would probably not result in direct regulatory moves against broadcasters' pocket books—but then again it might. As Federal Judge Warren Furgeson has noted, the root of goverment's power over broadcasters lies in "the vagueness of the standards which govern it" (quoted in Cole and Oettinger, 1978).

Over the years, the broadcast industry has spent much money to cultivate the backing of politicians and advertisers. However, circumstances clearly exist where the interests of these three sectors do not coincide, and response to organized public demands for changes in television material might sometimes be one of them. It stands to reason that network officials would try to stop such flareups from reaching advertisers and politicians, since the broadcasters would then be forced to expend valuable resources trying to convince powerful officials from those sectors that the network stand against the organized publics is worth sustaining.

In short, television network executives incur strong risks in either submitting to pressure groups or refusing their demands for change in television material. To predict how they are likely to deal with this dilemma, it pays to look at it in terms of the more general problem of an organization's response to unwanted demands from its environment. As Katz and Kahn (1966) note, a system that is constantly being disrupted by demands for change would tend to mobilize its forces to anticipate the disturbances before they disrupt normal operations and drain resources. March and Simon (1976) suggest that such a mobilization of forces would take the form of a highly complex and organized set of responses that will be evoked at the appearance of a particular environmental stimulus. They call this routinized set of responses a "performance program."

From this perspective, we can expect that each of the three television networks would have established routines for dealing with organized public pressures to change television programming. Too, we can expect that the procedure would be organized to carry out four general aims: (1) squelch or limit the influence of the advocacy organization on programming; (2) keep the demands from spilling over to the public arena, especially to the government or advertisers; (3) make sure that any programming changes that must be made do not depart from production routines and perspectives that encourage the basic predictability and profitability of the network-producer-advertiser relationships; and (4) deter other pressure groups from believing that their attacks on the networks will be successful.

SOME CASE EXAMPLES

Little systematic research exists on network responses to organized public demands for programming changes, and network executives as well as production firm executives are loath to discuss the subject in the press. Nevertheless, a close reading of academic and industry writings that do exist confirms the presence of performance programs with aims much like the ones derived from the resource dependence framework. The aims are carried out through (1) admitting the legitimacy of only those complaints that can be accommodated easily within standard programing routines; (2) attempting to actively delegitimize unaccommodable complaints by contending they violate core American values; while (3) sometimes making changes that appear broad but nevertheless accommodate traditional routines; and (4) contending that these broad changes were a response not to the organized public but to the audience.

The networks' responses center around their Program Standards and Practices Divisions, the "censors," as they are popularly known. Faced with complaints about programming from an angry public advocacy organization, network programming executives consult with the chief network censors to decide what to do. Typically, any instructions for programming changes are then conveyed to every program's creative personnel by the Standards and Practices executive who is the liaison to that show. The networks require that producers obey network censors, and challenges to their rulings must be taken up with high programming officials on the West Coast or in New York (see Russel, 1976; Traviesas, 1980; and Turow, 1981).

I saw the end of this chain of command when I studied the process of casting actors for television parts during the late 1970s (Turow, 1978). At the time, a number of Mexican American and senior citizen organizations were loudly and publicly dinning ABC, CBS, and NBC to increase the visibility of their constituencies in prime time. As a result, word had gone down through Standards and Practices in at least one network that producers ought to try to cast Mexican Americans and older actors, if possible. The producer of one show I studied relayed this suggestion to his director who, in turn, conferred with the casting director. The last two searched for parts in the script that would accommodate the casting of these two minorities while keeping the upscale, mainstream look of the show that they knew the networks and their advertisers demanded.

They concluded that a maid and a vineyard worker could be cast as Mexican Americans; that would constitute "credible" casting while it would help out the minorities. An older person, however, was not cast. The casting director and director had agreed that the part of a nurse would fit "a black or an older person, but not both"—and a black woman in her forties was chosen. In fact, before giving another black actor a small part, the production staff got concerned that there were too many minority representatives in that episode. Only after determining that the ratio of minorities to nonethnic whites was satisfactory did the producer agree that the black man be given the part.

This example shows that network executives sometimes do translate vociferous demands by ethnic, racial, and other minority groups into direct requests for programming changes. However, as the resource dependence framework suggests, the requests are clearly understood by production personnel as second in priority to the network mandate to produce a show that will attract advertisers and large audiences by using the "right" production values. Resolving these tensions typically means giving into public pressure for change only at or near the margins of a project.

The willingness by network and production company officials to hear public demands that do not really call for a reallocation of resources or a restructuring of activities may be one reason that spokespersons from all three networks told Montgomery (1981) that the National Gay Task Force has been the "most effective and well-organized of the special interest groups who lobby the television industry." Montgomery's research suggests that "effective" here means to a large degree internalizing the notion that when demands for change come from outside the industry they will have the greatest chance for acceptance if they do not threaten time honored formulas and the routines that create them. She shows that the demands gay activists have made have not really required fundamental reorientations in network and producer approaches to programming even in their use of gay program motifs. The advocates accepted "the rules of the game" for network television. In the case of dramatic series, for example, they agreed that

> the fundamental goal of garnering the largest possible audience necessitated that (a) the program [portraying gays] be placed in a familiar and successful television genre—the crime drama; (b) the story focus

upon the heterosexual male lead character and his relations to gay characters rather than upon the homosexual characters themselves; and (c) the film avoid any overt display of affection which might be offensive to certain segments of the audience (Montgomery, 1981: 56–57).

With its primary goal evidently being to squelch overtly negative portrayals, the National Gay Task Force found it acceptable to be influential near the margins of network projects. There are times, however, where pressure group demands on the networks cannot be defused by actions that so easily fit established routines and guidelines. In loud protests against such specials as *Playing for Time, Beulah Land,* and *Hanta Ho* and series such as *Bridget Loves Bernie, Soap,* and *Love, Sidney,* activist groups have demanded nothing less than the removal of a star, the reshaping of the entire program concept, or even the demise of the show itself. While the removal of one show or one actor need not indicate a general policy decision, network officials are clearly concerned that capitulating will invite an avalanche of similar protests. One network official confessed that giving into major demands might lead to an unprofitable "balkanization of the audience" (Montgomery, 1981).

Faced with such demands, executives in all three networks seem to have adopted a similar two-step approach. First, refuse to remove the show or its star even when it is not clear that the program will make money. Second, if the advocacy organization reflects a powerful constituency or if the advocates enlist the help of government or advertisers, try to work out a compromise. However, make the compromise one that transforms the changes protesters want into changes that mesh with tried and true television production routines.

An example of this approach can be seen in NBC's defense of *Love, Sidney,* a situation comedy starring Tony Randall that the network scheduled for the 1981–1982 season. The series pilot aired as a made-for-television movie the previous spring and raised the ire of the Coalition for Better Television. That fundamentalist organization objected to what its leader, Rev. Donald Wildmon, saw as *Love, Sidney's* theme: a quietly homosexual bachelor takes in a young actress and her daughter. He demanded that the series be removed from the lineup:

I'm concerned about why NBC decided to identify the man as a homosexual. . . . And why does the woman have to be promiscuous? Why couldn't the woman be a divorcee or a widow? Why does the child have to be illegitimate? . . . We urged our people to contact NBC and express their opinion (quoted in TV Guide, 1981).

NBC executives refused to abandon the program despite Wildmon's strong threat of a sponsor boycott. The network did relent publicly on one important point, however. The word went out that no episode after the pilot would "discuss" Sidney's homosexuality. This compromise was manageable, series producer George Eckstein insisted, because Sidney's sexuality was really necessary only in the background. Perhaps with some disingenuousness, Eckstein claimed that the charater's homosexuality was inserted simply to justify a modern twist on a time-honored situation comedy formula that dates to the *Bachelor Father* series of the 1950s, and before that:

> It [i.e., the homosexuality] is the raison d'etre for why Randall's character and the woman have a platonic relationship. It really is a story about a man and his surrogate family (*TV Guide*, 1981).

At times, however, finding compromises that can mesh with organizational perspectives simply is not possible. That was the case with *Playing for Time,* a dramatic CBS special embattled over the casting of Vanessa Redgrave, an avowed anti-Zionist, to play the central Jewish heroine in a story set at Auschwitz during World War II. Learning of the casting decision before the camaras began to roll, a number of Jewish leaders demanded that CBS officials order Linda Yellin, the executive producer, to find another actress for the part. Top network programming executives refused, and in the ensuing public arguments CBS spokespersons countered Jewish statements that the casting was insulting with pronouncements that the attempt to depose Redgrave represented threats to core America values that link private ownership to freedom of expression. The pressure groups, the CBS people said, were attacking freedom of the press and portending a resurgence of ideological blacklisting (*Newsweek,* 1980; *The Nation,* 1980; and Syrkin, 1980).

Seeing a stalemate, leaders of the Los Angeles-based Simon Wiesenthal Center for the Study of the Holocaust approached top executives in large advertising agencies and tried to persuade them that it would be insulting to the Jewish community to support the program. A boycott of products seems to have been only a half-hearted threat, but many agencies still chose not to use the controversial program as an advertising forum for their accounts. CBS, which had hoped at the start of the project to charge high ad rates for the prestigious vehicle, was forced to postpone its airing for lack of advertiser interest. Ultimately, the network sold off its advertising minutes at "distress" rates. The publicity lured a large audience to the program, but the network purportedly lost $4 million on the project (Cooper, 1983).

ADVERTISERS AND THE PROCESS OF RESPONSE

The *Playing for Time* incident underscores the determination by network officials to protect central aspects of their programming discretion, even at high costs. It also illustrates the nervous role that advertisers have played in network battles with advocacy organizations. Large and angry organizations, determined not to be stymied by network refusals to relinquish substantial programming autonomy, turned increasingly in the 1970s and 1980s to advertisers as a way to pressure the networks. Through implicit or explicit threats of product boycotts for sponsoring certain shows or certain types of shows, the protesters were hoping that advertisers and their agencies would use their clout to bring about the kind of shows protesters wanted. And, as the advertising director for General Motors told a closed meeting of television representatives in 1981, the pressured atmosphere did lead to decisions by sponsors to stay away from certain types of shows:

> "When it comes down to it [advertising executives] have to look through the eyes of what we think is General Motors or Procter and Gamble and what we stand for. We can be scared out of some things, yes, because we know that subjects can raise the rats, and we're not in the business of antagonizing people" (Margulies, 1981: A-29).

Not wanting to "raise the rats" can lead to broader consequences as well. For example, one can make a strong argument that threats by the Coalition for Better Television and the Moral Majority to boycott sponsors that supported programs the advocates considered sexually immoral and demeaning to traditional American values created a climate of fear among advertisers in the early 1980s. That influenced ad agencies' buying habits that, in turn, lead network programmers in a more compliant direction.

Of particular significance to the Coalition's cause was the public endorsement of its aim to "improve" television by the chairman of that giant consumer goods firm and largest television advertiser, Procter and Gamble. Word in the trade press was that Procter and Gamble executives had been nervous over reports that the Coalition was going to list it among companies that sponsor unacceptable prime-time programs. They were even more worried that the Coalition might later move to attack Procter and Gamble's ownership of six sultry daytime soap operas, a huge and important investment for the manufacturer. "P & G was afraid the soaps would be a problem down the line," said a network television executive. "By focusing [the Coalition's] attention on prime time, I guess they figured they'd get them off their backs" (Coates and Marich, 1981).

This comment reflects an awareness of the intricate strategies sometimes involved when advertising and advocacy organizations meet head-on over network television. The network response, spread over a number of months, reflects four interrelated strategies. One that emerged early was an attempt by network and production executives to publicly discredit, delegitimize, and downplay the power of the groups. Thus, for example, CBS TV Network president James Rosenfield "snarled" according to *TV Guide* when asked about the Coalition's crusade. "We have a fundamental aversion to pressure groups of all kinds," Rosenfield declared. He added that Wildmon's operation was "ridiculous," filled with "danger," and "dying" (Powers, 1981). At the same time, Norman Lear and other television producers attempted to garner moral support and public sympathy for sponsors' resistence by invoking the First Amendment and decrying censorship (Coates, 1981a, b).

The second network response strategy involved trying to convince advertisers and ad agencies that the advocacy organizations were really unrepresentative of the public at large and that, in any case, product boycotts tend to be ineffective. Rosenfield made both points in his interview with *TV Guide,* and ABC and NBC commissioned separate studies to support the contention (Coates and Marich, 1981).

The third and fourth response strategies stemmed from the fact that, despite their nervousness, sponsors still relegated to the networks the ultimate responsibility of delivering an audience to them in an effective selling environment. In other words, the networks still held the ultimate card: the ability to decide how to vary prime-time programming to reduce pressure group anger while disrupting as few of their basic programming routines and perspectives as possible.

From trade press reports, it seems that network programming decision makers decided to do that by reacting to only the most obvious and superficial demands for change on the part of the fundamentalist groups: those relating to sex and an absence of conservative political values. One way they did that was by toning down the most clearly racy aspects of the "sexy" comedies that worried advertisers, while still keeping the plot elements and comedic routines that they felt gave the programs high ratings and strong commercial recall scores.

So, for example, ABC quietly retained many of the sexual innuendos that formed the backbone of *Three's Company* and *It's a Living* while emphasizing to the ad industry that the female characters would wear less skimpy clothes. Many advertisers seemed satisfied. (Coates, 1981b).

Another way the decision makers reacted was to revive television's police and detective formulas. Network programmers had played down these formulas in the previous few seasons because of strong social controversy over television violence. By the late 1970s, though, the networks and producers had learned that they could reduce overt interpersonal violence on television while maintaining an action pace through substituting car crashes and stunt displays for more primitive gore; success of adventure-comedy shows like *The Dukes of Hazzard* had pointed in that direction. As a result, police and detective dramas looked attractive to network executives. Such dramas had drawn consistently strong ratings throughout much of television's history. Reliable production firms could turn them out easily. Many advertising agency executives liked them because they felt that their "action" orientation generated high commercial recall scores among viewers (Banks, 1978). And, the police and detective formulas were quite amenable to conservative social values.

One result of the network reorientation, then, was an updated reinstatement of program-related routines that had lain relatively dormant for a number of years. A clutch of new action-packed police and detective dramas emerged on the scene with explicitly conservative orientations. *Strike Force, T. J. Hooker, Cagney and Lacy, Hill Street Blues, Simon and Simon, Magnum, P. I.*, and others moved alongside the toned-down comedies to uphold the rights of citizens and police in an urban (and international) jungle ruled by criminals. This might not have been the kind of programming the Coalition and Moral Majority had demanded, expected, or even liked. But, as the resource dependence framework suggests, the organized demands of the public will constantly be refracted in the television networks by organizational and interorganizational imperatives that receive higher priority.

THE RHETORIC OF RESPONSE

Note that network executives did all that without really acknowledging publicly that advocacy organizations were the cause of program changes. In fact, network leaders continued to maintain a tough stance toward pressure groups. At the same time, they began to insist to advertisers that they had always chosen programs not simply because of ratings but because of a "desirability index" sensitive to audience attitudes as well. The implication was that the networks were being responsive to shifts in the general audience mood and that public advocacy organizations should not attribute program changes directly to their militance.

From the network standpoint, such an executive rhetoric must walk a line between calming the advocacy groups and advertisers by admitting change, on the one hand, and publicly signalling the success of the advocates on the other. It is an exceedingly thin line, and the difficulty of achieving full success was noted by Marvin Koslow of the Bristol Meyers Company (a major advertiser) in an industry symposium on "The Proliferation of Pressure Groups in Prime Time":

> Whether you announce a change in programming content, whether you just let it subtly happen, or whether you meet with Mr. Falwell [of the Moral Majority], he will claim credit for having achieved that change in programming content. . . . The organization is going to take credit for any kind of change. . . . That's the only way they can continue to survive (Margulies, 1981: A-32).

Writer-producer David Rintels noted in response, however, that the networks and production firms need not approach their public rhetoric regarding pressure groups as an acknowledgement of reality. Rather, he suggested, it should be used as a signal to society at large that organizations that try to force changes in network programming through public clamor and advertiser boycotts ought not and will not be considered legitimate:

> If, as I hope, we do improve television, I'd like to see us get credit for it, not Mr. Falwell. I do not want to legitimize a man whose tactics I fear and resent. . . . (Margulies, 1981: A-32).

CONCLUSIONS

David Rintel's remarks point to the broad range of pressures that urge creators and programmers toward both change and continuity in television fare. Many creators have personal, artistic, and social motivation for moving in new directions. At the same time, they know that industry pressures create a need to retain routines that work and that keep them working. When ideas for change originate from such producers, writers, or network programmers, they can be processed through the corporate system so that compromises fit industry requirements and arguments take place out of the public eye.

But when organized forces from outside the industry make demands, executives see the situation very differently. To them, public disputations endanger their control over the resources and routines that help them do their work. Industrial and organizational autonomy to pursue the resources and routines are so central to network and production firm assumptions that television executives view pressure group demands for all but marginal changes as major threats.

The resource dependence framework leads one to suggest that perception of such threats would ignite a series of industry responses to help the networks and producers keep control over the routines that govern their ability to deliver the right audiences to advertisers reliably and efficiently. And, in fact, a number of examples in this paper show the responses in action. Some consequences that these responses hold for program content can be determined much more clearly than can others. A most difficult one to gauge is whether threats of organized public pressure, even if not successful in the short run, nevertheless dampen network interests to pursue certain topics. One might argue, for example, that the *Playing for Time* and *Love, Sidney* controversies would make network executives think more than twice before again casting Vanessa Redgrave as a Jew or designating the lead of a situation comedy as a homosexual. In other words, the latent consequences of such pressures might be to further increase the hesitance of executives to opt for change over continuity.

But this paper has argued that deflecting pressures and continuing routines hold consequences that run much deeper than allowing people to do work more predictably or even placing conscious limits on change in television material. Because the routines that guide the creation of television programming are rooted in the fundamental values of U.S. society, the interaction of the television industry with public advocacy organizations becomes for the industry a rehearsal of the value and legitimacy of activities that reflect the core ideology of liberal capitalism, among other key values. In this sense, then, network responses to pressure groups work on two related levels: (1) They explicitly uphold the rights of the network as private producers of cultural material to protect their investments and to delegitimize as anti-American those who challenge them; and (2) they implicitly perpetuate the cultural system that reinforces the legitimacy of those rights by reinforcing the routines and formulas that enact that theme.

Clearly, a good deal more work must be done to corroborate, flesh out, and extend these notions. This paper has tried to show that the resource dependence framework is a good guide through this fascinating process.

REFERENCES

Advertising Age (1983) Report on sales and earnings, Procter and Gamble Co., September 8: 127–128.

Advertising Age (1983) Report on sales and earnings, J. Walter Thompson Agency, March 16: 38–40.

Aldrich, Howard (1974) Organizations and Environments. New York: John Wiley.

Banks, Seymour (1978) Personal communication, interview with vice-president of Leo Burnett Advertising, Chicago.

Barnouw, Erik (1976) The Sponsor: Notes on a Modern Potentate. New York: Oxford University Press.

Brown, Les, (1972) Television: The Business Behind the Box. New York: Harcourt Brace Jovanovich.

Cantor, Muriel (1980) Prime Time Television. Beverly Hills, CA: Sage.

Coates, Colby (1981a) "Coalition may not call boycott." Advertising Age, June 29: 1.

Coates, Colby (1981b) "Boycott pro and con." Emmy: The Magazine of the Academy of Television Arts and Sciences Summer: 39–41.

Coates, Colby and Robert Marich (1981) "P&G's rap at TV laid to fear of boycott." Advertising Age June 22: 85.

Cole, Barry and Mal Oettinger (1978) The Reluctant Regulators. Reading, MA: Addison-Wesley.

Cooper, Abraham (1983) Personal communication, interview with associate director of the Simon Wiesenthal Center for the Study of the Holocaust.

Cowan, Geoffrey (1978) See No Evil. New York: Simon and Schuster.

Evan, William (1976) Organization Theory. New York: John Wiley.

Gitlin, Todd (1979a) "Prime time ideology: the hegemonic process in television entertainment." Social Problems 26: 264ff.

——— (1979b) The Whole World Is Watching. Berkeley: University of California Press.

Katz, Daniel and Robert Kahn (1966) The Social Psychology of Organizations. New York: John Wiley.

Levin, Richard (1981) "How the gay lobby has changed television." TV Guide May 30: 3–6.

March, John and Herbert Simon (1976) Organizations. New York: John Wiley.

Margulies, Lee (1981) "Proliferation of pressure groups in prime time 1981." Emmy: The Magazine of the Academy of Television Arts and Sciences Summer: A–29.

Montgomery, Kathryn (1981) "Gay activists and the networks." Journal of Communication 31: 49–57.

Newsweek (1980) "The activist actress." September 29: 52–58.

Powers, Ron (1981) "The new holy war against sex and violence." TV Guide April 18: 12.

Rowland, Willard (1983) The Politics of TV Violence. Beverly Hills: Sage.

Russell, Richard (1976) "When it comes to slipping a questionable line or a touchy idea past the network censors. . . ." TV Guide December 16: 39–44.

de Sola Pool, Ithiel and Irwin Shulman (1964) "Newsmen's fantasies, audiences, and newswriting," in Lewis Dexter and David White (eds.), People, Society, and Mass Communications. New York: The Free Press.

Syrkin, Marie (1980) "Vanessa in Auschwitz." The New Republic October 18: 39.

The Nation (1980) "Death of a principle." October 15: 345.

Traviesas, Herminio (1980) "Bleep! confessions of a network censor." TV Guide August 30: 9–10.

Tuchman, Gaye (1971) "Making news by doing work: routinizing the unexpected." American Journal of Sociology 79: 119–131.

――― (1974) "introduction," in G. Tuchman (ed.) The TV Establishment. Englewood Cliffs, NJ: Prentice-Hall.

Turow, Joseph (1977–1978) "Another view of citizen feedback." Public Opinion Quarterly 41: 534–543.

――― (1978) "Casting for television: the anatomy of social typing." Journal of Communication 28: 18–24.

――― (1981) "Unconventional programs on commercial television: an organizational perspective," in D. Charles Whitney and James Ettema (eds.), Individuals in Mass Media Organizations. Beverly Hills: Sage.

――― (1982) "The role of 'the audience' in publishing children's books." Journal of Popular Culture 16: 90–99.

――― (1984) Media Industries: The Production of News and Entertainment. New York: Longman.

TV Guide (1981) June 6: A–1.

Williams, Raymond (1975) Television: Technology and Cultural Form. New York: Schocken.

PART II

INTERPRETING THE TELEVISION TEXT

Chapter 7

POPULARITY AND IDEOLOGY
A Structuralist Reading of *Dr. Who*

John Fiske

THE FIRST EPISODE of *Dr Who* aired on November 23, 1963, which makes it the British Broadcasting Corporation's (BBC) longest running fictional program ever. It is exported to over 40 different countries all over the world and has spanned a network of fan clubs and organizations: in Chicago in 1978, 100,000 fans attended a convention.

Its popularity, as argued by Tullock and Alvarado (1983) lies in the flexibility of its structure—the time can range over millions of years, the Doctor himself can be (and has been) played by a number of different actors who vary his personality, appearance, and age, and he can have a number of different helpers and companions. But this flexibility is always contained within a set of conventions. The Doctor is essentially good—he is nonviolent, selfless, and his missions in time and space are always to defeat evil, to free the oppressed, and to establish a harmonious free society in the worlds that he visits.

He is a "Timelord" with human form and human characteristics, but a nonhuman origin. He is a rebel, constantly ignoring the control of his masters in Gallifrey. His reliance on space-age technology is minimized. The Tardis, his space/time ship, is like a police box (a blue telephone kiosk) on the outside, but is an enormous network of corridors and control stations on the inside. It is extraterrestrial, and its operations therefore slide easily over that crucial boundary between magic and science. K9, the canine computer, is domesticated, friendly hi-tech, not technology to be in awe of or to wonder at. Dr Who wins his struggles not by superior technology (which in science fiction generally means superior force—technology is both totalitarian

AUTHOR'S NOTE: An earlier version of this chapter, under the title "Dr Who, Ideology and the Reading of a Popular Narrative Text," appeared in *The Australian Journal of Screen Theory,* 1983, 14 pp. 60–100.

and imperialistic) but by reason, fearlessness, humor, and curiosity. Science, for him, is not a means of controlling the world or taming nature, but an expression of man's eternal curiosity—the desire to find out and to understand. His is a humane, mentalistic science, not a hi-tech, antihuman one. This paper uses a structuralist analysis of one particular story in order to raise some issues about its specific popularity and about popularity in general. Structuralism and semiotics avoid terms like escape or diversion to describe the television genre to which Dr. Who belongs because they imply that the symbolic world of television drama is disconnected from the social world of the audience. The notion of popularity, however, suggests connections between the two worlds, and it is these connections and their ideological effect that this paper seeks to explore.

The story whose analysis enables me to raise these theoretical issues is called "The Creature from the Pit." It is by David Fisher, and was first broadcast in Britain in 1979, and consists of four 30-minute episodes. Let me summarize the plot briefly.

The Doctor, Romana, and K9 are brought by the Tardis to Chloris, a planet overrun with vegetation and short of minerals. They have picked up a distress call from what the Doctor identifies as a huge egg. During their investigation they are captured by soldiers and a "Huntsman" who controls "the Wolf-weeds" (large balls of vegetation that kill by rolling over their victim). They are taken to Chloris's ruler Lady Adrasta, but before they reach her they are attacked by bandits in the forest and Romana is kidnapped. Adrasta is surprised that the Doctor has identified the mysterious object, as the best brains in her kingdom have been unable to. Her chief engineer is condemned to death for his failure to solve the mystery. His execution consists of his being thrown into the pit where the Creature exists ready to devour any human being with whom he comes in contact. Meanwhile Romana, with the aid of K9, has escaped from the Bandits but is rapidly recaptured by Adrasta's men.

As a strategy to save her, the Doctor jumps into the pit. In the pit, which is a series of worked out mine galleries, the Doctor meets Organon, an astrologer who has been thrown in there by Adrasta. He has made himself comfortable in the galleries and has learned how to keep out of the Creature's way. He explains to the Doctor that Adrasta owns the only mine on Chloris and thus all its mineral wealth. By means of this monopoly of metal she maintains her power. The Doctor guesses that the Creature is not a native of Chloris.

Adrasta keeps Romana alive because of what she knows about the egg and because of K9's abilities. She, Adrasta that is, has discovered the capabilities of the Tardis, which she wants to use to fetch metal from other planets, thus preserving her monopoly. She now has no use for the Creature; previously she had used it as a means of terror for maintaining her power, but the strengthening of her mineral wealth will serve the same function. So she takes K9 to the pit to kill the Creature.

Down in the pit the Doctor has followed the Creature to try and learn more about it and discovers traces of minerals that have not come from Chloris. He befriends the Creature, who draws the shape of a shield that the Doctor has seen in Adrasta's palace.

The bandits meanwhile attach Adrasta's palace in order to steal her metal, including the shield that the Creature has drawn. The shield mysteriously hypnotizes them, and makes them carry it towards the Creature. The Doctor places the shield on the Creature who then uses it to communicate through the Doctor's voice. We learn that the Creature is called Irato and that he is an Ambassador from Tythonis on a trading mission to exchange vegetation (the food of the Tythonians, of which they are short, for metal, of which they have plenty). The mysterious "egg" is, in fact, his spaceship. Adrasta saw that free trade would break the power that her monopoly had given her so she imprisoned him in the pit.

The Huntsman shows doubts about Adrasta's autocratic leadership and after an argument sides with the Doctor and turns the Wolf-weeds against Adrasta. Irato kills both Adrasta and her Wolf-weeds. He is naturally cross about his long imprisonment and plans to leave Chloris immediately in the egg. But the Doctor has "borrowed" his photon drive without which he cannot leave. He is then forced to disclose the information that in 24 hours a neutron star will hit Chloris. The Doctor uses the photon drive as a bargaining counter to persuade Irato to spin a web of aluminium around the star and then use the Tardis's gravitational field to yank it off course. Reluctantly Irato agrees, but Karela (Adrasta's henchwoman) has stolen the photon drive and tries to make an alliance with the bandits to preserve the metal monopoly with them.

K9 is called in to destroy the metal that the bandits have. This simple lesson in economics that metal is not of intrinsic value but that value is a function of scarcity, shows the bandits the fragility of their theory. The Doctor returns the photon drive and departs with Irato for Tythonis. He returns with a draft contract for a trading agreement, which he hands to the Huntsman who has now taken over power and will, by implication, establish a progressive, democratic, *good* government.

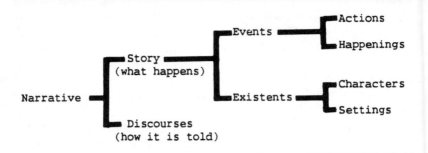

FIGURE 1   Structural Model of a Simple Narrative

In this paper I intend to explore two closely related concerns: (1) the relationship between the syntagmatic, onward thrust of the story through time and the paradigmatic, atemporal discourses through which it is realized, and (2) the notion of popularity, which I define as "an easy fit between the discourses of the text and the discourses through which its model readers articulate and understand their social experience."

Let me use a simple structural model of a narrative as my starting point (Chatman, 1978). The reader should consult Figure 1. The top half of the model identifies first the comparatively unproblematic elements that can be schematized by a straightforward analysis of the manifest content. But the significance of these elements does not lie in their identification and nomination: but rather in the ways in which they are, or can be, interrelated.

And what is really at issue here is the relationship of discourses. For a number of discourses are used to realize the Doctor and his adversaries in the narrative. In this story, we find centrally the discourses of politics, morality, economics, and individualism used to establish the identity and difference of heroes and villains, while that of science and reason provides the common ground between them. The Doctor is realized by a neat interplay between the values of liberal democracy and those of "good" science, while his adversaries signify the values of totalitarianism and "bad" science. We will return to this point later, at the moment I wish only to establish the structuralist truism that significance lies in relationships, not in entities.

And these relationships are those among elements in the story (the top half of the model), among the discourses used to realize them, and between the elements and the discourses. Central to all these interrelationships is the notion of discourse, and this is one that I find most fruitful for it enables us to link text and society in a way that leads toward a theory of popularity.

A discourse, then, is both a topic and a coded set of signs through which that topic is organized, understood, and made expressible. Discourses, according to O'Sullivan et al. (1983), are "the product of social, historical and institutional formations, and meanings are produced by these institutionalised discourses. It follows that the potentially infinite senses any language system is capable of producing are always limited and fixed by the structure of social relations which prevails in a given time and place, and which is itself represented through various discourses." Discourse is the social process by which sense is made and reproduced. A discourse may be manifest in a text, but its origins and destinations are always social. It functions both in the production and reception of texts and in the production of meaning in social experience. Making sense of our social experience is at least a parallel activity to reading a text: indeed, I am tempted to go further and claim that the two are, in essence, identical. The notion of discourse is essential to both, for it is this that explains how we bring our social experience to bear upon our reading of texts and how we use our reading of texts to feed back into our social experience. In this, I differ only in emphasis from Morley (1980a):

> Thus the meaning of the text must be thought of in terms of which set of discourses it encounters in any particular set of circumstances, and how this encounter may restructure both the meaning of the text and the discourses which it meets.

The discourses available to the reader are obviously those available to the author for giving sense to the chain of events that constitute his story. And the interplay between textually located and socially located discourses is the process by which meaning is achieved in both text and society. And the interplay is two-way.

In the discourse of politics, for example, our social experience and our textual experience confirm each other in, for example, the positive connotations of democracy and the negative connotations of autocracy. But cultural consensus within a discourse can also be an agreement to differ: we agree that Marxism and monetarism, for example, can have positive or negative connotations within the same discourse depending on the speaker and context.

This points us to one of the crucial differences between discourses in society and the same discourses in a text, especially a popular text: those in a text operate with a higher degree of consensus and tend to exclude signs with alternative connotations. Popular texts are constructed from those areas of a discourse where consensus is high enough to be taken for granted—thus we find Dr. Who defined partly through democracy in the political discourse and his adversaries through totalitarianism, because these signs can be taken for granted.

Interestingly, and most importantly, this assumption of consensus is transferred to more controversial areas, such as free trade and individualism. But we will return to this later. At the moment I wish to make the point that it is in the nature of popular texts to operate within the high consensus areas of a discourse and then to extend this assumed and unquestioned consensus to more controversial areas.

Our social experience is, therefore, harder to read than a text, because it is fraught with the internal contradictions and sites of ideological struggle that are disguised, if not excluded from a popular text by its conditions of production and reception. Reading social experience is a struggle, and because of its open nature we find it difficult to be finally sure that our reading is adequate: Reading a text, however, is easier by far, and the greater closure within it is constantly working to reassure and convince us that this easy reading is adequate—totally adequate. A text, then, becomes popular when its readings, which are confidently believed to be adequate, fit neatly and naturally with readings of social experience that we use the same discourses to understand, but which are by definition, more complex, contradictory, and thus harder to read. Popular narratives prove in their own closed world the adequacy of discourses as explanatory, sense-making mechanisms: This adequacy is then transferred to the use of those discourses in the social world to the ultimate relief and reassurance of the reader. In this Dr. Who text, for example, we will see how the discourses of politics, economics, and morality enter into a mutually validating relationship within the narrative; this validity is then, through the sociotextual nature of discourse, itself transferred to the appropriate institutions that form their prime locations in society.

So discourses are not just social topics and a system of signs for realizing them: they are the means by which social experience is constructed and by which the social being is constructed. My history is the process by which I have acquired the range of discourses that enable me to exist as a social being.

Structuralism is concerned with the way that members of a culture make sense of their experience. It stresses that this sense derives not from any intrinsic meaning of an individual unit of experience, but from the relationship between the various units. Thus, later on in this article when I discuss the potential meanings of characters and settings in this story, I am able to do so only in terms of diagrams that relate characters and settings together according to certain criteria and value systems. The "meaning" of the character of *Dr. Who* emerges from two key sets of relationships—one with Romana and K9 (see Figure 1) and the other with Adrasta, Irato, and the bandits (see Figure 4). Similarly the meaning of the discourse of politics can be understood only in its relationship with the discourses of economics, morality, and individualism, and these in turn can be understood only in their relationships with the discourse of science/reason and the way it functions to transform nature into culture. Thus, for structuralism, meanings are not fixed or set either in a text or in an abstract system of language: meanings are constantly generated and negotiated both by the structures that are dominant in any one text or in any one society at a particular period, and by the relationship between the discursive structures in a text and those in society as they come together in the crucial moment of reading. These various structures, and the relationships within and between them, are not arbitrary or random. All structures result from the operation of the human brain. This means that they all have something in common, and thus we should expect to find similarities between those found in, for instance, language, and those in, for instance, the kinship system, and those in, for instance, the cooking system (see Levi-Strauss 1955). The repeatability, or parallelism, of structures is the way that a culture produces a unifiable or coherable world view for its members. Structures that make sense of one facet of experience fit with those applied to another: this apparent harmony is essential to the smooth working of ideology. For without it, that is when contradictions and disunities are perceived, the arbitrariness of ideology, and therefore its partiality, is made apparent.

Developments in structuralism, which go under the name of poststructuralism, tend to emphasise the role of the reader in the construction of relationships both within structures and between structures. This sets structuralism on a different path from more traditional modes of textual analysis in that it prioritizes the reader over the author. The author's intention and even his "creativity" are demoted from objects of crucial interest. The meanings of a text are not what the author intended or wished to put into it, but what the reader finds when using that text in a particular moment of space and time. Thus, the text can have different meanings for different readers at different cultural moments. This is not to say that the text is a wide-open potential of any meanings; far from it, for the structures of the text itself prefer some potential meanings over others and delimit the space within which meanings can legitimately be found.

Within this emphasis on the role of the reader can be found three main theoretical positions. The first, and this is one associated largely with Screen Theory, is that the reader is produced by the text. By cooperating with the text, the reader positions himself or herself in the appropriate discursive and social position to make the easy sense that the text itself prefers. This view has been challenged by work such as that of Morley (1980b), which asserts that the reader's social and cultural experience has at least as much bearing upon this negotiation of meaning as have the structures in the text. Both these positions differ from the third, which asserts that readings or interpretations exist in empirically definable individuals and are therefore assessible to empirical analysis.

Structuralism insists that meanings are located ultimately in subjectivities not in individuals. Subjectivity is the site of consciousness, which is produced by a number of cultural and textual agencies. O'Sullivan et al. (1983) write: "Subjectivity is a way of conceptualising text/reader relations without reproducing either as fixed unitary categories. At the level of analysis a lot of work has been done to show how cultural products (especially films and television) employ textual analysis and strategies like point-of-view, mode of address and narration to propose or fix a subject position from which they can be made sense of when read." This position of the reading subject need not coincide with the position of the biographically defined individual: classic Hollywood films position their readers as middle-class, white males. That is to say that they prefer to be read by the discourses that make sense of social and textual experience in a way that serves the interests of that particular social category. This means that blacks, or the working class, or women are positioned by the film in ways that contradict their social experience and are led to make sense of both the film and their experience via discourses that are not "theirs." In this sense, then, individuals are seen not as self-possessed and self-possessing entities, but as subjects in ideology constituted by the range of social discourses available to them (and these discourses, as we have seen, are both social and textual).

Barthes (1975) explains subjectivity as the "I" who reads the text: "This 'I' which approaches the text is already itself a plurality of other texts, of codes which are infinite or, more precisely, lost (whose origin is lost. . . .. Subjectivity is a plenary image with which I may be thought to encumber the text, but whose deceptive plenitude is merely the wake of all the codes which constitute me, so that my subjectivity has ultimately the generality of stereotypes." He goes on to explain that "my task (as reader) is to move, to shift systems whose perspective ends neither at the text nor at the 'I': in operational terms, the meanings I find are established not by 'me' or by others, but by their *systematic* mark" (1975: 10–11). System, for Barthes, is a central term that refers to the structural properties of codes and discourses.

Subjectivity is thus available to analysis only via discourses, texts, and cultural practices, not by empirical investigation of individuals. Interpretation now becomes not a matter of matching an individual reader's response with an individual author's intention, but one of discovering within the text relationships of discourse, of characters, of settings, of narrative moments that parallel and reproduce structures found elsewhere in the culture and that will be available to the reader to bring, via the reader's discursive practices, to the making of the text.

This approach follows the priorities set by Todorov (1977) when he points out that there are two lines of force in a narrative: the vertical, which consist of the discourses of knowledge (e.g., the hidden cultural laws of class, politics, and sex roles), and the horizontal, which is the sequence of events. For Todorov, the vertical is the more significant.

Of the discourses of knowledge in this narrative, the first, and most obvious, is that of science; but science is not the value-free objective discourse it claims to be in society. As Tulloch (1982) has suggested, pure science is finally totalitarian—it allows no alternative, no oppositional view. In story after story in Dr. Who, "pure" or "cold" science is used to maintain or establish a totalitarian political order. Science is a means of power in an intergalactic version of feudal society. The Doctor typically defeats a totalitarian, scientific antagonist and replaces him or her with a liberal democratic humane scientist to take over and bring justice and freedom to the oppressed serf class.

While it is easy to oppose the values of liberal democracy to those of totalitarianism in the political discourse, it is less easy to oppose the values of totalitarian or "cold" science with the "warm" humane science whose values are embodied in the Doctor, and this is what the narrative works hard to achieve.

In this particular story, both types of existent, characters and settings, are used to structure our values, both within the discourse of science and in its relationships with other discourses such as politics or "humanism." In using this word we need to cut out many of its traditional associations with the "humanities," but to maintain its

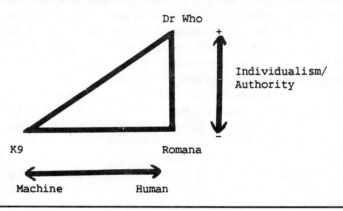

FIGURE 2   Triadic Structure of Hero Relationships

central concern with the "human," the nature of man (defined according to, as we shall see later, a postromantic, individualistic, capitalist set of criteria).

And at the heart of this humanism is the concept of the individual. Science, in our culture's common-sense understanding of it, at least, is anti-individualist: the objectivity of empiricism distrusts the individual in any role other than that of observer, analyst, or computer. Value-laden scales such as morality or politics are anathema to it.

The text then faces the inherent ideological problem of its genre—science fiction. It needs to reconcile the objective of inhuman values of science with the individualistic and moral values of popular fiction. It does this by a careful structuring of heroes, villains, and discourses.

The triadic hero in this story consists of Dr. Who, Romana, and K9. Their basic relationships are structured on the dimensions of first, machines (controlled) to human (controller), and second, of degree of individuality, which goes with authority. The structure can be visualized as presented in Figure 2.

K9 is pure, technological science with two major exceptions—he is "domesticated," controlled by man, whom he constantly refers to as "Master" and "Mistress," and he is programmed to kill only in self defense. He has not only rigid scientific principles—he will not accept incompatible data, but also rigid, if fragile, moral principles. He can be significantly opposed to the Daleks in that he is science with the proper relationship to humanity, whereas they are antihuman. He is a domesticated Dalek, and this concept of the domestication of science is an important one. It is no coincidence that one of our commonest computer systems is called a PET. This is a similar pun to that contained in the name K9/canine, and both illustrate the ideological function of puns in bringing together opposing discourses and defusing the opposition either by laughter or by demonstrating similarity of the signifier that overrides the more fundamental difference: in this case that between science as threatening to take over humans, and pets that are wild animals or nature domesticated, tamed and brought into households under human control. Science and nature become one in the K9/canine pun: the inherent threat in each is defused by the domestication common to both.

K9, then, is clearly a machine: Dr. Who and Romana are both Timelords in human form, but the Doctor is more "human" than Romana. Tulloch (1982) shows convincingly how the Doctor's ability to err is a way of structuring human or individualistic values into a "cold" scientist. He has other character traits that perform the same function: one is his schoolboyishness (Romana chides him for his untidiness and his collection of "useless" junk: he is also reading a child's book when the story opens), another is his hint of teenage rebelliousness (he will not plug in the transceiver so that he can receive orders from Gallifrey), similar to this is his trait of "randomness" (the Tardis is liable to materialize and land the Doctor almost anywhere: the acceptance of "chance" or "luck" seems another key value of the human when opposed to the coldly scientific) and another, of course, is his sense of humor. His eccentric dress performs much the same function. The romantic echoes of Bohemia in his hat and coat and the long scarf (apparently knitted by a myopic maiden aunt) both serve to individualize him. This individualism is set against the "objectivity" of cold science where the subjectivism of the individual observer/worker is distrusted and minimized: Dr. Who must, for ideological reasons, have a marked individualistic dimension.

The fact that his basic science is medicine—the most human and least objective of the sciences—is also significant, not least because it allows us to call him Doctor rather than Professor. Gerbner (1973) has shown how scientists in popular fiction tend to have negative connotations: they are usually evil and working against the common good of humanity. The Doctor, however, is essentially a healer, particularly of sick societies. Think how much colder the connotations would be if he were called "The Professor" instead of "The Doctor." Romana, however, lacks the Doctor's human frailties or imperfections and, therefore, lacks the flashes of inspiration and insight that in the Doctor's case accompany them. She works by pure logic, either when calculating their chances of survival (74,384,338 to 1) or when

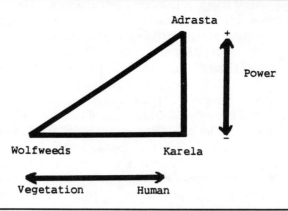

FIGURE 3   Triadic Structure of Adversarial Relationships

reasoning her way out of the captivity of the bandits. She is, finally, less individualistic than he, for his eccentricity is a signifier of individualism.

A structure similar to that of the heroes relates the adversarial triad of Adrasta, Karela, and the Wolf-weeds, as depicted in Figure 3. The Wolf-weeds are tamed nature in the same way as K9 is tamed science. (Note that they are *Wolf*-weeds, i.e. *canine* and they are used for actions that are the evil equivalents of K9's good ones; for instance, they can and do kill whereas he merely stuns.) Twice the Wolf-weeds overpower K9 and render him helpless, paralleling Adrasta's capture and recapture of the Doctor and Romana, but more importantly reflecting the unbalanced situation on Chloris where nature is overpowering culture. Adrasta has power rather than the authority that the Doctor has. Her effectiveness relies on force, not on respect for her as an individual, and she therefore lacks the Doctor's touches of individualism, which are necessary to define his authority as a dominance achieved by individual worth exercised within a socially granted power role. Karela is an evil helper of the villain as Romana is the good helper of the hero.

But the two triads of heroes and villains do not operate alone; their values are extended and elaborated in their relations with minor characters and the settings of the story, that is, in its existents. The four main settings and the four main character groups are given identically structured relationships, as illustrated in Figure 4. The greater complexity of this model reflects the fact that negative and oppositional values have come into play as we take account of char-

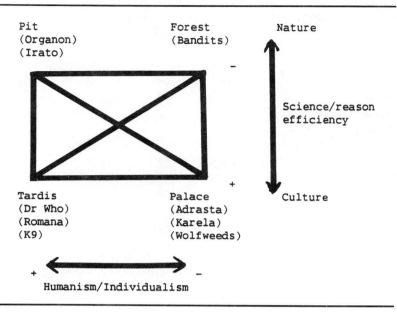

FIGURE 4   Relationships of Minor Characters and Settings

acters' roles other than the protagonists, that is, helpers and adversaries. The bottom left of Figure 4 is where humanism and science meet at the site of the heroes.

The Tardis exemplifies this meeting perfectly: on the inside it is pure science, on the outside idiosyncratically individualistic (see Tulloch, 1982); it is the mechanical equivalent of the Doctor, who also clothes his science in the garb of eccentric individualism. It is also a metaphor for control—spatial physics expands its interior presumably *ad infinitum,* whereas externally it is not only compact, but a police box—a metonym of social law and order.

The conflict in the narrative is between the left and right of this structure, that is between the humanistic and its opposite, not between science and nonscience. Indeed, the astrologer (nonscientist) Organon is the Doctor's only helper, and Irato becomes "friendly" by the end of the story. The pit itself was once mine workings, but now has become the underground equivalent of the forest. This structure elaborates our understanding of science, because it is seen as a site of conflict only in its relationship with the humanistic discourse, and this humanistic discourse merges into the political. Those on the right of the structure are totalitarian in that they are concerned to gain and exercise power over others for their own ends. All those on the left, including K9, are captured at one time or other by those on the right. The bandits are inefficient, deviant members of the same totalitarian ideology that Adrasta embodies. They are less evil and less of a threat than she is only because they are less "scientific" and therefore less logical. This means that they cannot organize themselves efficiently into a leader and followers and they cannot understand how the economics of metal shortage is the key to political power.

Their social structure is a parody of the democratic. They have shapeless discussions that never reach a decision: they vote and then ignore the result, and they have a leader whose constant slips of the tongue show that he is in fact concerned solely with his own interests while pretending to have those of his followers at heart—"Bandit Leader: Metal, metal, metal, it'll make me—er, *us*—the most powerful people on Chloris." The bandits share with Adrasta a disregard for human life, both kill easily and callously, and after Adrasta's death they join with Karela to try and maintain the evil despotism based upon the monopoly of metal. They are properly on the right of the structure for they are binarily opposed to the "true" democracy embodied in the Doctor.

As the bandits are opposed to the Doctor and therefore aligned with Adrasta, so Organon is opposed to Adrasta and aligned with the Doctor. Adrasta threw him in the pit for his inefficiency, his nonscience, as she did with the hapless engineer at the start of the story. But he is properly on the left of the diagram because of his respect for the individual and his desire to help the hero. Irato has also been thrown into the pit but this is because he provided an opposition to Adrasta not on the science scale but on the political and economic scales.

On the left of the structure are the democrats, that is, those who value the rights and abilities of the individual, for the use of reason and persuasion rather than force to achieve social ends, and the belief in negotiation to arrive at a consensus. Irato is a diplomat from Chloris on a trade mission charged with the responsibility of achieving a trading agreement beneficial to both parties.

This brings us to another crucial discourse—the economics. Adrasta's power is maintained partly by her guards, but mainly by her manipulation of the economy so that she can maintain a monopoly of metal. In the past she owned the only metal mine: now this is worked out and she jealously guards the small remaining quantities of metal. The bandits' one aim is to steal as much as they can, not because of its use-value—they do not care if it is in the form of swords, drinking cups, or ornaments—but because of its scarcity value. The shortage of metal has meant that the land cannot be cultivated, so the vegetation has run riot and the planet is almost completely overgrown.

Irato is a huge green shapeless monster who survives largely on chlorophyl from vegetation. He was sent from Chloris, which is a planet with a surplus of metal but a shortage of vegetation, in order to arrange trade with Chloris—a simple example of free trade that should, according to basic capitalist economics, have produced two balanced economies each supporting prosperous bourgeois democratic societies. But Adrasta saw that the end of her monopoly in metal would mean the end of her power, and that the increase in its availability would destroy her wealth by removing the scarcity value of her metal. She therefore captured Irato and threw him into the pit before any of her subjects could learn of his proposals. Adrasta's power, maintained by her "artificial" monopoly, is unbalanced because it is undemocratic, and is lacking the influence of the individual upon the ruling process. This social and political imbalance is "naturalized" by the rampant vegetation, which is nature out of balance with man. Both are the result of the artificial monopoly, both will then be cured, the implication goes, by natural free trade. The naturalizing of free trade into the obviously right system, indeed into the only possible system, is a central part of the ideological force of the narrative.

Towards the end of the story, Irato, the symbol of free trade, rolls over and kills Adrasta, the symbol of monopoly, and her Wolf-weeds. When he rolls off they are dead and monopoly is vanquished. The final action of the Doctor before dematerializing the Tardis is to produce a "mutually beneficial trading agreement" between Chloris and Tythonis. The actions in the narrative prove the structuring of the discourses.

The structure of Figure 4 illustrates that those on its left are free traders, whereas those on the right are monopolists. The discourse of economics exhibits a precise structural match with that of politics, and both fit with the underlying one of individualism. All three bear the same relationship to the discourse of science and, in fact, become the criteria for evaluating between "good" and "bad" science. The use of these value-laden objectives brings us on to the fourth crucial discourse, that of morality. The BBC is specific and precise about the morality of the show—the Doctor must be clearly good, and his adversaries clearly bad. The story admits of no blurred value judgments in the main characters, though minor ones may undergo a transformation through their meeting with the Doctor from apparently bad to really good (e.g., the Huntsman and Irato).

The significance of the Doctor lies partly in his structured relationship to gods and man. He is an anomalous creature in that he is neither God (or Timelord) nor man but occupies a mediating category between the two. He has a nonhuman origin and many nonhuman abilities, yet a human form and many human characteristics. In other words, he occupies the same space between humans and God as does Christ. Other Christ-likenesses include his consistent function of cleansing a society of evil and setting it on the paths of justice and goodness; the intergalactic timelessness of the Doctor is not unlike eternal heaven of Christ; his dislike of violence and his sexual abstinence are other shared characteristics, as is the fact that both are leaders. The fact that both are part of a trinity may be stretching the parallelism too far, but again, it may not.

Other motifs in the story support the theory that the discourse of morality is not just a humanistic one, but one with a strong religious base. Romana (echoes of Pax Romana?) is always dressed in white flowing robes with connotations of angels or vestal virgins and as such is structurally contrasted with the black of Adrasta who thus takes on Satanic connotations. We can also note here the traditional Christian motif of the bringer of evil into the world being a woman. The Huntsman's turning against his former mistress echoes the repentance of the sinner, and the defeat of Adrasta is the spiritual purging of the planet.

This structure of moral values, underwritten as it is by religious connotations, is the final naturalizing force in the ideological practice of the program, "the good" and "the bad" are clearly distinguished in the text, both by appearance, nature, or setting (that is as existents) and by behavior (that is by actions) as Figure 5 shows. Tabulated like this the fit between actions and existents is striking in its simplicity. In the narrative, however, the constant killing and capturing by the villains takes a variety of exciting forms that disguises the fundamental monotony or at least homogeneity. But this is typical of television where an attractive variety of signifiers commonly overlays a restricted range of signifieds and a simple repetitive self-reinforcing structure. Indeed, the attractiveness of the signifier is essential for the ideological effect because without it, the internal repetition of the structure would become manifest with the result that it would cease to be the hidden organizing device, and would then become apparent and therefore propaganda. In the discourse of morality the good is so

The Heroes			The Villains		
Actions	Existents — Settings	Existents — Characters	Existents — Characters	Existents — Settings	Actions
Sharing information Befriending Caring Helping	Pit Decayed culture Reverting to nature			Forest Rampant nature Hostile to culture	Killing Taking captive Stealing Monopolizing
		Long hair and beards indicate inefficiency, lack of science, and deviation from the social norm			
Setting free Befriending Reasoning Revealing the truth Sharing	Tardis Futuristic culture	 White, Humanistic Individualistic	 Black, Conformist De-individualized	Palace Old-fashioned culture	Killing (including threats + orders to) Taking captive, lying Concealing the truth Monopolizing
Stunning (ie. not killing) Information storing Computing		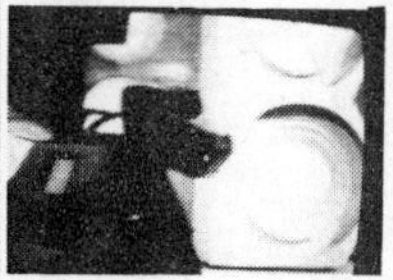 Tamed science	 Tamed vegetation (nature)		Killing Capturing

FIGURE 5 Parallel Relationships between Actions and Existents in Text

181

clearly distinguished from the bad because its rightness is tested, found true, and finally rewarded by the narrative, and our affective sympathy with hero and villain is constructed to coincide with it, so that finally we are afforded practically no opportunity to question the basis or implications of this morality either in the text or in society. The ideological closure of the moral discourse is more final and complete than it can be of the political and economic discourses that would on their own admit of radically opposed or negotiated readings (see Hall, 1973).

The discourse of morality however allows little or no space for negotiation. It is difficult, if not impossible, to imagine a frame of reference that could be brought to bear upon Adrasta that could evaluate her as anything other than evil, and that therefore rejects her political, economic, and anti-individualistic values. The apparently innocent agreement of all discourses to fit the same structure and thus to support each other makes the text highly resistant to any other than its preferred reading. To clarify this we need to add the other discourses onto Figure 4. This elaborated structure is presented in Figure 6.

Here the discourse of morality functions to close off those other discourses whose values are more open to question, particularly those politico-economic ones that are by definition specific to a Western industrialized democracy. And this is where the ideological effect of the onward drive of the narrative is so crucial. The constant unravelling of the mysterious or the flow of tension and release within suspense also functions to close off alternative readings. In nonnarrative television texts such as quiz shows (see Fiske, 1982) or current affairs shows (see Morley, 1980a), the relationships between discourses are more open, and therefore more variable readings are possible.

Here the onward syntagmatic flow of the narrative serves to restrict the potential range of the discourses, and thus the range of positions from which the reading subject can make sense of the text. I do not wish to take up the overdetermined position of some of the early screen theorists, which overemphasised the power of the text to construct the subject, but I do agree with them in their identification of the hegemony of the text in the enterprise of making sense. This text, in common with other popular narratives, constructs a restricted space within which the reading subject must be positioned if she/he is to make the preferred sense, which is the easy natural sense of the text. The limits of this space can be determined by identifying in more

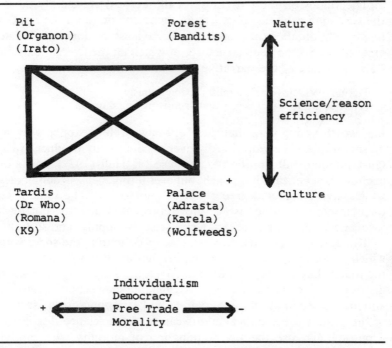

FIGURE 6   Revised Relationships of Minor Characters and Settings

detail the binarily opposed values by which the four main discourses
are articulated. We can tabulate them thus:

Discourse of politics: Democracy : Totalitarianism
Freedom : Slavery
Authority : Power
Progress : Stagnation
Peace : Violence
The Individual : The Ruler or State

Discourse of economics: Free Trade : State Monopoly
Use Value : Scarcity Value
Plenty : Scarcity
Balance : Imbalance

Discourse of individualism: Freedom : Captivity
Individuality/Eccentricity : Conformity
Life : Death

Discourse of morality: Truth : Lies
Good : Evil
Christ : Devil

The values on the left (those of the heroes) are clearly those of the Christian capitalist democracies, whereas those on the right are, by implication, those of communism (or at least the dominant Western view of it). So the deep structure, of which all the events, existents, and discourses of the narrative are transformations, is

Heroes : Villains : : Capitalism : Communism
(Heroes are to Villains as Capitalism is to Communism)

It is worth noting here that the story never refers explicitly to capitalism—indeed the word hardly ever occurs in any product of capitalist popular culture. This is because, as Hall (1977) points out, capitalism never calls itself such, but uses terms such as "democracy," which have a higher degree of social valorization. The same is true for communism, which is also not represented directly, but by the associated values of totalitarianism, state monopoly, and so on.

This text may be closed in its sense of delimiting the space within which a preferred reading can be arrived at. But within this space the reader has a certain amount of freedom. Schoolboys can use the discourses of science and morality to validate their school experience, and may subordinate those of politics and economics to the suspense of the plot. More skeptical adults can read the science discourse as a parody, but use the text's conflation of morality with capitalist democracy to validate their social experience. Different readers can place the discourses in a different hierarchical order, foregrounding them and relating them differently within the limits proposed by the text. But these limits are crucial: The text does not encourage us to correlate despotism with free market economics via the concept of the slavery of the one who may be exploited in the trading deal; neither does it allow us to perceive that the Doctor's liberal democracy requires dominant and subordinate classes just as clearly as does Adrasta's totalitarianism. These readings are radically opposed, ones that would be produced by readers who *dislike* the text, that is who put themselves outside the realm of its popularity.

The reading I am giving in this paper, one that derives from an academic discourse, is also radically opposed, in that it refuses to accept the ideological closure of the text; such radically opposed readers bring to bear on it discourses from their extratextual experience, or they find relationships among the textual discourses that the text itself does not invite. They look for the contradictions between the text and the world, or at least evidence of the arbitrariness of that relationship that the realism of the text seeks to hide. They see the text as a social construct that is the product of a particular social consciousness in a particular historical epoch whose laws and dominant values they may well not accept.

They would therefore read as significant the general absence of class identities. All characters speak with "classless" (i.e., middle-class) accents with the exception of the bandits. The bandits are criminals or deviants, and the opposed reader would note how the text displaces the working class into the criminal class: both are deviant from the middle class consensus. Dorfman and Mattelart (1975) have identified the same ideological practice in Donald Duck comics where criminals are consistently given working class characteristics— and they are the only characters who are. This displacement of class identities into criminal identities is a powerful tool in the naturalizing of the middle-class point of view from which to read the text.

Feminist oppositional readers would note a similar practice in the Adrasta-Romana opposition. Adrasta is female-dominant-evil; Romana is female-subordinate-good. The text emphasizes morality as the significant difference, and by so doing naturalizes the culturally more important value of subordination.

Interestingly, the individualizing character traits of the Doctor (e.g., inspiration, intuition, randomness) are ones normally associated with the feminine in our culture. Romana is therefore denied them, and her distinctive character traits are limited to femaleness—subordination, objective reasoning, and a proneness to victimization and captivity. Similarly, this feminist reading would note sardonically, if not angrily, that Adrasta's power is portrayed as unnatural not only because it depends on an artificial monopoly, but also because it is political power, which is traditionally confined to the male. The restoration of a male, the Huntsman, to dominance at the end is a hidden factor in the ideological closure, just as the trading agreement is a narratively foregrounded one.

But these "readings against the grain" require a conscious effort that can only be motivated from outside the text, or by the perceptions of contradictions between text and world. They deny the easy fit between the textual and social discourses of the reader, and refuse to allow the smooth harmony of the text to disguise the contradictory nature of material reality. They are produced by readers who insist on bringing extratextual discourses to bear in a way that opposes the inscribed preference of the text. They therefore define themselves in opposition to the "model readers." These are defined by Eco (1979) as ones who are "determined by the sort of interpretive operations they are supposed to perform." Model readers are subjects predicted by the text who willingly cooperate with that text in their own construction. They accept the textual hegemony by assisting in its ideological closure.

This notion of the relationship between the text and an active reader differs crucially from that posited by uses and gratifications theorists, who also assume an active reader. In uses and gratifications theories the media are seen as means of gratifying social or personal needs in the individual, and these needs frequently, if not normally, stem from lacks or absences in the lives of viewers: the media are seen as compensatory. Uses and gratifications theory finds its data in the stated gratifications of viewers: it ignores the content of the programs and prioritizes the viewer's ability to seek gratification for often unarticulated needs.

Structuralist/discourse theory, on the other hand, gives high priority to the text and seeks to discover in the text structures or discourses that can make sense of both it and the (potential) social situation of the reader. The subjectivities of readers are formed largely by their discursive experience, that is by the discourses available to them to make sense of their social experience, and of the multitude of texts that they meet. Culture is the process of making sense, and discourses are central to this process. The individual reader's conscious or subconscious does not determine the meaning of the text, as uses and gratifications theory implies; rather, the reader's consciousness is determined by the discourses that produce him or her as a social subject, as a member of a culture (see Barthes, 1975). The model reader of the popular text relates to (or understands) authority, for instance, via particular forms of political and moral discourses. The belief that these same discourses in broadly similar articulations can make sense of Dr. Who's preference for the Huntsman over Adrasta, of the British actions in the Falklands, of the behavior of the father in the Western middle-class family, of the teacher in the school or of the policeman in his locality, makes the structured relationship of discourses in both text and society of greater importance than the individuality of any reader. Texts and social experience are both made and understood by discourses, and the reader's subjectivity, the site of this understanding, is equally a discursive product. A radical feminist, to take an instance already quoted, has/is a consciousness, a site of understanding, formed by the way that feminism interacts with the discourses of politics, of economics, of the family, of education, of work, and of all the formally and informally constituted institutions that form the framework of our culture, and that produce the discourses that produce the same. This consciousness, or structure of discourses, thus determines the sense she will make of a television program such as this one, or of a moment of social experience such as a man opening a door for her, or of the language system with its characterization of the human as the male.

This emphasis on the discourse as the "maker of sense," rather than on the individuals (whether author or reader) involved in the process of communication is shared by many contemporary theorists.

Kristeva (1970) talks of a closed text as being one where the author disguises the productive work and tries to convince the reader that author and reader are the same. The insight is valuable here, though her emphasis differs slightly from mine. Her implication is that the author, whether an individual or an institution, as in this case, is in some way being dishonest or underhanded in this enterprise. Barthes (1979) makes a similar point, though more positively, with regard to texts in general:

> The text requires an attempt to abolish (or at least to lessen) the distance between writing and reading, not by intensifying the reader's projection into the work, but by linking the two together in a single signifying process (*practique signifiante*).

My point is that the popularity of the text is directly attributable to the collapse of the difference between author and reader: the appropriate discourses by which the text is constructed and read are part of the commonsense experience of both. But popularity (then) is not just the willing consent of the model reader to the hegemony of the text, it involves a more active assessment of the effectiveness of the discourses in making sense of both the text and the world. And this fit between world and text is the prerequisite of what Genette (1968) calls verisimilitude or, more commonly, realism. Genette makes the point that the basis of a text's verisimilitude is to be found outside it, in the sociocentral assumed consensual values of society, that is in the intextuality between the text and social behavior seen as a constructed text. The overall mode of this story is realism, despite the obvious fantasy of the characters and settings. This verisimilitude derives partly from the logic of cause and effect by which the actions are strung together, partly from the anonymous narrator evidenced in the objective camera work and motivated editing, but more importantly from the way that the discourses by which the text articulates its narrative structures are also those through which its model readers live their lives. The model reader and invisible author merge into one in the joint activity of making sense. The text is believable, it is verisimilar, because its discourses are part of the ideology of common sense. This cooperation denies any contradictions between world and text because it prioritizes the realism and, as McCabe (1974) points out, a defining feature of realism is its inability to deal with contradictions:

> The unquestioned nature of the narrative discourse entails that the only problem that reality poses is to go and look and see what *things* there *are*. The relationship between the reading subject and the real is placed as one of pure specularity. The real is not articulated—it is. These features imply two essential features of the classic realist text:
>
> (1) The classic realist text cannot deal with the real as contradictory.
> (2) In a reciprocal movement the classic realist text ensures the position of the subject in a relation of dominant specularity.

Realism facilitates the easy interchange of discourses between text and world. If we assume that making sense of our social experience involves writing a narrative about it, that is making a text of it, then this text will, for the well-adjusted majority at least, be a realistic one. Realism is the most easily available mode of apprehending the world around us, particularly if we inhabit a science-based culture. For realism and science both assume an empirically verifiable universe with an objective existence that stands independent of the perception of it and which texts can refer to and signs can denote. Kristeva's author disguising the productive work is twin to the scientist observing natural phenomena objectively: both pretend their work is untainted by the stain of subjectivity or social consciousness, but instead attains a state of universal objectivity, of factuality.

The classic realist text of which this Dr. Who story is an example, is by definition a closed text, and it therefore becomes politically necessary to prize it open by the sort of semiotic or structuralist analysis. Let us return to these discourses, which are so crucial to the structure and the popularity of the text and which are shown in Figure 6. Those on the horizontal scale are culture-specific in the way that those on the vertical scale are not; they are instead assumed to be universal. Mankind is essentially rational, logical, scientific, and science and reason are the means by which man imposes himself on the world and in so doing turns Nature into Culture. Science and reason become central to the definition of human nature. But the culturally specific moral and political values of the horizontal dimension are the crucial ones in determining what sort of culture and what sort of identity this rational mankind actually creates for itself. The determining values of the narrative are those on the horizontal dimension; the vertical values provide the ground upon which the conflicts of the narrative and the oppositions of the other discourses are enacted.

An analysis of a scene from the story (see Table 1) will demonstrate how densely interwoven are the discourses of politics, economics, morality, and individualism, and how they are used to articulate the conflicts and the sequences of suspense and resolution in the narrative. The scene occurs towards the end of the story and is the crucial one in which Adrasta is finally overcome. It opens with K9 having been overpowered by the Wolfweeds and Adrasta apparently in control.

The camera work exemplifies Kristeva's hidden productive work of the closed text. There are 36 shots in this four-minute, twenty-eight-second scene, and every one is changed by a cut—there are no dissolves, fades, or wipes. Every cut is motivated by the dialogue or action. The camera is objective, though placed slightly below eye level. Chatman (1978) suggests in his analysis of a frame from *Citizen Kane* that the low angle shot at crucial moments connotes the foregrounding of ideology, in that characters are seen from a less than realistic viewpoint. This may be true here, though the distance of the camera below eye level is less marked than in the *Citizen Kane* example, in fact none of my students have commented on it until the second or third viewing of the scene. The other piece of constructed camera work is that Adrasta is consistently shot in tighter closeup than the Doctor or his helpers. An unpublished study by one of my students has found evidence to suggest that villains are conventionally shot in tighter closeup than heroes in popular television fiction, and that this code is even extended to newspaper photographs. This sort of connoting, and therefore value-laden, camera work is subtle enough to escape conscious notice on first viewing but nonetheless signifies on the ideological level. The author in the realist text may be invisible but he is not absent. Discourses are visual as well as verbal, and ideology is the framework of meaning that holds the discourses together.

Here ideology is a pluralistic, as well as a slippery, concept. Though its final effect is to impose a false unity upon a contradictory world, it can perform this work in different ways. In Figure 6, for example, ideology functions differently in each of the two dimensions. In the vertical the ideology of our science-based world, with its concepts of

TABLE 1 Examples of Dialogue and Discourse from Dr. Who

	Dialogue	Discourse
K9:	I am immobile, I was overpowered by the Wolf-weeds.	Hostile Nature overcoming tamed Science (Culture)
ADRASTA:	Order your dog to kill Tythonian.	Totalitarian disregard for life/the individual.
DOCTOR:	No.	
ADRASTA:	If you will not, your friend Organon dies.	Attempt to exploit the democrat's care for others.
DOCTOR:	Organon. Goodbye, old man, so sorry about this. Thanks for all the help.	The Doctor parodies totalitarian callousness, knowing Organon will be safe. Unexpected reaction = individualism.
ORGANON:	Doctor!	
DOCTOR:	If my deductions are correct, the well-being of two planets is at stake. Irato must not die.	The Doctor concerned for the health of societies.
ADRASTA:	Huntsman, set the Wolf-weeds on the Doctor.	Wild Nature (Wolf-weeds)/Death opposed to Science (the Doctor)/Life.
DOCTOR:	Now wait, that's all you've got on this planet, isn't it—weeds, weeds, forests, and weeds! You scratch about for food wherever you can, but you can't plough the land can you? You can't do anything until you've mastered the forest and the weeds, and you can't do that without metal.	Nature-Culture opposition articulated in discourse of Science (albeit primitive) that sets up the terms for an identical opposition in the discourse of Economics (see below).
ADRASTA:	Don't listen to him. It's just the ravings of a demented space tramp. Set the Wolf-weeds on him.	Attempt to discredit Doctor's reason/science. The falsity allies morality with science, repeated in the structure:- Nature::Culture, Death::Life, Lies::Truth, Wolf-weeds::Doctor.
DOCTOR:	Do that and you hurl this planet back into the dark ages, and for what? To satisfy the petty power cravings of that pathetic woman.	Economic and political progress dependent on the transformation of Nature into Culture by Science.
ADRASTA:	Have a care, Doctor.	Care = pun: care for self versus for others.
DOCTOR:	Have a care yourself. Care for your people for a change.	Democracy and individualism enter the fray!
ADRASTA:	Kill him!	Totalitarianism = anti-individualism (again).

HUNTSMAN:	Let him speak.	A convert to democracy and the rights of the individual.
ADRASTA:	Huntsman! I order you.	Totalitarian tone.
HUNTSMAN:	Let him speak.	First signs of conversion to democracy/free speech.
DOCTOR:	Now if my deductions are correct. . . .	Logic/reason allied to economics. . . .
ADRASTA:	They're not.	Another example of totalitarianism = falsity.
DOCTOR:	Irato came here 15 years ago to propose a trading agreement. Tythonis is a planet rich in metallic ores and minerals. Am I not right, K9?	Economic discourse articulated identically to the scientific (see above).
K9:	Checking data bank. Affirmative Master.	Scientific confirmation = truth of democrats contrasted with falsity of totalitarianism.
DOCTOR:	That was a good guess.	Individualism = inspiration.
ADRASTA:	Fool! You listen to the opinions of an electric dog.	Totalitarian misconception of science/truth.
DOCTOR:	Typhonians exist on ingesting chlorophyll, large quantities of it judging by their size. Now there is a superabundance of plant life on Chloris.	The universal objective logic of free-trade economics proved by its rationality and therefore scientificness.
ROMANA:	So, Irato came here to offer you metal in return for chlorophyll. Of course!	NB "offer"—free trade is generous "in return"—and fair.
DOCTOR:	Right. And who was the first person he met?	
ORGANON:	The person who held the monopoly of metal here.	Monopoly = totalitarian power. Free trade = democracy.
DOCTOR:	Right. And did she put the welfare of her struggling people above her own petty power? No. She's tipped the ambassador into a pit and threw Astrologers at him.	Politics, economics, and morality in one.
HUNTSMAN:	Is this true, my lady?	Wit = individualism
ADRASTA:	Not a word of it. It's a pack of lies.	Conversion to democracy marked by desire for truth. Totalitarianism = falsity (yet again).
DOCTOR:	Let's see if Irato agrees with me, shall we?	Irato : symbol of free trade.
ADRASTA:	That won't prove anything. You just take hold of that thing and say exactly what you like. You expect intelligent people to fall for your childish tricks?	Doomed appeal to reason.
DOCTOR:	Well, it's very simple really. Why don't you come over here, take hold of the communicator, and we hear the truth from you.	

Continued

TABLE 1 Continued

	Dialogue	*Discourse*
ADRASTA:	What. No. Don't talk such rubbish. Huntsman, I order you to kill the Doctor.	The despot lies and kills.
HUNTSMAN:	My lady, I think we want to hear the truth of this. Go and speak with the creature.	The new democrat and his desire for truth.
ADRASTA:	No. I refuse. I utterly refuse.	
HUNTSMAN:	I think not, my lady. (He sets the Wolf-weeds on her).	The conversion is complete, even Nature turns against the despot in the end.
ADRASTA:	No! Back! Back!	
DOCTOR:	Just take hold of the communicator.	
IRATO:	Thank you, Doctor. Your deductions are of course correct. We are running dangerously short of chlorophyll on Tythonis, and have more metal than we need. Reports reached us of this planet Chloris, which has precisely the opposite problem, and we thought that a trading agreement would be mutually beneficial.	A mutually beneficial trading agreement—there are no losers, no one profits at another's expense—free market economics minus competition, minus exploiters and exploited, minus losers, minus anything that might disturb the ideological homogeneity.
ADRASTA:	It's lies, lies. It's all lies.	There she goes again!
IRATO:	No, it is you who are lying. Unfortunately I ran foul of this evil woman who tricked me into the pit. If you will forgive me, I have a score to settle.	Truth and free trade go together.
HUNTSMAN:	So, I think, have we. (The Wolf-weeds knock Adrasta down).	Nature destroys the one whose unbalancing and therefore unnatural monopoly gave it its unnatural power.
ADRASTA:	Aaaaaah! (Irato rolls over Adrasta and the Wolf-weeds).	The symbol of free trade and freedom crushes the symbol of monopoly and slavery, and ingests the Wolf-weeds, the symbols of unbalanced Nature. Free trade becomes culture.
DOCTOR:	Dead!	
HUNTSMAN:	Yes. And with her die the dark ages for this planet.	Progress. Chloris moves into the "renaissance" and the birth of science, reason, individualism, free enterprise and trade, capitalism and the middle classes!

history as progress, of man's right to impose himself upon and exploit nature, and of the supremacy of human reason, is placed beyond the possibility of conflict or doubt.

But on the horizontal dimension the values are clearly open to opposition. In the social world, as in the text, the dominant values of capitalist democracy are struggling to establish, defend, or extend themselves. The events of the story maintain the plot's constant forward drive from one expression of this struggle to another. This plot, in its outcome and closure, proves the supremacy of these values, as does our constructed sympathy for the characters and their settings on the left of the structure. The two dimensions come together in the effectiveness of science both in the value system and in the plot.

Though science and reason are common to both sides, the heroes are effective and finally victorious apparently because their science and reason are superior. At the start, the Doctor discovers the nature of the mystery object where Adrasta's engineers have failed, and at the end Irato and the Tardis together manage to save Chloris from destruction by a neutron star on a collision course. The Doctor's reason (together with the occasional flash of inspiration) is the means by which he controls the forward drive of the plot. As he uncovers each piece of the mystery, so one more battle against the opposition is won. The hero's science is not only more moral and humane than the villain's, but it is also more effective. It is this demonstrated effectiveness that brings together the twin ideologies of science and of capitalist democracy. They finally become the same ideology because the narrative demonstrates that they both work.

The only conflict is that between opposing ends of the horizontal scale, and its resolution is achieved by the superiority of the science of those on the left. The universality of science and reason naturalizes the culturally specific values of democratic capitalism and in so doing performs the mythic function of transforming history into nature (Barthes, 1972). For this story transforms the culturally specific (i.e., history) into the universal (i.e., nature). Its final point of equilibrium is that point where science and democracy come together in an uncontradictory harmony at the bottom left-hand corner of the structure. If we take Todorov's (1977) definition of narrative as a sequence of events by which one state of equilibrium is disturbed and then transformed into another similar but different state, then we can see that the original equilibrium disturbed by the arrival of the Tardis was unnatural and therefore located on the right of the structure. The events of the story function to naturalize the restoration of the equilibrium to its "proper" place on the left. The mythic function of naturalizing history and the ideological practice of denying contradictions are one and the same, a similarity identified by Levi-Strauss (1955) when he proposed that "the purpose of myth is to provide a logical model capable of overcoming a contradiction." Here, the contradictions are those between science and politico-economic-moral values. The events of the story demonstrate that the Doctor and his helpers are successful because they are better scientists, but the structure of the discourses proposes that their success derives from their morality, politics, economics, and individualism. The story acts mythically in that the logic of its chain of events overcomes the contradictions inherent in a society whose ideology reconciles apparently unproblematically the totalitarianism of science with democracy and individualism. As Davies (1978–1979) points out, "narrative is a major agency in realism's attempt to deny contradictions." The popularity of the text derives from the reader's ability to transfer this uncontradictory reconciliation easily between text and society, a transference that becomes conventional because it is generic to the series of Dr. Who and even to the genre of science fiction.

This postulates an identity between an aesthetic/psychological need in the reader that is gratified by the deep structure of the text, and the ideological practice by which the text proffers dominant readings to its model reader. This need can be defined as the need to make unproblematic sense of an inherently self-contradictory area of the culture, and the practice can be identified as the conventional practice of realism. This similarity between reader's need and textual structure exists only in the reader's perception of the ease with which the text's power in overcoming contradictions and society's denial of structurally similar contradictions enter into a mutually validating relationship. The aesthetic structure of the text is satisfying only to the extent that it performs an ideological function in society.

This theory implies that popular art is not escapist, but mythic. It does not merely provide an imaginative refreshing alternative to the hard grind of an industrial existence, rather it enables and encourages the reader to make a particular kind of sense of that existence. The reader and the text are both active, and the text becomes popular only when the two activities are mutually supportive and when they can be replicated to make sense of that much broader, more open text that is our social experience.

There is a vast difference between the signifiers of these two texts (Dr. Who meeting shapeless green monsters on distant planets is not exactly an iconic reproduction of our daily commute into the city).

The extent of this difference almost guarantees the effectiveness of the ideological work, which the similarity of the discourses performs. Because the same discourses can be related in similar ways to produce similarly satisfying structures of common sense out of such apparently diverse representations of reality, they must have a universal applicability. The divergence of the signifiers is yet another naturalizing force, which denies the historicity of the text's production and reception, and therefore of any difference between them. The only conflict is between opposing ends of the horizontal scale, and its resolution is achieved by the superiority of the science of those on the left.

Davies (1978–1979) makes a similar point:

> The creation of a narrative almost always entails the shaping of awkward materials into a smooth, closed structure. And this is the essence of myth. Like bourgeois ideology, most narrative cinema denies history, denies material reality as contradictory and denies the fact of its own production.

There is little doubt that this Dr. Who story is guilty of all the charges laid by Davies on narrative cinema. The big question is how effective the texts are in turning the reader into a passive consumer/spectator who willingly, though unknowingly, consents to the hegemony of the text. Davies (1978–1979) argues that they are highly effective, and many others working within the tradition of Screen Theory would agree with her. My disagreement rests on her negation of the role of reader in the negotiation of meaning. The text may well not invite reader activity, and may well prefer consumer/spectators to readers, but this does not account for its popularity, nor why some texts are more popular than others. For a text to be popular its discourses must fit those used by the reader in social experience, and thus it must be open to socially derived, as well as textually derived, inflections of meaning.

Here my position diverges also from McCabe's (1974), quoted above, in that I do not see the realist text as limiting the reader-subject to a position of mere specularity, but agree rather with Morley's (1980b) refusal to allow the textually constituted subject complete dominance over the socially constituted subject. The reader has a social life that is a structure of discourses just as the reader has a text that is also a structure of discourses, and reading is the activity in which the two are brought together. Work, as yet unpublished, by researchers at Murdoch University lends some support to this position. They investigated the finding of the 1981 Australian Broadcasting Tribunal that *Prisoner* and *Sale of the Century* were the two most popular shows amongst schoolchildren. They found that the appeal of *Prisoner* lay largely in the way that children could use it to validate and make sense of their school experience. The warders paralleled teachers, with a parallel hierarchy and parallel roles: some hard, some soft, some young and inexperienced, some hard-bitten. The prisoners were like students, with their own code of ethics and behavior, their own pecking order, and their variety of forms of relationship with the staff. The prison was seen as the equivalent of school—an institution to which people were sent for a fixed term where there was a sense that real life existed only outside and where the inmates were made to think and behave in the way that society wanted them to. These discourses of social relationships, of power and authority, and of institutional behavior enabled the students to find in text and world a similar kind of sense by similar discursive means.

It is easy to hypothesize similarly about the appeal of *Sale of the Century*. It demonstrates how knowledge or education can be turned into immediate reward: it collapses the temporal dimension of the sequence that children are constantly reminded of—a good education means a good job means good material rewards. Here the results flow instantly from the right answers. The discourses of education and economics bear a similar signifying relationship in the quiz text and the school world.

These relationships between discourse, text, and world constitutes a system, for each element affects and is affected by the others. Texts and social experience enter a mutually supportive relationship, and each, and both, affect the discourses by which they are structured and understood. Barthes (1979) stresses this system of society, text, and discourse (or language): "A test is that social space that leaves no language safe and untouched." The fit between text and world not only tests each item, but also the discourses by which that fit is established.

Prisoner, Sale of the Century, and this Dr. Who story all illustrate how active readers can bring to bear upon the text discourses that they use to make sense of their social experience. The texts, with their neat closures and purified structures, prove the efficacy of the discourses as interpretative strategies, and reassure the reader that this effectiveness is transferrable to the extratextual world. The relationship between world and text is not one of iconic reflection, nor a relationship of content or appearance. Rather it is a homologue of form, where what is shared is a structured relationship of discourses, so the realism, the verisimilitude, resides not in what is represented, but in how. The final satisfaction of viewing is not escapist, nor a gratification of individually or socially generated needs, but a reassurance of the adequacy of the social discourses of the reader. And this is where a structural analysis is so important, because it reveals the ideology that is at work within the text and therefore the limits of the corresponding ideologies in society that can be validated by it within this relationship that we term "the popular."

Before I close, I must point out a possible weakness in my position: it could be seen to encourage a reactionary complacency. This is certainly not my intention. As much as anyone, I wish to encourage students and others to develop the distancing that defends them against the hegemony of the text. But I also wish to defend them against a possible misunderstanding of the work of some of the Screen Theorists whose high priorizations of the text can be seen to imply that the production of questioning, radical, contradictory tests will finally produce a radical audience. This inference that texts can change the sociopolitical structure of society is one that I find unacceptable because it ignores the fact that an art form that is radically opposed to dominant social discourses would not be popular, but would appeal largely to the converted, that is to those whose social discourses fit a priori, with those of the text. It would lose the mass appeal necessary for effective social change.

I would argue, conversely, that social change can start only in society. Socially responsible popular art can, in theory, articulate and thus encourage that change, but it cannot originate it. Nor can it hasten it too quickly or it becomes in danger of losing its audience and thus its categorization as popular.

Popular art works generally, but not, I believe, necessarily, in favor of the *status quo*. What we now need is an understanding of popularity, of the intertext between work of art and social experience, and that is what I have attempted to move towards in this paper. The next enterprise is, for my money, the crucial one: it is to discover and analyze just how a work of popular art can be other than reactionary.

198 Popularity and Ideology

REFERENCES

Barthes, Roland (1972) Mythologies. London: Paladin.
_____ (1975) S/Z. London: Jonathon Cape.
_____ (1979) "From work to text," in J. V. Harari (ed.), Textual Strategies. Ithaca: Cornell Univ. Press.
Chatman, Seymour (1978) Story and Discourse—Narrative Structure in Fiction and Film. Ithaca, NY: Cornell Univ. Press.
Davies, Gill (1978–1979) "Teaching about narrative." Screen Education 29.
Dorfman, Ariel and Armand Mattelart (1975) How to Read Donald Duck: Imperialist Ideology in the Disney Comic. New York: International General.
Eco, Umberto (1979) The Role of the Reader. Bloomington: Indiana Univ. Press.
Fiske, John (1982) "TV quiz shows and the purchase of cultural capital." Australian Journal of Screen Theory 13.
Genette, G. (1968) "Vraisemblance et motivation." Communications 11.
Gerbner, George (1973) "Teacher image in mass culture," in G. Gerbner, L. Gross, and W. Melody (eds.) Communications Technology and Social Policy. New York: Wiley-Interscience.
Hall, Stuart (1973) "Encoding and decoding in the television discourse," in Occasional Papers No. 7. Birmingham University, Centre for Contemporary Cultural Studies.
_____ (1977) "Culture, the media and the ideological effect," in J. Curran, M. Gurevitch, and J. Woollacott (eds.) Mass Communication and Society. London: Edward Arnold.
_____ , Dorothy Hobson, Andrew Lowe, and Paul Willis [eds.] (1980) Culture, Media, Language. London: Hutchinson.
Kristeva, Julia (1970) La Texte du Roman. The Hague: Mouton.
Levi-Strauss, Claude (1955) "The structural study of myth." Journal of American Folklore 69.
McCabe, Colin (1974) "Realism and the cinema: notes on Brechtian theses." Screen 15.
Morley, David (1980a) The Nationwide Audience. London: British Film Institute.
_____ (1980b) "Texts, readers, subjects," in Stuart Hall et al. (eds.) Culture, Media, Language. London: Hutchinson.
O'Sullivan, Tim, John Hartley, Danny Saunders, and John Fiske (1983) Key Concepts in Communication. London: Methuen.
Todorov, Tzvetan (1975) The Fantastic. Ithaca, NY: Cornell Univ. Press.
_____ (1977) The Poetics of Prose. Oxford: Blackwell.
Tulloch, John (1982) "Dr Who: similarity and difference." Australian Journal of Screen Theory 11–12.
_____ and M. Alvarado (1983) Doctor Who: The Unfolding Text. London: Macmillan.

Chapter 8

TELEVISION NEWS AND THE
CLAIM TO FACTICITY
Quebec's Referendum Coverage

Gertrude Joch Robinson

NEW PARADIGM IN THE SOCIAL SCIENCES

In his *Social Sciences Since the Second World War*, Daniel Bell shows that most disciplines have undergone paradigm changes in the past forty years, many of which occurred sometime around 1970. Communication studies, too, participated in this development, and the larger picture is therefore instructive in explaining the emergence of alternative approaches such as semiotics and "critical theory" in our field. Bell demonstrates that the social sciences up to the sixties believed that comprehensive paradigms to order human knowledge could be developed through quantitative techniques. He points to the yoking of cybernetics and linguistic theory with cognitive psychology and computer science. The resulting "systems theory" promised a model capable of explaining both mind and society. Talcott Parson's development of structural-functionalism also aimed at integration by identifying the mechanisms of social cohesion and change.

The growing optimism about the efficacy of the social sciences was fueled by a number of postwar developments. Among these were the introduction of the computer and statistical techniques, which permitted the statement of social propositions in testable form. During the late forties and fifties, furthermore, U.S. universities underwent a transformation through the GI Bill and the Cold War scientific rivalry with the Soviet Union. This for the first time melded governmental and foundation resources into a huge research and development effort that included the social sciences. In the sixties, finally,

AUTHOR'S NOTE: This research was sponsored by Social Science Research Council grant #410-81-0398. This funding for the research assistance on the news segment of Paul Attallah and William Straw is gratefully acknowledged.

199

the rediscovery of social problems like discrimination, poverty, race riots, and environmental issues drew attention to the expertise of social scientists and gave them an identifiable role in the building of the great society (Bell, 1982: 12–21).

By the early 1970s most of these promises had gone unrealized and the social sciences began to reevaluate their paradigms. More "hard core" oriented researchers in economics, psychology, sociology, and political science refined their quantitative approaches and retreated into the analysis of smaller-scale problems. Others, mostly, in anthropology, linguistics, and social psychology went the opposite route in search of new overarching paradigms. Two of these, neo-Marxism with its various "critical stances" and semiotics, have had a resonance in communication studies. Neo-Marxist approaches have raised questions about interconnections between media and other social institutions as well as the class nature of ideological outlooks (Gitlin, 1978). They have also investigated multinational corporations and their influence on international news flows and data exchanges.

The thrust of the semiotic and symbolic approaches is more difficult to classify because they lack a common label. Horace Newcomb refers to his perspective as the "humanistic" approach (Newcomb and Hirsch, 1983), Clifford Geertz (1973) calls his "interpretative anthropology," while James Carey (1975) uses the term "cultural studies." Despite this diversity of labels, these researchers do have one thing in common: they assume that human beings live in a symbolic as well as physical environment, both of which must be accounted for in understanding social behavior. Geertz's apt description that "human beings float in a sea of symbols" draws attention to the fact that whatever the nature of external reality, humans perceive it only through their own concepts, and therefore always "construct" it. This means that creation is thus an integral and constitutive element of human behavior, not an afterthought tacked on to existence. In Carey's words, "Communication is a symbolic process whereby reality is produced, maintained, repaired and transformed." (Carey, 1975: 6) All media analyses, these researchers believe, must account for this interpretative process.

THE "SEMIOTIC APPROACH" IN TV NEWS STUDIES

Interpretative news approaches first surfaced in the mid-1970s and have appeared through two channels. One of these is European, the other is North American. The European contact has been with three sources: the French structuralist writers (Levi-Strauss, Foucault, and Derrida); the British Film Institute, and the Birmingham School of Cultural Studies, of which Stuart Hall was the original director (Robinson and Straw, 1984). The North American channel is grounded in literary criticism and humanistic studies and is exemplified in the work of Horace Newcomb. Articles in his *Television: The Critical View* introduce semiotics as an analytical tool, and draw attention to the aesthetic dimensions of the medium. At about the same time, Robert Darnton (1975) raises issues about story formats in the news and Molotch and Lester (1975) explore how events are framed to generate newsworthy accounts. By 1978, Gaye Tuchman develops a phenomenological approach to "news," and Michael Schudson (1978) and Herbert Gans (1979) investigate the philosophical bases of journalistic ideology.

All of these researchers agree that, if human beings are unable to get at reality through their own concepts, a distinction must be made between historical events and reports of these events. Media contents, as reports, must be studied like any other "text" for their surface and their underlying meanings (Geertz, 1973). News stories, like other reports, are fictitious reconstructions with a unique structure that displays such attributes as "realism" and "facticity." To analyze them, one must focus not only on what is *talked about,* but on *the way in which* television news goes about telling its stories. Consequently, something analogous to linguistic rules of verbal construction become important in determining how hierarchies of message presentations are created and interact to form a "story line." Hall notes:

> The raw historical event cannot in that form be transmitted by a television newscast. It can only be signified within the aural-visual forms of the television language. In the moment when the historical event passes under the sign of language, it is subject to all the complex formal "rules" by which language signifies (Hall, 1973: 2).

Our case study of the Quebec referendum campaign as a television news text is designed to explore systematically the relationship between a television sign and its meaning and how television signs are combined into a code. It is often argued that signification processes are hierarchical and develop on three levels (Barthes, 1967). On the first level, meaning accrues from the identification of the sign with its signifier. Prime Minister Trudeau's television image stands for the man. This sign however carries additional social meanings (second and third order) that derive from the way in which Canadians evaluate "premiership" of this particular incumbent as well as "political leadership" in general. The comprehensive world view undergirding this concept is surely quite different for an audience member who is a Liberal than for a Conservative.

Analyzing how signs are combined into a "code" in television news has proved to be extremely difficult for a variety of reasons. To begin with, the television code lacks discrete and quantifiable units. Cinema semiology demonstrates that within the moving image of television discourse there is no unit that corresponds to the word in verbal language. The minimum discrete unit is the shot, which is a particular sequence of images and therefore already a construction of syntax. Another methodological difficulty is that the construction rules are not well understood. We know that television discourse joins images sequentially, and furthermore articulates sound and image with each other in multiple ways. Consequently this discourse has at least two levels: sound and image. Mostly these two have been analyzed separately, a procedure that is clearly inadequate. We will try to deal with the combined levels, adopting a "correlational typology" that utilizes *news personnel roles* to interlink the verbal and visual discourses.

Preliminary observation suggests that the sound-image relationship varies from program to program. Dramatic series like the Québécois *téléroman* have different hierarchical relationships of sound to image, than television news. Yet exactly how television news is structured no one knows. We are, however, aware that this program format provides a paradox. While television is regarded as an essentially visual medium (this being what differentiates it from print and radio) sound dominates image in news broadcasts. Gans has therefore aptly called television news "visual radio." (Gans 1977: 147) What he means by this is that the verbal element allows for the semantic fixing or binding of images by the spoken text in television news. This accords with Raymond Williams's idea that television is, above all else, the maintenance of a *flow*. This continuity is possible only through the predominance of verbal links. Without sound, many of the visual segments of television news make little or no sense. The verbal, then, functions on the side of continuity and intelligibility, the visual on the side of heterogeneity and semantic dispersion. To explore how the verbal functions as a metadiscourse for the visual, constitutes one of the primary foci of our subsequent case study (Williams, 1974: 86).

One final point bears mention; namely, the fact that news production does not occur in a vacuum. It is at this point that our approach differs from that of pure "semioticians." It places the text in a work situation and is sensitive to production moments in its creation.

For the production personnel, news-making is framed by "knowledge in use" about routines, technical skills, and professional ideologies, as well as meanings and ideas that are shared by the audience. All of these influence the selection of events for topical description and determine their particular treatment. In the political as in other realms, "knowledge in use" must harmonize with the "definitions of the situation" provided by different audiences making up the complex society in which we live (Berger and Luckmann, 1967). Production requirements divide newswork into beats, geographical territories, and topics. They also define certain people as "hard news" and others as "human interest" sources. These two categories of occurrences are retold in different ways, using identifiably different formats, languages, and imagery.

Our case study will indicate that both journalistic and audience roles must be redefined. Journalistic roles are not passive or opaque; rather they are powerful, occupying what Sahlins (1976) calls the "synaptic" creative space shared by artists, advertisers, and market researchers. All of these must be sensitive to the latent correspondences in the cultural order in which they live in order to be successful (Newcomb and Alley, 1983: 32). The success of news producers and personnel thus depends on their ability to "read" accurately their audiences' perceptions through the "knowledge in use" that is generally shared. This meaning grid is based on the political attitudes and values arising from the social signification levels of signs and codes already mentioned. These define the meaning of leaders, followers, causes, strategies, and goals of campaigns in relatively predictable ways, precisely because they are *socially* determined. This social determinacy comes from the fact that these concepts mean what they do, only because there is agreement between the members of a culture. They are centered in the ill-defined area of intersubjectivity, which is not yet well researched.

The shared meaning grid indicates as well that the audience's role in the signification process is also an active one. Audiences do not respond like a "tabula rasa" to programs, but rather like the multi-refracting convex eye of a huge insect that interprets its surroundings within certain parameters. Exactly what these parameters are is not yet known. Neither class, nor gender, nor the socioeconomic variables so dear to the heart of the sociologist are linearly related to the interpretative capacities of individuals, although they *do* form the larger context for such interpretations (Morley, 1980).

Our case study will finally show that the notion of "individual" journalistic bias is much too simplistic to describe the interpretative role of news personnel. The truth value of a story is not in its match to some kind of reality. It lies rather in its success at *expressing* underlying and widely accepted core values about the political process as it unfolds in a particular society and campaign. As Michael Robinson has aptly noted, political analysis "has focused too closely on parties and candidates and has ignored the more subtle definitions of politics" (Robinson, 1978: 209). If television news representations are not the actions of living men, but stories about their actions, the evaluation of a leader's role and importance must be established through more than a headcount that merely records mentions in newstories. To use a theatrical metaphor, it suggests that a campaign and a leader's role in it is built up and constructed through many different scenes. All of these taken together contribute to a scenario in which different presentations of leaders, followers, and dramatic encounters are possible, depending on what the *whole story* is believed to be "about." Fiske and Hartley aptly summarize this distinction when they note that "the metaphoric real world shown on television does not *display* the actual real world, but *displaces* it" (Fiske and Hartley, 1978: 48; emphasis in original).

In deciphering our television news text, issues of validity cannot be dealt with in the usual way, because processes of meaning creation are neither linear nor amenable to other types of statistical analysis. The main purpose of this case study is consequently *not* the testing of the assertion that our reading is the only right one. Instead we are engaged in discovering whether there is an *overdetermination* of visual and verbal signs and codes in this news text that encourages certain systematic interpretations based on binary oppositions to be applied to campaign leaders, followers, and issues. These binary oppositions may be represented through such things as the color attributes of parties, the emotional tones evoked with respect to leadership styles, the visual framing of political personalities, as well as the language used in interviewing them or reporting their actions. Though the illustration of such sign overdetermination also cannot prove that our reading of the text is either "intended" by the creators, or necessarily "shared" by all audience members, it does enable us to posit that these systematic textual configurations constitute one of the components that determine Quebec producers' as well as Quebec audiences' contexts for interpreting the claims of those seeking sovereignty in the referendum.

The 1980 Quebec referendum provides a particularly good occasion for studying television news reporting because it was a well-defined and circumscribed political event in which the positions of the two sides were clearly marked. It was furthermore a campaign with colorful and articulate leaders. In addition, the intensity of the debate proved to be much stronger than in ordinary election campaigns, because of the importance of the decision Quebecers were asked to make with respect to the destiny of Canada. All of these factors combined to submerge all other political occurrences under the grid of referendum coverage in which everyone had to take sides.

REFERENDUM DISCOURSE ON CFCF-TV

To begin to elucidate the basic characteristics of the television news discourse we chose to analyze CFCF's *Pulse* news program on Friday, March 7, 1980. This show was methodologically rich because it included not only interviews, but also an opinion poll, as well as a description of a "campaign issue" that arose out of the error in judgment of the NO campaign. Most of the same narrative devices are found on other channels and the analysis that follows should therefore not be construed as singling out this show, network, producers, or reporters for praise or opprobrium. We simply use it to begin to illustrate how television newscasts "made sense" out of the referendum for Montreal's English languge audiences and how it suggests "preferred readings" for its viewers.

DESCRIPTION OF THE NEWS SEGMENT

The syntagm lasts 11 minutes but attention will bear mostly on those items specifically related to the referendum. What follows is a summary of the verbal transcript, adding those visual details that affect signification.

The segment opens with the last few seconds of the show immediately preceding the 6 p.m. news (*The Price Is Right*). As the credit sequence for this show rolls, a TV voice-over announces the evening's television line-up and a graphic announces a show for later in the week. The station's musical logo ("CFCF 12 Montreal. . . .") is sung, and then the news begins. The news opens with white lettering on a black background giving the day and date—FRIDAY MARCH 7, 1980. It immediately cuts to an image of a car struggling up a slippery hill. The dramatic theme music has also begun. In the upper righthand corner of the image of the car is a computer-graphic headline relating this shot to the city's longstanding strike of blue collar workers. Snow is still not being cleared from Montreal streets. The next shot is of people walking on a sidewalk. The headline links this image to the results of a new referendum poll released that day. Then, a brief shot of the referendum statistics chart and the newscast's visual logo—a revolving globe with the word PULSE written over top. Cut to the main newsreader who introduces himself, the headlines, and his two colleagues, sports, and weather, who in turn give five-second intros to their topics. The first item deals with the blue collar strike. This is a lengthy report highlighting the effects of the strike, a rejected injunction against the city, and an interview with city councillor Nick auf der Maur.

Then follow four items related to the referendum. The main newsreader seated in front of a graphic of a ballot box announces that a new poll has been released. A report showing the poll result follows and the same reporter does an interview with Claude Ryan about the poll. The main newsreader, before the same graphic, then introduces an item on René Lévesque's reaction. The report shows Lévesque's reaction and then fills us in on his day's campaigning on a radio open-line show. The main newsreader, still seated before the same graphic, reads a short item about PQ house leader Claude Charron who "admits" that his party members try to be disciplined before the National Assembly cameras. This is followed by the main newsreader, now seated before the party PQ logo, introducing an item about a new PQ booklet that is a "simplified version of confederation" designed to "sell" sovereignty-association. The reporter in this item goes to great lengths to point out the red and blue figurines used throughout the book to represent Canada and Quebec respectively.

As a television syntagm by definition consists of words and images, specific methodological tools must be developed to deal with the correlations between the two. We cannot, for instance, proceed with a computer word count that is frequently used for a purely written text, because this method does not take account of how viewing occurs, the pictures presented, or the image/sound relationships, all of which are important factors in electronic meaning creation. As noted earlier, visual semiotics, as well as discourse analysis indicate as a first assumption that television news makes sense to us because the verbal dominates the visual. This verbal dominance is represented in the continuous flow of commentaries, reports, and interviews emanating from anchor persons, reporters, and commentator's voice-overs. This flow is linear in time and thus quite different from meaning creation in newspapers that is partially fixed by a visual matrix, which McLuhan (1965) has called a "mosaic."

NEWS AS FLOW

The syntagm begins with the last few seconds of the program immediately preceding the 6 o'clock news (*The Price Is Right*) and ends with the presentation of the referendum items proper. In the few seconds between the end of the previous program and the beginning of the news, the evening's television line-up is made known, either through the use of graphics or through the voice of an off-screen announcer. This is the first instance of flow. Commercials and self-promotional material (promos) are programmed into the overall sequence of images such that there are never any gaps and such that the viewer, once his curiosity has been aroused by the promise of shows to come, will stay tuned to the same station to find out what happens next. Programs and commercials form a whole, and it would be a mistake to speak of commercials as an interruption. It is rather the absence of a commercial or of some other material, indeed the presence of a gap, which constitutes the interruption. In fact, programmers work so as to avoid dead air time. One need only think of the effect produced when a news clip fails to roll on cue or when the screen goes blank for a few seconds. The absence of material is an interruption. The presence of material, visual or verbal, is the desired flow. Commercials, promos, or music are just another way of filling up space, of suturing potential gaps.

The flow elements that have just been defined as existing within the space between two programs (commercials, graphic and voice-over promos, the promise of more to come) are reproduced in exactly the same way within the news program proper. The news program opens with a graphic showing the day and date. Immediately, one hears dramatic music accompanied by illustrative news clips and by computer-graphic headlines. Then, however, something else very important happens: the main newsreader introduces himself, the headlines, and his colleagues, sports and weather, who give 5-second intros to their items. This introduction of the three well-known personalities provides a visual link between the journalistic working space and the audience's living room. It also creates a meaning grid between journalistic roles and their use in the television news discourse. At least three different newscaster roles can be distinguished utilizing different visual and verbal formats. They are the anchor, the reporter, and the interviewer roles, as well as weather and sports. The differing amounts of time that these roles appear on the screen, and their different visual and verbal styles, indicate that they form a hierarchy in which professional status and signification levels complexly interrelate. In this hierarchy the anchor is at the top, not only professionally but also in visual display time. He usually is presented seated facing the camera, while the reporter and interviewer often stand in front of identifiable locations. Verbally the anchor voice uses direct address, that of the reporter makes comments or voice-overs, and the interviewer voice asks questions of nonstudio personnel. How these three voices constitute and affect the news narrative will be further discussed in the next section.

For the present it is important to complete our scrutiny of the way in which news personnel behavior functions as a suturing device. The naming by one reader of his colleague who is about to appear is a voice-over suture of the gap between two images. Its function is to make the transition so smooth as to be invisible, so that the flow remains uninterrupted. When newsmen call each other by their first name in order to introduce news segments, it obviously also signifies cosiness and camaraderie, but the banter serves as well to fill up potentially dead air space. The gaps between images are further sutured by the fact that the readers will comment upon the news. This happens especially frequently in sports and weather reports, but also in the juxtaposition of anchor with reporter statements. In the meaning hierarchy these are designed as an elaboration of the original point of view presented by the anchor.

Numerous other suturing devices are used to link the physical space of the studio with the physical space occupied by the viewer, all of which make the news show seem more "realistic" than a situation comedy. Frequently readers will look towards an off-screen monitor before the film clip is rolled, thereby implying that they see what we see and our look is equivalent to theirs. This off-screen look is a visual suture of the gap between two images as well as the gap between two spaces. The habit that reporters have of naming themselves and the station for which they work at the end of every report ("This is So-and-So for CFCF News. . . .") is again a suture: it connects the space of the report with the space of the studio; it connects the on-camera gaze of the reporter with the on-camera gaze of the newsreader. He, in turn, is the familiar and respected visitor in the homes of the audience that is accustomed to watching *Pulse* news. Anchor people and newsreaders thus not only help maintain the flow of images, they also forge a direct and intricate visual link with the viewers. This link is further reinforced by the way in which the television news narrative is structured and presented.

VERBAL SIGNIFICATION IN THE NEWS NARRATIVE

Television news discourse creates a narrative that is intrinsically different from other narrative forms. Some of its formal characteristics are obvious, others much less so. Stories are recounted in the past tense, headlines are in the present. Items are short and presented in a linear manner like beads on a chain. The threads that hold this narrative chain together require careful scrutiny, because they are not yet well understood.

Like all languages, the language of news prose contains a special relationship to the everyday world; it both frames and accomplishes discourse. In television news, the discourse creates an aura of "actuality" rather than "fantasy" and this represents a claim to "facticity." Our segment indicates that this facticity is achieved in a variety of ways. The use of the past tense for retelling stories indicates to the viewer that real time and studio time are one and the same. It links the anchor with the viewer at home who is encouraged to feel that he is participating in a public event. What is not emphasized is that this participation is not active, but vicarious, that it entails listening to the retelling of the day's news, rather than influencing it.

"Facticity" is further enhanced in television news by the station's not seeming to rearrange time and space in the interviews it presents. In this way the viewer is led to believe that his space, the political space, and the studio space are one and the same continuum. Photographic images finally respect the visual perspectives of the seated viewer behind a camera. This gives the impression of "seeing for oneself" (Tuchman, 1979: 111–113). All devices together suggest that television as a medium is a neutral transduction, that it presents a "window on the world." The medium's continued "believability" is supported by the fact that audiences are usually unaware of the editorial restructurings, the visual patching of archival with other kinds of filmed material, and the ways in which anchors and reporters affect the suggested meanings that are to be placed on public events.

The four referendum-related items permit us to explore in greater detail how visual restructurings and editorial commentary set up a context that suggests "preferred descriptions" of political events to the viewer. The four items making up the topic of the referendum on March 7, 1980, were: (1) the opinion poll results and Claude Ryan's reaction; (2) René Lévesque's reaction and his day of campaigning; (3) Claude Charron's "admission," and (4) the PQ booklet on sov-

ereignty-association, using red and blue graphics. The meaning creation for these four disparate items proceeds on two levels: verbally
and visually. Within these two, furthermore, various types of signification processes can be discerned. We will use the referendum segment as a whole to analyze and distinguish the broad processes of
the verbal and visual meaning creation. The individual items in turn
illustrate the various types of signification that are involved.

The first thing that one notices is that in the television news discourse the verbal dominates the visual and is used as a metadiscourse
in a variety of ways. In our segment this metadiscourse involves three
voices with different functions. The anonymous off-screen voice an-
nouncing the different segments functions as a station's "emblem"
giving it its specific tone and color. Whatever this voice says invariably
happens, which means that it regulates the flow of the metadiscourse.
The anchor's voice connects specific items into meaningful topics like:
the blue collar strike, the referendum campaign, sports, and weather.
His metadiscourse is reflexive, it comments not only on the content
of the event, but the event itself. This is illustrated in the treatment
of the opinion poll where the anchor first gives the major result of
the poll, an increase for the "NO" side, and then comments, "*Pulse*
news managed to reach Quebec Liberal leader Claude Ryan this
afternoon, and he said that the job of painting Sovereignty-Association as independence is having some good results, but some work
still needs to be done. . . ."

The reporters' voices in turn add specific details that are designed
to relate events to what the audience personally knows. In our example, a reporter's voice reads specific poll results and notes that
there is still great ignorance among the electorate about the referendum. He ends with, "The recent Liberal convention and the debate
in the National Assembly have probably changed all that." The sequence shows that the construction of the meaning grid is participated
in by all three voices and is self-consciously reflexive, melding visual
interviews with the poll results. The news narrative thus becomes a
tale within a tale. Everything that happens is presented as though it
is a story of that day's television programming. Within the newscast
the story of the day's events are retold with the news operation as a
whole "managing to reach Quebec Liberal leader Claude Ryan."
Individual reporters doing interviews are framed into this whole and
do not draw attention to themselves. Since everything takes place at
the level of "telling," the "tellers" and their story versions are in

command. They not only choose the items to be reported, but provide the perspectives for the viewer as to how the political events they are reporting are to be interpreted.

VISUAL SIGNIFICATION IN THE NEWS NARRATIVE

Meaning creation on the visual level is secondary to the interpretative grid, created by the anchorperson's and reporter's voices. It functions in a support capacity to reinforce the initial decision that the four disparate referendum items are to be treated as part of the same topic. One graphic, which consists of a blue ballot box covered with a maple leaf on the left and a fleur-de-lis on the right, plus a hand depositing a ballot, is used as a backdrop for all but the fourth item. The discussion of the PQ booklet is accompanied by the PQ party graphic, which shows striking similarities with the *Pulse* graphic and is displayed in the same space. In this case, therefore, discourse (what is shown and said) and metadiscourse (what is said about what is shown and said) converge. There is a conscious attempt to construct an isotopy that will lend a pattern of intelligibility to the four items.

Within both the verbal and the visual "frames of reference" that have been established by the voices and the graphic, semiotic theory suggests there are three levels of signification that are operative (Barthes 1967). On the first, a sign stands for itself, while on the second and third, signs and signifiers come in contact with cultural meanings. Let us illustrate the signification process by looking at the way in which the graphics "make sense" out of the four disparate referendum items. Since graphics have to be simple, they contain all the important oppositions valorized by a given point of view. In a sense, then, they are the concentrate of their user's imaginary universe.

Closer analysis of the two graphics indicates that they set up a series of oppositions that result from second and third order significations. The blue ballot box with a red maple leaf on the left and a fleur-de-lis on the right, plus a hand above depositing a ballot, signifies a variety of things. As a sign it is self-contained, and the viewer reads it as a particular ballot box with decorations. In Canada, however, the maple leaf and fleur-de-lis signs also have cultural meanings and stand for Canada and Quebec as symbolized by their flags. Furthermore, depending on which political world view (ideology) or comprehensive outlook the viewer subscribes to (third order signification), the ballot box graphic additionally symbolizes the NO and the YES forces; the Liberals and the Péquistes, the federalists and the sovereignty-associationists, the English and the French.

The semiology of images thus suggests that one can go a bit further in elaborating the "web of facticity" set up in the news discourse, by exploring the signifying frameworks that are employed. The television news discourse is constructed in terms of recurrent isotopic oppositions, which operate at three levels. The ballot box graphic illustrates that levels two and three of the signification process are generally unnoticed by the audience, because they depend on the ways in which both the signifier and the signified are valued. Obviously these evaluations will be different for a federalist and a Péquiste viewer. Signification on these levels is not mentioned or even brought into consciousness, because a consensus in outlooks is assumed. These significations are thus "latent." They are furthermore assumed to be shared by both the English language station and the viewers for whom it programs.

It is only when these "latent" grids of intelligibility are ambiguous or challenged for one reason or another that they rise to the level of consciousness and are commented upon. This is the case in item four, the coverage of the publication of the Parti Québécois booklet. In this item the reporter is visibly upset by the fact that the booklet uses the same color symbolism utilized by the *Pulse* ballot box graphic— red figurines to represent the federal position and blue ones to illustrate the PQ stance. In flipping open the PQ booklet, the camera scans the pages displaying large red figurines seeming to menace smaller blue ones. The reporter makes such comments as "TV coverage has a great impact on how the PQ is planning its campaign. . . . Of course the booklet oversimplifies the federal case. . . . According to this the reds are exploiting the blues. . . . the duplication of federal and provincial services is displayed as waste . . . the apparent solution to all of these problems is equal representation." The sequence indicates clearly that the PQ also opposes red to blue as Canada versus Quebec, yet for the PQ, the blue term is extensively valorized while the red is not. This is in exact opposition to the *Pulse* news station's valorization system.

In this case, then, the same red/blue opposition changes meaning completely depending on whether it is embedded within a federal or a sovereignty-association discourse. The task of the *Pulse* reporter's metadiscourse is therefore to take hold of this other signification and to point out that it lacks the calm and reason of *Pulse's* web of signification. By pointing out that it bears values different from those of the television station, it is discredited. The metadiscourse must make viewers aware of the PQ's alternative meaning grid (ideology) while assuming that they agree with CFCF's own signification framework. A latent web of signification, the color symbolism, is therefore used to construct a conscious signification. In this operation of meaning stabilization, ideologically determinate interests are made to look natural and universal. They are linked to the "commonsense" ways of doing and seeing things shared by reporters and audience. Smith notes that this linking has the effect of making the fundamental features of our own society mysterious, because it prevents us from recognizing them as problematic. "Ideology as contrasted with knowledge identifies . . . the interested procedures which people use as a means not to know" (Smith, 1974: 3, 12).

PRESENTATION MODES IN THE NEWS NARRATIVE

The coverage of the referendum campaign and the development of patterns of intelligibility (isotopies) is at base the semantization of the sociopolitical values of the NO and YES sides. If, after Roland Barthes, we define a narrative character as a proper name or other signifier to which various units of meaning are attached, then the NO and YES camps may be viewed as primary signifiers. Additional units of meaning develop out of the various contexts in which the leaders and followers are covered. These configurations of attributes develop diachronically throughout the campaign and synchronically in opposition to each other. Their elaboration requires the analysis of individual segments as well as the discourse of various channels as a whole. Here we have already indicated some of the basic oppositional signification schemes set in motion by the ballot-box graphic and by color. The two interviews with Claude Ryan and René Lévesque indicate that the way in which their leadership behavior is portrayed provide additional units of meaning that enlarge on, as well as reinforce, the already established oppositional signification framework.

The two interviews appear after the poll, which is an event that has to be retold and interpreted within the larger opposition established between the NO and the YES sides. More important, however, is the fact that the poll is immediately reinserted into the private lives of the party leaders. In doing so the television news discourse is merely following a narrative paradigm that personalizes important events. This is what has been called the Americanization of the Canadian and Quebec political discourse. This so-called Americanization, however, seems to be not so much dependent on Canada's geographical nearness to the United States, but rather on the systematic use of Manichean narrative paradigms. These are common in all television news discourses because they help to enhance viewer understanding of complex events. This paradigm effaces historical comprehension and replaces it with opposition. It draws attention to, rather than explains, political events. It conveys "acquaintance with" rather than "knowledge about" (Roshco, 1977). A recent study by Patterson supports this contention, indicating that in the 1940 elections, Lazarsfeld, Berelson, and Gaudet found that about 35% of election news dealt with the fight to gain the presidency and 50% with the subjects of policy and leadership. In 1976, these proportions were reversed and the majority of reports concentrated on the strategic maneuvers of the contenders (Patterson, 1980: 26). The same study also found that television news utilizes this narrative paradigm more extensively than print.

As already mentioned, the anchor links the increasing poll support shown for the NO side by stating *"Pulse* news managed to reach opposition leader Claude Ryan this afternoon, and he said that the job of painting Sovereignty-Association as independence is having some good results, but some work still needs to be done. . . ."* The "managed to reach" phrasing suggests both a difficult accomplishment and one probably achieved by *Pulse* alone. The news discourse thus moves quickly to incorporate a less time-bound event with the up-to-the-minute framework of the day's news. The anchorperson's concluding phrase, "some work still needs to be done," is followed immediately by the image of Liberal party leader Claude Ryan and his voice, which begins, "But I'm quite optimistic we'll achieve that."

The conclusion of the anchorperson's introduction and Ryan's opening words appear as parts of a single phrase. This is not only a common method for establishing flow, but also valorizes the anchorperson's interpretative discourse as factual inasmuch as it leads so smoothly into (and therefore is compatible with) that of Ryan. The reporter interviewing Ryan speaks only midway through the interview, and is not seen clearly until the interview is well underway. Thus, Ryan's remarks seem originally to be directed at, or in response to, the anchorperson's introduction, and the reporter replaces him (as representative of the news operation) only part way through. This produces a much greater effect of continuity between the station's metadiscourse and Ryan's direct discourse than if the anchorperson's introduction had been followed by a reporter-originated question to Ryan.

Following the interview with Mr. Ryan, less significant results of the opinion poll (i.e., those not related to the referendum itself) are presented by a commentator other than the previous anchorperson. This sequence itself is clearly bracketted: the change in voices signals a change from actuality to the analytic, almost academic commentary, which in this case takes on a public-service air. This segment is followed immediately by coverage of Lévesque's response to the poll results. There is an almost perfect A-B-A symmetry here, in the sense that partisan statements are divided by a neutral analysis, "event" stories by commentary, and anchorperson's discourse by that of the commentator.

The coverage of Lévesque's response is introduced as follows:

Premier Réné Lévesque says he hasn't had time to study the Radio-Canada poll. He refused to make any specific comment when shown the results by PULSE's Bob Benedetti today in a Sherbrooke radio station. . . ."

Lévesque then begins: "Well, the only thing I'll tell you is this. . . ."

At one level, the introductions to coverage of Claude Ryan and Réné Lévesque here are similar: a reporter is dispatched to each and manages to "reach" him. However, while the impression is given that Ryan was tracked down and proceeded to deliver a reasoned response, the presentation here is more one of the reporter having confronted Lévesque with the results, than of his responding to them. The confrontation becomes the event covered, rather than, as in the case with Ryan, the content of the response.

The visual presentation of the Liberal leader features him alone, shot at eye-level, in front of a Caisse Populaire. There is no indication of his reason for being there, and the interview is thus isolated from any meaningful context. The Premier is shot from a somewhat higher angle, surrounded by reporters in a crowded, chaotic situation, which is clearly not the organized one of a press conference or prearranged interview. The manner of shooting evokes the reason-emotion opposition recurrent throughout the referendum campaign in the coverage of Ryan and Lévesque. Here, it is transformed more precisely into a *rational, collected* versus *confused* and *irritable* opposition.

An even more important distinction, however, lies in the manner in which these interviews function as events. Ryan's interview is of interest for its content; it could easily be presented in written form and lose none of its intelligibility. In the case of Lévesque, however, the event does not lie in what he is saying—a series of challenges, quips, and refusals to speak—but in the whole of the situation itself.

There is a subnarrative of Lévesque's confrontation with reporters, his attempts to escape them, and his defensive questions as to the source of *Pulse*'s early information on the poll results.

The intelligibility of this sequence depends on the combination of verbal and visual discourses, and there are no phrases that could be isolated and meaningfully paraphrased or transcribed from the event of the interview itself. However much it may be presented as a "scoop" of sorts, it is a direct discourse whose content is primary. Lévesque however lacks such control in the presentation of his responses, and is submerged within a visual-oral situation of confrontation that is itself the event. In this case, two phenomena having a radically different status as events, are presented in a linear and logical sequence—that of the responses of the two leaders to the opinion poll—which suggests they are on the same level of intelligibility. In fact, as we have shown, they are not.

CONCLUSION

"JOURNALISTIC VALUES" AND "CONSTRUCTION RULES" FOR THE REFERENDUM NARRATIVE

In his essay (1975) Robert Darnton notes that four things are needed to understand how newspaper reporters function as communicators. These are: the structure of their milieu, the city room; their relation to editors, other reporters, and sources; the way they get "broken in" as reporters; and how standardized techniques of telling "stories" influence their writing of news. As previously mentioned, North American news "selection" theories have concerned themselves extensively with the first three, but have failed to deal with the fourth. This is because "story-telling" modes fall into the "ritualistic" domain of communication, which deals with the way in which cultural meaning is created. According to Darnton the journalist learns about this ritualistic domain in covering the *fait divers*.

> To turn a squeal sheet into an article requires training in perception and in manipulation of standardized images, cliches, "angles," "slants," and "scenarios," which will call forth a conventional response in the minds of editors and readers. A clever writer imposes an old form on new matter in a way that creates some tension—will the subject fit the predicate?—and then resolves it by falling back on the familiar. . . . The trick will not work, if the writer deviates too far from the con-

ceptual repertory that he shares with his public and from the techniques
of tapping it, that he has learned from his predecessors (Darnton, 1975:
189–190).

Since this ability is based on story-telling modes that are usually taken
for granted, anchored and displayed in such high- and low-culture
forms as fairy tales and penny novels, it is understandable that most
journalists are unable to describe this talent. They simply say they
have a "news sense."

Our case study indicates that television news and its counterpart
in the press, differ from each other both in presentation mode and
in their signification processes. While this is not the place to compare
these in detail, it is important to note that television news text is
presented as "flow," while press news is presented as "mosaic." The
television flow is made up of picture and sound sequences sutured
together, where the printed page uses static suturing techniques and
lacks sound. The television flow, furthermore, is linear while press
presentation juxtaposes columns, ads, and empty space, syncopated
by headlines. Our analysis has indicated how the voices of news
personnel are hierarchically organized and how they function as framing and linking devices to create flow. The television news text is
additionally presented in a "factual" mode, in which the time and
space dimensions are seemingly not altered and in which people speak
in their "own" voices. News personnel roles, we found, make person-
to-person linkages with the audience, which are interpreted as being
similar to those in interpersonal communication settings. This occurs
because they utilize visual conventions rather than phonetic rules.
Since these are taken for granted, television news seems more "real"
and easy to understand than print. These visual conventions include
first-order gratification processes that identify news personnel roles
as "real people." They also include the linking of news personnel
with "real" audience members in a shared setting that replicates the
face-to-face situation. As such, they and especially the anchor become
stand-ins for *us* in the television discourse. In this discourse, furthermore, the verbal dominates and fixes the meaning of the visual
image. The visuals thus become illustrations of verbal points made
by the anchor whose interpretations are hierarchically at the top and
thus dominate. No wonder people identify with Bill Donovan and
not *Pulse* news in the abstract.

A second point clarified by our semiotic analysis is the news
values that guide the referendum coverage proper. According to Gans,
news values are made up of three different kinds of value consider-

ations. He calls them journalistic importance judgments, editorial reality judgments, and reportorial views about the nature of society and leadership (enduring values). Together these produce an inter-pretative framework (Gans, 1979: 280–82). They specify the "angles," "slants," and "scenarios" that Darnton refers to above. Preliminary analysis and previous research suggest that five of these news values seem to guide the referendum coverage of both the English and French Canadian media. They include the "initial importance judg-ment" that the referendum is to be covered as an "election," not as a constitutional crisis or a federal-provincial struggle. Such a decision, we propose, tends to underplay the revolutionary/disruptive potential of a majority for Quebec sovereignty, by suggesting that the outcome of the referendum will be like any other regional no-confidence vote. Such an initial decision led to the editorial "reality judgment" that the story will be framed as a "contest between parties." Our news segment indicates that this approach features leaders and followers and tends to describe the referendum in military metaphors.

In a "contest between parties," story line and "style" are more important than "substance." "Style" reporting provides the founda-tion for consensus government as it is practiced in Canada and the Untied States. This emphasis on "style" manifests itself in the re-porting of gains, losses, and strategies, rather than the issues on which leaders disagree. "Style" reporting thus dampens polarization of the audience by obscuring fundamental power and status differences in the political arena. The use of polar oppositions such as the "rational" Mr. Ryan and the "emotional" Mr. Lévesque, the Reds and the Blues, federalists and nationalists to describe the leaders, followers, and goals in the referendum, simplifies and heightens the color of the story-line. These oppositions also provide the primary interpretative grid into which news occurrences can be easily integrated. The ref-erendum segment shows that these five news judgments function as "construction rules" for the coverage. Not only do they "screen" what will be selected for presentation, they also "frame" how the selected event will be played. Single items are not judged on their *intrinsic* merit, but on how they define and advance the contest as a whole.

Another set of value judgments affecting coverage are shared by news personnel and audience alike. They include views about such things as the "good" nation, society, and leadership. Of course these depend on the news channel's and audience's attachment to the "fed-eralist" or the "sovereignist" cause. How differences in evaluation of Canada/Quebec (the Reds and the Blues) provide different meaning hierarchies for news events, is particularly well illustrated in *Pulse*'s presentation of the PQ booklet sequence. Here the underlying judgment is that Canada represents the good nation and the good society. Its goodness is measured by such things as its presumed tolerance for individual rights, as opposed to a sovereign Quebec's supposed intolerance. Claude Ryan spoke Italian on more than one occasion precisely to underline this tolerance by Canada and suggested frequently that a sovereign Quebec would not preserve civil liberties. Enduring values, the segment demonstrates, are included unconsciously in news judgment and therefore do not conflict with "objectivity." As a matter of fact, Gans argues they make "objectivity" possible. Since these values are part of news judgment and have shown remarkable temporal stability (Roshco, 1979), they can be interpreted somewhat differently by each news organization. They also make journalists feel detached and comfortable in the knowledge that in adherence to such values they are protected from charges of bringing personal values into their work.

What we have demonstrated is that attention to the way in which news makes "sense" contributes to our understanding of the news production process in a variety of ways. To begin with, it shows that "news" is a "discourse" and not an "event." It is made up of news personnel roles, voices, and visual representation styles. All "discourses" are constructed from a point of view, because they must make sense for a particular audience. The journalistic work context that shapes the content of the news consequently includes not only the influences of peers and journalists' images of the public, but also inherited techniques of story-telling that are efficacious in conveying meaning to a particular social group. News rendition as a communication process is consequently not closed, but accessible to the audience by virtue of shared enduring values and story-telling techniques. These are partially structured through binary oppositions that encourage "preferred descriptions" of social and political reality. These in turn guide the audience to "see" things in a particular way (Hall, 1974). We have traced some aspects of this point of view in the coverage of the PQ booklet.

Initial importance and editorial reality judgments plus the enduring values to which a news organization subscribes form a consistent view of the political world, or ideology. The question of bias must consequently be reconsidered. It exists in everyone's mind, not only in the mind of reporters. It is, as a matter of fact, the sine qua non of human existence. Human beings have no way of apprehending social reality except through the meanings they attach to their surroundings (Burke, 1963). These meanings are influenced by the actor's status and power, the actions he is attempting, and the goal to be achieved. Though total objectivity remains an ideal, a greater awareness of one's own particular bias lies in recognizing the historical contingency of one's own discourse and in the recognition of other ways of telling the same story. Semiotic analysis facilitates the identification of symbolic oppositions and other narrative strategies, all the while remembering that we humans create and re-create the "reality" we call our everyday lives through such narration.

REFERENCES

Barthes, Roland (1967) Elements of Semiology. London: Jonathan Cape.

Bell, Daniel (1982) The Social Sciences Since the Second World War. New Brunswick: Transaction Books.

Berger, Peter and Thomas Luckmann (1967) The Social Construction of Reality. Garden City: Doubleday.

Burke, Kenneth (1963) The Grammar of Motives. Los Altos: Hermes Publications.

Carey, James W. (1975) "A cultural approach to communication" Explorations in Communication II 2(1): 1–23.

Darnton, Robert (1975) "Writing news and telling stories." Daedalus 104: 175–193.

Derrida, Jacques (1967) De La Grammatologie. Paris: Seuil.

Fiske, John and John Hartley (1978) Reading Television. London: Methuen.

Foucault, Michael (1969) The Archeology of Knowledge. Paris: Gallimard.

Gans, Herbert (1979) Deciding What's News: A Study of CBS Evening News, NBC Nightly News, Newsweek and Time. New York: Random House.

Geertz, Clifford (1973) The Interpretation of Cultures. New York: Basic Books.

Gitlin, Todd (1978) "Media sociology: the dominant paradigm." Theory and Society 7: 205–253.

Greimas, H. (1971) "Elements d'une grammaire narrative." Du Sens, Paris.

Hall, Stuart (1971) "Television as a medium and its relation to culture," in Stencilled Occasional Papers No. 4. Birmingham University, Centre for Contemporary Cultural Studies.

————— (1974) "Encoding and decoding the television discourse," in Stencilled Occasional Papers No. 7. Birmingham University, Centre for Contemporary Cultural Studies.

Lazarsfeld, Paul, Bernard Berelson, and Hazel Gaudet (1968) The People's Choice: How the Voter Makes Up His Mind in a Presidential Campaign. New York: Columbia University Press.

Levi-Strauss, Claude (1976) Structural Anthropology, Vols. 1 & 2. New York: Basic Books.

McLuhan, Marshall (1964) Understanding Media: The Extensions of Man. New York: McGraw-Hill.

Molotch, Harvey and Marilyn Lester (1975) "Accidental news: the great oil spill as local occurrence and national event." American Journal of Sociology 81 (September): 235–260.

Morley, David (1980) The "Nationwide" Audience. London: British Film Institute.

Newcomb, Horace [ed.] (1976) Television: The Critical View. London: Oxford University Press.

_____ and Paul Hirsch (1983) "Television as a cultural forum: implications for research." Quarterly Review of Film Studies 8 (3).

Newcomb, Horace and Robert S. Alley (1983) The Producer's Medium: Conversations with Creators of American TV. New York: Oxford University Press.

Patterson, Thomas E. (1980) "The role of the mass media in presidential campaigns: the lessons of the 1976 election." Social Science Research Council 34 (2): 24–30.

Robinson, Gertrude Joch (1981) "Binational news: the social construction of world affairs reporting in the French and English Canadian press," in G. J. Robinson, News Agencies and World News. Fribourg: University of Fribourg Press.

_____ and William Straw (1984) "Semiotics and communication studies: points of contact," pp. 91-114 in M. Voigt (ed.) Progress in Communication Sciences, Vol. 4. Norwood, NJ: Ablex.

Robinson, Michael J. (1978) "Future television news research: beyond Edward Jay Epstein," in W. Adams and F. Schreibman (eds.) Television Network News. Washington, DC: George Washington University School of Public Information Affairs.

Roshco, Bernard (1979) Newsmaking. Chicago: University of Chicago Press.

Sahlins, Marshall (1976) Culture and Practical Reason. Chicago: University of Chicago Press.

Schudson, Michael (1978) Discovering the News: A Social History of American Newspapers. New York: Basic Books.

Sebeok, Thomas A. [ed.] (1978) Sight, Sound and Sense. Bloomington: Indiana University Press.

Smith, Dorothy (1974) "Theory as ideology," in R. Turner (ed.) Ethnomethodology. Baltimore, MD: Penguin.

Tuchman, Gaye (1974) "Making news by doing work: routining the unexpected." American Journal of Sociology 79 (July) 110–131.

_____ (1978) Making News: A Study in the Construction of Reality. New York: Free Press.

White, David Manning (1950) "The 'gatekeeper': a case study in the selection of news." Journalism Quarterly 27 (3): 383–390.

Williams, Raymond (1974) Television: Technology and Cultural Form. London: Collins and Sons.

Chapter 9

THE UNWORTHY DISCOURSE
Situation Comedy in Television

Paul Attallah

EVER SINCE television was made commercially available in the late 1940s, a great deal has been written in North America about it. Oddly enough, however, most of that writing has been heavily marked by a high degree of sameness. Not only are the contents and the conclusions of most television writing remarkably similar but, more importantly, so are their fundamental presuppositions about the very nature of television. The most widely shared and tenacious presupposition insists on seeing television almost exclusively as a technology producing both social and psychological effects. Indeed, most television research has been devoted to exploring precisely that proposition. Whatever its merits, this fundamental presupposition springs from the following factors: (1) the introduction of television as a privately-consumed commodity within the family rather than along the lines of other popular attractions such as movies, vaudeville, or the circus; (2) the consequent concerns about child rearing and psychology, social propriety, and education; (3) widely shared attitudes towards science and technology and their place in society; and (4) the predominance of behaviorist and positivist modes of thought in the institutions most likely to study television.

These factors are important to bear in mind because what is said about situation comedy, as about any type of television, will be dependent on what is believed about television and society as a whole. Clearly, if you believe society and individuals to operate in a certain way, your television will in all likelihood display contents and formats consonant with your presuppositions; and so will your television research. Indeed, the reader need only refer to the vast body of literature known as effects studies in order to see how certain conceptions of human psychology, of the relationship between mind and machine, and of the place of technology in society lead directly to highly specific and particular types of research and to no less specific conclusions and policy recommendations.

These presuppositions are also operative in the case of situation comedy but they naturally assume a form appropriate to that type of television show. What I wish to argue is that situation comedy can be understood as a *genre*. To understand a genre, however, one must also understand the institution that produces it. No genre exists or has meaning independently of its context. The context of situation comedy includes basically not only the institution of television and all that it produces but also the social meaning and values upon which it draws and which it reformulates.

SITUATION COMEDY

As a rule, one does not talk about situation comedy. To quote Mick Eaton: "There has been virtually nothing written about television situation comedy as a specifically televisual form" (Bennett et al., 1981: 26). This is due to the way television is talked about in general, to the unworthiness that accrues to it and its products, to its institutional functioning, and to the various modes of availability of its products. In a sense, the absence of sitcoms in television writing can be seen as an effect of the institutionalization of television, which prefers to draw attention to its other achievements. Nonetheless, one may adopt a number of points of view in order to talk *around* the subject of situation comedy.

One may take, for example, an industrial perspective and discuss the situation comedy as an economic proposition: is it successful and does it earn money? In this case, only its status as a commodity is of interest and one might just as easily be talking about any other commodity; the situation comedy has no specificity.

One may adopt a social scientific and critical point of view and choose simply to ignore situation comedy either because it has no discernible effect or because it appears to be generally irrelevant and to make no contribution whatsoever to society. This goes a long way towards explaining the dearth of material on situation comedy.

One may also, on the other hand, occasionally take the inverse stance and talk profusely about certain "quality" or "relevant" situation comedies such as *MASH, All in the Family,* or *The Dick Van Dyke Show.* These shows are seen as important precisely to the extent to which they do not resemble situation comedies, because they make significant social statements, or because of strong characterization and good scripting. In this case, it is the content of the situation comedy that is singled out for praise and attention, and especially that content's resemblance to "serious drama." One may also talk about *I Love Lucy,* for example, as an incomprehensible social phenomenon: why do people watch *Lucy*? She just must be a very talented/zany/gifted lady. Again, it is the content (star) of the show that is singled out and, again, questions of textual specificity or of audience reception are neglected.

Finally, one may adopt an historicist point of view and attempt either to classify types of humor or to retrace the origins of the situation comedy through films, radio, vaudeville, and the theater, as Raymond Williams has begun (1974). Both of these can be interesting but they do tend to deny the situation comedy's *televisual* specificity and to see it as a variation on a preexisting form, which it may not be, and on a previous content, which it may not share.

Occasionally, sitcoms are approached genealogically with all the attendant pitfalls of unproblematized genre theory (see Mitz, 1980). But on the whole, one does not talk about situation comedy as a mode of address or as a televisual form. This is due, primarily, to the unworthiness of the object.

UNWORTHINESS

There is a strong sense in which television and everything connected to it is seen as unworthy: unworthy certainly as a serious intellectual pursuit, unworthy as a source of ideas or of stimulation, unworthy of critical evaluation, unworthy even as a pastime. The entertainment it provides has long been considered inferior to the entertainment provided by books or films or plays; its information more ephemeral and less substantial than that provided by newspapers, books, magazines, or journals. In short, in the classic dichotomy between high art and low art, television definitely occupies the region of low art. And, as innumerable books proclaim, television is a "mass" medium, a business and not an art, which consequently obeys the law of the lowest common denominator. As an activity, television is generally held to induce both passivity and violence, and ranks far behind sports, play, or socializing, and especially reading. Furthermore, there are few television theorists or scholars in the sense that there are film theorists and literary scholars, that is to say people inspired by a genuine passion for their object of study above and beyond its content, supposed effects, and presumed uses. There is no television equivalent of an auteur or of an auteur theory, nothing that might correspond to film or literary theory. There are very few journals devoted to television, there is exceptionally little inquiry into the forms and language of television, no network of references, debate, and response. If, like film and literature, television does spark love in some people, the love that fuels inquiry, debates, and theory, then it is a love that dares not speak its name, for it is almost nowhere present.[1]

Instead, television is studied as a technology: effects studies, uses and gratifications studies, sociological and psychological studies, impressionistic studies, and these are clearly overdetermined by its unworthiness. Does anyone attach electrodes to opera lovers in order to determine the behavioral effects of an aria? Does anyone claim that the meaning of poetry can be exhausted by knowing the economic state of the publisher, or that sculpture corresponds to certain uses and gratifications? The whole approach to television is akin to saying that if you write with a typewriter, that is to say with a machine, your writing is more objective or more likely to have an effect. Such positions are clearly only possible because of the maintenance of certain untenable theories of high art and television's relegation to the status of low art.

Television is, in fact, so undeserving of our interest that only two types of people may legitimately attend to it. The first type consists of people who may be defined as suffering some lack: children, housewives, old people, the poor, off-duty laborers. They lack either the knowledge to know better, or they lack in other activities, or they lack resources. For them, television is obvious and self-explanatory, if still undesirable. Their very social status exhausts their relationship to television and television's relationship to them. As a matter of course, we expect children to like television precisely because they are easily amused and do not know any better, but we also expect them to grow out of it. Television is definitely a phase in life. The other type that may legitimately attend to television consists of people who may be defined as having a surfeit: social scientists, commentators, reformers. They have a surfeit of knowledge and typically apply it to explaining what the first type is doing. Their social status gives them a privileged and authoritative view on television. They approach the object through a forest of precautions and justifications: "We wished to find out why . . ."; "We were commissioned by X to discover . . ."; "It is our aim to explain that . . ."; and so on. One of the major purposes of these is to sanitize the object as much as possible, to objectify it, and to demonstrate manifestly that they themselves, the researchers, take no pleasure in it. The first type's relationship to television, then, is entirely personal and insignificant, whereas the second type's is entirely social and authoritative. The second type provides a metadiscourse on the first.

This is the dominant attitude toward television. The immediate temptation is, of course, to say exactly the opposite, to say that television is good and wonderful and enlightening and valuable. Such a reaction would, however, merely confirm the terms of the original debate and set us off on a search for the quality of television, hoping to prove that representations of peace on television cause peace in society. In fact, it is the terms of the debate themselves that need to be understood and modified.

My original object of study for this paper was *The Beverly Hill-billies,* and one can imagine how the unworthiness of the object was greatly amplified by that fact, for, though it was probably one of the most watched programs in the history of television, it was also one of the most vilified and despised. Its unworthiness stems from two causes: the type of program that it is (situation comedy), and the specific program that it is. It appears that in an undeserving medium, situation comedy constitutes a particularly undeserving form equalled only perhaps by the game show and the locally produced commercial.

As a sitcom, *The Beverly Hillbillies* is particularly interesting on a number of levels. Some sitcoms are much discussed (*All in the Family*); some are loved and fondly remembered (*I Love Lucy, The Mary Tyler Moore Show*); some are honored and praised (*Dick Van Dyke, MASH*). In every case it is because of some element extrinsic to the show's status as sitcom: the issues raised, good acting, or good casting. *The Beverly Hillbillies* apparently had none of that. On the contrary, it remained doggedly at the level of sitcom, refusing to rise above its status or to transcend itself. Consequently, very little was written about it, and almost all of that was uncomplimentary. Within the institutional blind spot that designates situation comedy, *The Beverly Hillbillies* seems to stand out as one of the greatest absences of all.

This silence is surprising, and one should try to make it speak. In its inclusions and exclusions, in what is spoken and in what is not, one detects a pattern or a system, an order of regularity, a recurrent way of approaching, ordering, and constituting objects, in short, a discourse.

GENRE

One of the most useful ways to discuss situation comedy in general and *The Beverly Hillbillies* in particular, which I shall use as a somewhat privileged example, is from within genre theory. An excellent discussion of genre in the cinema is to be found in Stephen Neale's monograph (1980).

There is no doubt that situation comedy exists for us as a category quite distinct from westerns, newscasts, police dramas, documentaries, or even variety. The *TV Guide* listings even go so far as to identify shows according to their generic type: *Three's Company*—situation comedy; *Dragnet*—police drama; *Carol Burnett*—variety. Television writing, as a whole, easily categorizes shows into generic groups. Nonetheless, most of us can easily imagine which shows would properly belong under the rubric "situation comedy" and which would not. There would undoubtedly be some problematic entries, a few test cases, but by a large, the sorting process occurs quite smoothly. It seems, in fact, that the entire television industry is organized around the production of specific genres. Everything that appears on television effectively fits into one genre or another. Television could be said not to exist outside of its genres. There is nothing that is just "television." It is always a specific "type" of television: police show, soap opera, and sportscast. Genres would appear, then, to be a fundamental institutional category. Certain production companies, actors, directors, writers, or producers, specialize in making only one type of show and come to be known and appreciated for precisely that reason. Quinn/Martin Productions, for example, specializes in police drama *(The FBI, Barnaby Jones, The Streets of San Francisco, Quincy);* Norman Lear productions specializes in "relevant" situation comedy *(All in the Family, Maude, The Jeffersons, and so forth)*; and Hannah-Barbera specializes in cartoons. It might even be possible to sketch a history of television through the rise and fall of different production companies and their corresponding generic cycles, from MCA-Revue Studios in the fifties, to Filmways and Screen Gems in the sixties, to Norman Lear and MTM in the seventies. This is, of course, highly reminiscent of the history of Hollywood wherein certain small studios and certain units within large studios made nothing but certain types—genres—of films. And much like current television production, the films of these studios or units all had the same "look"—similar production values, characters, and situations.

So, it is probably fair to say that the concept of genre has a certain sociological resonance. It is something with which we feel comfortable and that helps us organize the output of television. It also has a certain institutional and industrial resonance. Shows self-consciously offer themselves as belonging to specific genres, and production is organized around them. Beyond that, however, genres seem also to have a life of their own; they exercise a determinate and clearly visible pressure. For example, if I were to make a western tomorrow, its final shape would not be determined solely by institutional organization, by the industrial mode of production, distribution, and exhibition, or by economic, ideological, and other interests, but also, and perhaps more importantly, by the history of the genre itself. I would want to argue, therefore, that genres have something that might be called "relative autonomy" and that the variations in and between generic cycles can be explained by it.

We would probably all agree that *The Beverly Hillbillies* belongs to the genre known as situation comedy. Very few books have been written about situation comedy and none about *The Beverly Hillbillies*. This is the zero degree of unworthiness. The one book devoted entirely and solely to sitcom is Rick Mitz's *The Great TV Sitcom Book* (1980). It is essentially a large coffee-table book abundantly illustrated with photographs. Overall, the book is sociologically interesting in that it represents what gets written about television and certainly about situation comedy. Nonetheless, the interest of the book resides in its explicit though inadequate use of the concept of genre. This is not so surprising, as other books on popular phenomena also seem spontaneously to adopt the genre approach. For example, Will Wright's *Sixguns and Society* (1977) and Gary Gerani's *Fantastic Television* (science fiction, 1977) also root their observations in a generic understanding of the object of study. Why they should turn to this methodology is a moot point. Perhaps it is the popular appropriation of what is seen as "scientific" structuralism. Perhaps it is only the mirror image of television's own institutional organization around the necessity of genre. Whatever the reasons, and whatever the value of the generic approach, it remains fraught with serious theoretical difficulties that must be negotiated before it can be said to be of any use. Most writers do not successfully negotiate them.

THE PROBLEM OF CONTENT

The greatest danger of all lies in the conflation of genre with content. It is often thought that genres can be defined on the basis of their content: a western is a western because it contains horses, guns, cowboys. As Mitz states:

> A sitcom has its own special set of characteristics. . . . There's [sic] the credits, then a commercial, then the show, then a commercial, then more of the show, then more commercials, then a short "tag," then the closing credits. . . . There's the sit—the things that happen—and the com—the laughs that, hopefully, come out of the sit (Mitz, 1980: 3).

Here, Mitz's emphasis is placed on the content of the show. He refers to the sit and the com, the commercials, the show, the tag, the credit sequence, all elements that refer us to content. The problem with content is that it can cut across genres. A cowboy can be in a documentary, a horse in a sitcom *(Mr. Ed)*, a gun in a cop show, and so on. This is the single, most monumental error of those who would adopt genre theory. It rests on a fundamental misunderstanding of the institution of which genre is a component. How then can we define genre?

Whenever we look at a western, for example, the most studied genre, we realize that it is not exactly like everything else we can see on television or at the movies. We define it by difference. We begin, then, by positing a background against which are played out a number of differences, and which gives these differences their meaning. The answer to what constitutes difference is what gives us the notion of genre.

Usually, the difference of the western is answered as follows: the western is different from the nonwestern because of its subject matter (the settlement of the western United States between 1860 and 1880, order versus disorder, civilization versus barbarity), because of its treatment of the subject matter (use of space and natural elements, actors whose demeanor suggests ruggedness), and because of its supposed effects (reaffirmation of the triumph of good over evil, pride, patriotism).

It is clear, however, that the important element is the second: the treatment of the subject matter. If the settlement of the western United States were not treated with a particular use of space and nature, with the establishment of specific types of hierarchies between all the show's elements, then it would not be a western but possibly a documentary.

It is usually argued that the manner in which subject matter is treated constitutes a convention and that certain conventions signify certain genres. And yet, as with content, the same conventions can cut across generic boundaries. The good guy can get the girl in any genre, black and white can symbolize good and evil in any context, and so on. The definition of genre as a bundle of conventions remains unsatisfactory because it does not get away from the conflation of genre and content, and ends up either imposing an a priori category or turning genre into an ahistorical and transcultural essence. Let me explain.

Conventions are the element upon which most genre theory fastens as definitive of the very concept of genre. If we say that the western is characterized by x and y conventions, we have, besides returning to the level of content, selected out a number of arbitrary characteristics and said that all objects exhibiting these characteristics will be westerns. What is the justification for selecting those characteristics and not others? There is none. A given choice of characteristics can only be justified on the basis of preexisting conceptions of what the western is. That is to say that in order to select those characteristics and in order to know that they are the definitive ones, we must already have a definition of the genre before the selection occurs. There is no necessary link between the category (western) and its characteristics (whichever conventions we may choose) other than that we have chosen to see a link. To proceed in this manner says more about the selecting agency than it does about the object of study. This then constitutes an a priori category.

In order to deny the charge of imposing an a priori category on the genre, it is sometimes argued that such categories are not arbitrary but are in fact derived from actual observation. The "actual observation" sends us even deeper into content analysis and totally fails to answer the question of why the observer actually observed some characteristics and not others. Nonetheless, it is argued that any category naturally groups dissimilar objects and that when the same dissimilar objects are found together time and again, they form a category and thereby become similar objects. One of the problems with this is that categories are never natural and are always constructed, so that to say that a category naturally groups anything is simply naive. Furthermore, such a category, if it could be said to exist, could only be applied to a closed system for, if a category were observed to contain all the usual dissimilar objects save one, or one too many, then it would cease to be the category in question. To say, therefore, that all westerns share certain characteristics is to imply that all westerns have been produced and that no new ones will ever be produced. This is essential lest a new western introduce a new characteristic and thereby destroy the existing category. On the other hand, it also implies that should any new western ever be produced, it will somehow partake of the essential nature of all previous westerns. If one begins to define the category "western" as soon as the first western is produced, then either the category contains only that one western or it is constantly being destroyed and modified as a category in order to accommodate all the new westerns that bring new elements into play. Or else, all those other "things" are not really westerns. Since, obviously, all westerns may not yet have been produced, we are not dealing with a closed system and such a category (the western) cannot yet exist.

In order to avoid such a logical obstacle, it is usually argued that a category such as the western exists above and beyond all the specific instances yet to be or that have been produced, that is to say that there exists an *essence* of the western. Bazin argued along precisely those lines when he posited the existence of a "superwestern" from which all other westerns derived and of whose essence they all partook (Bazin, 1961: 147). How did Bazin know a film was a western? Because it partook of the essence of westerns. What was the essence of westerns? It was composed of the mass of all western films. The essence justified the corpus and the corpus justified the essence. Bazin began by assuming the existence of that which he set out to prove and then, upon having discovered that which he had constructed in the first place, congratulated his logic for having been so effective. We are then arguing that all westerns share some common third element, across all their similarities and dissimilarities, which marks them unmistakably as westerns. That third element has to be some ideal-perfect state of the genre that all specific instances of the genre only approximate to a greater or lesser degree. This establishes genres as a tautological essence and mystifies them more than it explains them. It fact, by essentializing them, it places them beyond the realm of explanation.

THE PROBLEM OF THE SITCOM

If we were to take all this and apply it to the sitcom, what would we call its subject matter, which distinguishes it from the nonsitcom, what would be its treatment of that subject matter, and what would be its presumed effects? The difficulty with using the sitcom as an example can be seen immediately. It would be fairly easy to state the supposed effect of the sitcom: laughter, the feeling that all is well with the world, that our problems are not that important, and that they are not insurmountable. It might even be fairly easy to say what the treatment of the subject matter is: the resolution of conflict in the mode of humor. We would be rather hard-pressed, however, to say what the subject matter or pretext of the sitcom is. Is it zany, exaggerated, or eccentric characters? Not necessarily. *Leave It to Beaver, Father Knows Best, Family Ties, My Three Sons,* and *The Brady Bunch* are hardly notable for the eccentricity or outrageousness of their characters. On the contrary, they, like most sitcoms, insist on the utter normality of their characters. Is it a certain type of situation? Not necessarily. Sitcoms have been set in prisoner of war camps *(Hogan's Heroes),* in police stations *(Barney Miller, Car 54 Where Are You?),* and in other historical eras *(Happy Days, Laverne and Shirley, It's About Time).* Is it the presence of certain types of conflict? Possibly, but one would be hard pressed to argue that the conflict of *Gilligan's Island, Mork and Mindy,* and *Maude,* was of the same order or intensity, or concerned with the same themes or issues, or even, at times, worth calling conflict. And at any rate, are any of these elements—zany characters, situations, conflict—specific to situation comedy? Hardly. In fact, the subject matter of sitcoms is very difficult to define, and when we come to it, it will retroactively redefine many of the other categories we shall have been using.

All this might seem to add up to a convincing argument for the dismissal of the concept of genre: it is tautological, essentialist, a priorist, content-laden, and unspecific. These are genuine dangers but they spring from a misunderstanding of the institution of television and not from some inherent flaw in the concept of genre. What I want to draw attention to is the question of treatment, the way in which the elements of a genre are handled. *Genres are ways of organizing, regulating, and hierarchizing themes, signifiers, and discourses.* To reject genre on the basis of the objections raised above is to misunderstand the institution of which genre is a regulator. For though these are serious dangers, they stem from a misuse of the notion of genre. They stem from a belief that genre is a reified category. They fail to see genre in relationship to the large institution of television. Instead of seeing genre as a feature of the institution, they try to make genre exist absolutely, independently of the institution. How does the institution of television work, what is characteristic of it? Why should its manifestations be genres?

INSTITUTION

Television as an institution is a highly complex phenomenon. It is perhaps first and foremost an industry, with all the problems of specialization, capital, technology, production, and distribution that implies. As an industry, however, it is crucially dependent upon audience appreciation for its very survival. Indeed, if audiences do not watch the shows offered, the shows become unprofitable, and the institution must ultimately cease production altogether.

The problem for the institution of television is to link its output to audience approval, to get the audiences somehow to want to watch its shows. This is not necessarily an easy task to accomplish as the enormous number of flops attests. And obviously, the production of desirable shows does not happen in a pure or unmediated manner. It is subject to the constraints of competition, of habit, of the socially acceptable, and so on.

Television, furthermore, like any institution, produces a discourse. That is to say that in an ordered and regular manner it constructs representations. The content of its representations can vary enormously but the manner of their construction is consistent. It is this regularity or redundancy that is a discourse. For example, television sitcom can include everything from *I Love Lucy* to *All in the Family,* and within that range any number of contradictory and even antagonistic positions can be assumed. Yet, across these various specific instances, there are certain invariants:

(1) The same tropes reappear. This can be something as banal as the physical appearance of the characters, the necessity of a funny look or gesture.
(2) The same ways of setting up arguments or points to be resolved recurs.
(3) The same mode of address (wit) recurs.
(4) The same way of imagining a situation that will be both funny and significant recurs; hence the necessity of establishing a homeostatic situation with well-defined, nonevolving main characters who nonetheless encounter an endless stream of minor, outside characters.
(5) The same relationship between the product (sitcom) and the institution (television) recurs; the various products must all achieve the same goal; hence, the same mode of address.
(6) The same relationship between the product and the empirical reality it is said to represent recurs. The same theory of representation is at work in all sitcoms; the way reality is thought to look and operate is heavily coded into every aspect of the representation from the construction of narrative space to the definition of character types.
(7) Ultimately the same conception of the audience recurs.

These indicate of course the recurrence of a certain conception of the audience. The discourse of the institution of television, which, like all discourses, is intended to someone, systematically arranges, orchestrates, and constitutes its audience through its construction of representations.

In a social context, however, in which no constraints compel television viewing, it is necessary that television as an industry produce products that will provide some form of satisfaction to large numbers of people. Therefore, though on the one hand the television industry seeks to produce shows for profit, it must also simultaneously produce a certain pleasure in the viewer. The viewer must want to watch television, and the television program must, to a certain extent, meet the viewer's wish.

Furthermore, the viewer's past experience of television will inform his future choice of programming and future viewing patterns. If the industry failed to produce pleasure, the viewer would be unwilling to watch, and without the viewer's attention, the television industry would be unable to sell commercial time and hence unable to maintain itself. It must present itself, institutionally, as something desirable. Television must present itself as a body to be loved. All its products must attempt to produce pleasure such that the pleasure of the past will be inducement for the pleasure of the future. Clearly, then, for television to be successful, to establish itself as an industry with a public wanting its product, it must get the audience to like it. And the best way to do that is to have the audience internalize and expect the repeated experience of pleasure. This process occurs over time and is therefore an historical internalization of the institution by the audience.

The institutionalization of television occurred quite rapidly. This is because the audience had already internalized the experience of pleasure from movies, radio, novels, and so on. The institutional, economic, and psychological structures upon which television depends were already largely in place by the time it was introduced. Naturally, television inflected those structures in its own way and as a function of the constraints that surrounded it. Television brought certain tropes and devices together into configurations that began to acquire, or had already acquired from earlier institutional settings, standardized meanings that came to be expected and recognized. The persona of a Walter Cronkite is a good example of how a specific configuration of personal style, institutional setting, and the constraints of journalistic professionalism, comes to be stabilized, generalized, recognized, and expected. These configurations that provided forms of stabilization and coherence also produced enough pleasure and found sufficient resonance within viewers, for whatever reasons, for them to want to watch them again and again, thereby making it profitable for the institution to repeat them again and again.

One of the most successful inflections of the institution was the production of genres. Different segments of the audience responded more or less favorably to certain configurations. It was possible to refine these configurations and in the process attract viewers willing to attend to them because they offered a special type of satisfaction. Genres appear out of this process of specialization. A genre is a highly specialized configuration requiring an equally specialized viewer who knows how to expect pleasure from it. And though the genre may fragment the market, it also strengthens it. Those viewers not likely to watch a soap opera might watch a detective story instead.

The institution, then, in the sense given it by Christian Metz in *The Imaginary Signifier* (1975), is not just a technology or an industry but also a set of mental or psychological practices that are, to a certain extent, an internalized mirror reflection of the outside institution. The history of American primetime network television, which arguably represents one of the most successful attempts at historical internalization, is, in fact—with its adoption of the ideology of realism, its insistence on continuous flow, the dominance of narrative as a form for virtually everything, a television star system, the fragmentation into genres, and the development of highly specialized production processes—a collection of strategies designed to increase the viewer's pleasure.

Like cinema, television is

> not only a set of economic practices or meaningful products (but) also a constantly fluctuating series of signifying processes, a "machine" for the production of meanings and positions, or rather positions for meaning; a machine for the regulation of the orders of subjectivity (Neale, 1980: 19).

In other words, it is an institution constituted at the site of the intersection among several discourses, strategies, positions, and interests, but also inflecting these and producing its own. What every institution does by virtue of the historical internalization of its discourse is to provide meanings and subjects for those meanings, literally positions for meaning. And those meanings and subject positions are imbedded in and constituted through and through by *narrative*.

Television produces endlessly, across the totality of its output, countless stories—tales that may be funny or tragic or exemplary or slices-of-life. In this it is hardly different from the other cultural institutions of the current social formation. Everything on television is given narrative form, that is, the successive posing and resolution of enigmas. Even this paper is structured as a narrative, with an original enigma (what's wrong with sitcom studies), followed by its eventual resolution. Sports events are the confrontation of opposing camps and the resolution of their conflict is offered as narrative closure. Newscasts are structured as the telling and retelling of the day's events. Educational programming is usually presented as the posing and subsequent resolution of an enigma. Even commercials are routinely constructed as microscenarios. Narrative is the massively dominant form of television, and one can say of television exactly what Stephen Neale says of cinema:

> The focus of the cinematic institution, of its industrial, commercial and ideological practices, of the discourses it circulates, is narrative. What mainstream cinema produces as its commodity is narrative cinema, cinema as narrative. Hence, at a general social level, the system of narration adopted by mainstream cinema serves as the very currency of cinema itself, defining the horizon of its aesthetic and cinematic possibilities, providing the measure of cinematic "literacy" and intelligibility. Hence, too, narrative is the primary instance and instrument of the regulatory processes that mark and define the ideological function of the cinematic institution as a whole (Neale, 1980: 20).

It is my contention that television, for a variety of reasons having to do with its greater availability, its insertion within the family, and its greater turnover of images, has taken over the position in North America, here assigned by Neale to the cinema. As for narrative, it may be defined as

> a process of transformation of the balance of elements that constitute its pretext: the interruption of an initial equilibrium and the tracing of the dispersal and refiguration of its elements. The system of narration characteristic of the cinema is one which orders that dispersal and refiguration in a particular way, so that dispersal, disequilibrium is both maintained and contained in figures of symmetry, of balance, its elements finally re-placed in a new equilibrium whose achievement is the condition of narrative closure (Neale, 1980: 20).

The difference between genres, that which characterizes them, will then reside at least partially in how they conceive the initial equilibrium—what discourses make it up, in what order or sphere they situate it—in what disrupts the equilibrium—and in how a new equilibrium is achieved. *Genres, then, are specific ways in which equilibrium is conceived, disrupted, and replaced.* They are, quite literally, regulators of televisual narrative.

We may turn now to any sitcom to see where this concept of genre gets us. What is the nature of the original equilibrium in, for example, *The Beverly Hillbillies?* Here, the equilibrium is situated in the social order. The discourses that make it up have manifestly to do with class, wealth, and modes of social interaction; in short, those discourses that go to make up the social order of most television shows, the look of normality. The disruption is then provided by the arrival of outsiders clearly marked as belonging to another social class into a world of which they are entirely ignorant. Here, then, we have the confrontation of two discursive hierarchies and the question becomes, How will these people insert themselves into their new class?

If in *The Beverly Hillbillies* the disruption is figured by the intrusion of a new discursive hierarchy, this is not necessarily so in other genres. In the western, for example, the equilibrium is usually figured by some state of society disrupted specifically by violence: Indians disrupted by white men, settlers by Indians or bad guys, farmers by ranchers, and so on. In the musical and the melodrama, the disruption is figured by the irruption of desire. Stephen Neale states:

> For example, in the western, the gangster film and the detective film, disruption is always figured literally—as physical violence. Disequilibrium is inaugurated by violence which marks the process of the elements disrupted and which constitutes the means by which order is finally (re)established. In each case, equilibrium and disequilibrium are signified specifically in terms of Law, in terms of the presence/absence, effectiveness/ineffectiveness of legal institutions and their agents. In each too, therefore, the discourses mobilised in these genres are discourses about crime, legality, justice, social order, civilisation, private property, civic responsibility and so on. Where they differ from one another is in the precise weight given to the discourses they share in common, in the inscription of these discourses across more specific generic elements, and in their imbrication across the codes specific to cinema (Neale, 1980: 21).

In *The Beverly Hillbillies,* and indeed in situation comedy as a genre, equilibrium and disequilibrium are signified specifically in terms of social class. The situation comedy as a genre may then be said to rest upon the encounter of dissonant or incompatible discursive hierarchies. Each hierarchy mobilizes different values, different codes, different modes of social interaction, different semantic fields, different ideas about sex, art, religion, and politics. These latter can be said to be the discourses that make up the discursive hierarchies. The disruption, then, occurs and operates in terms of the discursive hierarchies themselves. Whereas in the western, disruption happens in terms of violence, and in the musical and melodrama it happens in terms of desire, neither violence nor desire is a discourse. They are events or forces that cause an activitation or a reorganization of the discourses involved. In the situation comedy, disruption and discourse are conflated, it is the discourse itself that is the disruption. And that is the specifity of the situation comedy, to organize disruption in terms of discourse. This further specifies the difficulty in establishing the subject matter of situation comedy. That subject matter is discourse itself. This in turn can cause us to view the "subject matter" of other genres in terms of discourses that are mobilized and that come into conflict with each other.

Disruption as discourse or discourse as disruption can take two forms. It can set into play forms of behavior or of linguistic usage that become nonsense and gibberish (Lucille Ball, Jerry Lewis, the Marx Brothers), or it can set into play forms of behavior and action that are simply incommensurate with the situation (*The Beverly Hillbillies*, Charlie Chaplin). These two forms of humor are simply what have been called the screwball or crazy comedy and the social comedy. They have also been called American and British humor, respectively. As Stephen Neale again states:

> Crazy comedy tends to articulate order and disorder across the very mechanisms of discourse, producing incongruities, contradictions and illogicalities at the level of language and code, while social (situation) comedy, on the other hand, tends to specify its disorder as the disturbance of socially institutionalised discursive hierarchies. It is important to stress that these two forms are indeed only tendencies (Neale, 1980: 24).

The Beverly Hillbillies, with its love of puns and sight gags, draws on both types of comedy. Most sitcoms fit somewhere between the two extremes of discursive disruption. *I Love Lucy*, for example, tends towards the screwball comedy. When Lucy gets her head caught in a vase, for example, the disruption is figured in terms of incongruous or illogical behavior. In fact, it is possible to see screwball comedy in "linguistic" terms. Elements are brought into contiguity and turned away from their intended or expected use much as in the word plays of screwball comedy. The elements (Lucy, the vase) are discrete units inscribed into new semantic fields much as the dialogue between the Clampetts and any outsiders. *Barney Miller* tends more towards the social comedy. Discourses of law, justice, and morality, which are very close to those held or believed in by the viewers, are brought into continuity with individuals or institutions who order those discourses differently. In *Barney Miller,* furthermore, the prisoners are usually "crazies." This allows the discursive hierarchies to remain closed to each other and dispenses with the need for any of the characters to gain experience by integrating elements of another discursive hierarchy into their own, and thereby allowing the basic situation to continue. *Leave It to Beaver* is clearly the encounter of dissonant discursive hierarchies: that of the children and that of the adults. The children gain experience but always inflect it through their own discourses such that it remains childish. Only Beaver's biological aging determined the end of that situation. *Mork and Mindy* is likewise clearly about the encounter of radically other discursive hierarchies, though the emphasis is again heavily on the screwball elements. Like Beaver, Mork gains experience but only through the filter of his own discourse, again allowing the situation to remain essentially unchanged.

So, whereas other approaches to situation comedy attempt to define it in terms of its antecedents (vaudeville, radio, film, theater), or in terms of its types of humor (as in Freud, Bergson, and the like), it is my contention that situation comedy can be dealt with and defined from within genre theory in terms of the discourses it sets into play. I would further contend that specific instances of situation comedy can be specified by the precise weight given each of the discourses in play and that generic cycles are largely explicable in terms of the weight given specific discourses in specific socioeconomic and institutional circumstances.

It is a narrative necessity of situation comedy that the "situation" remain unchanged. If the program is to be repeated week after week, the characters and their mode of interaction must not be allowed to evolve. Were they to acquire experience, then evolution would occur and the show could not continue. The ideal situation, therefore, is one that is both open and closed at the same time: open to outsiders or to other discursive hierarchies but closed to experience or to the modification of discursive hierarchies. This is usually handled by establishing a character or group of characters (the stars) whose discursive hierarchy is the one that will be repeated again and again. The privileged site for the establishment of a discursive hierarchy is the family, both literally and metaphorically. There are the "real" families of *Happy Days, Father Knows Best,* and *Donna Reed,* and the "metaphorical" families of *MASH, Hogan's Heroes,* and *Taxi.* But then, the family is probably the dominant metaphor for all North American television. In this, the sitcom shares an important element with other genres. Nonetheless, once the discursive hierarchy that is to be repeated weekly has been established, the ideal situation requires that it come into contact with other discursive hierarchies. Narratively, this is handled through a device such as the family or the place of work wherein a number of repeatable characters can come into contact with nonmembers. Usually, on a narrative level, the situation manages never to be resolved through some "natural" or diegetically motivated obstacle: Hawkeye will never leave Korea because of the army, Gilligan will never get off the island because of a number of accidents, and Uncle Martin will never fix his spaceship because the parts are not available on earth. Narratively, then, a small closure is provided to each week's episode while never providing a larger narrative closure to the fundamental situation.

Sitcoms use a number of strategies in order to preclude the possibility of the characters acquiring experience and thereby altering the fundamental situation. *The Beverly Hillbillies,* for example, frequently fails to provide even a microclosure to each weekly episode such that any number of questions (what happened to Elly May's boyfriend, what happened to the horse Jed bought, what happened to the man who fell into the swimming pool?) remain unresolved. The narrative has no real ending so that the question of experience cannot even be posed. Also, because of their discursive hierarchy, the Clampetts systematically and tenaciously invest a private semantic field; they literally do not understand what is said to them and therefore cannot acquire experience. Likewise, other characters do not understand what the Clampetts say to them, and the "situation" can therefore remain stable.

The narrative nonclosure of *The Beverly Hillbillies* also dispenses with the need for *vraisemblance* (real-seemingness). *The Beverly Hillbillies* makes little or no attempt to claim that it is a faithful representation of reality. In this respect, it is significantly different from many other so-called "relevant" sitcoms that not only make that claim but use it in order to establish some type of value. *MASH* and *All in the Family,* for example, are clearly intended to have a beneficial effect on the viewer such that the viewer will be a better person after having watched those shows.

THE "RELEVANT" SITCOM

This raises briefly the issue of the so-called "relevant" sitcom. Many writers have noted that sitcoms in the seventies seemed to become more socially aware, seemed to deal with much more delicate issues, and to deal with them more sensitively. There can be no doubt that the sitcoms of the seventies are experienced differently by their audiences than were the sitcoms of the sixties. Indeed, it is the opposite that would be surprising. The real problem with the so-called "relevant" sitcom lies in whether or not it represents some sort of qualitative shift as some writers have suggested.

A very good sense of the newness and importance of the "relevant" sitcom is provided by Horace Newcomb when, comparing the old comedy of the sixties to the new comedy of the seventies, he says:

> When the problems encountered by the families become socially or politically significant (the sitcom) form can be expanded. The frame of the ordered world is shattered. Families find themselves living in the world of the present without magical solutions and, to some extent, without the aid of peaceful and laughing love. Comedy, in the form of *All in the Family* or *Maude* or *MASH,* is changed into the perfect vehicle for biting social commentary. Clearly this has long been the case with traditional comic forms. . . . For television, however, the sense of satire and commentary was long in coming. When it did begin to present answers that were not totally acceptable at the mass cultural level, a new stage had been reached (Newcomb, 1974: 57–58).

The idea that the new sitcoms were biting social commentary beyond that which was generally acceptable gives a good sense of the excitement and interest that they generated. It might, furthermore, seem that the relevant sitcom by virtue of its very relevance somehow breaks with the type of generic considerations discussed so far, as though relevance really did break with discursive hierarchies by having some sort of direct hold on reality. There is, however, a slight problem with the concept of relevance.

When people talk about the relevance of sitcom, they are invariably talking about its content and not about its form or any specifically televisual trait it might possess. The very issue of relevance returns us, therefore, once again to the problem of content. Relevance is hardly a defining characteristic of sitcom. News shows, police dramas, documentaries, made-for-television movies all lay claim to relevance. Relevance cuts across genre, it does not constitute it.

Nonetheless, it is maintained that the "relevant" situation comedy marks a new stage in television comedy because it is socially and politically aware. And yet, does not a generic study of sitcom suggest that every sitcom, precisely because it is concerned vitally with class, is already socially and politically aware? Obviously, the distinction being argued between *MASH* and *Father Knows Best,* is that the former is conscious of its class implications whereas the latter merely acts them out. But it seems to me that the question of awareness in sitcoms is largely a question of fashion and that if some sitcoms are indeed more conscious of their liberalism, it is as part of an attempt to capture an audience. The extent to which all sitcoms deal with social and political issues can be measured by the frequent condemnations of sitcoms. There have also always been those who have objected to the inanity of *I Love Lucy* or of *Gilligan's Island* precisely because of its sociopolitical implications. But this again returns us to content analysis and effects studies. Does *Gilligan's Island* lull viewers into a false sense of happiness and deaden them to the really important issues of the day; and does *All in the Family* encourage bigotry or not; and does *MASH* glorify war or denounce it? The most sophisticated response possible is that for some viewers under some circumstances, they do, and for others they do not. Indeed, the extent to which social relevance is merely another discursive hierarchy, subject to infinite permutations as are all discourses, can be deduced from the emergence of shows such as *Family Ties* and others that attempt to make traditional conservative values seem cool and fashionable. *Family Ties* is about hippies of the sixties whose children in the eighties turn out to be right-wing Republicans. The liberalism of the seventies is the conservatism of the eighties, and both types of social awareness are equally "relevant." The only difference is that the relevance of the seventies came to liberal conclusions on social issues whereas the relevance of the eighties comes to conservative conclusions. The discursive hierarchy of relevance remains quite unperturbed by its specific content; it continues to construct its arguments in the same manner.

It is ultimately more fruitful to see the emergence of the so-called "relevant" sitcom as an industrial strategy. People with somewhat different concerns from those of the sixties came to positions of prominence within the television institution and discovered that it was still possible to ensure the institution's survival by a reordering of its discourses. Of course, television has always worked that way. If this makes the sitcom more relevant it is debatable. The presumed relevance of modern sitcom is but another effect of the institution of television, part of the way in which it maintains its currency as the most important and relevant medium of our time and its purchase on our attention. Advertising uses exactly the same content and concerns as socially relevant sitcom. Is it therefore more relevant? The more important question to ask is whether the sitcoms of the seventies structure their humor differently, whether they use a different mode of address, whether they conceive of disruption and equilibrium in new terms. Clearly, they do not. *All in the Family, MASH,* and *Maude,* to name but three, all conceive of disruption in class terms. This is the whole point about Archie Bunker: that he is a blue-collar worker. And also the point behind Maude: that she is an overbearing liberal. And one would be hard put to ignore or deny the importance of the class origins of the various characters on *MASH,* each of whom is stereotypically middle class and good, or upper class and boorish, or socially mobile and untrustworthy.

Relevance is merely another discursive hierarchy that has come to prominence because of a certain historically contingent articulation of the personal, the social, and the institutional. It will no doubt change as that articulation changes. At most, one might wish to detect a generic cycle built around the prominence of the discursive hierarchy of relevance but it would be an error to claim any qualitative shift in sitcom on the basis of that discursive hierarchy.

So far, we have said that situation comedies mobilize a discourse on class. The other extremely important discourse they mobilize has to do with sexuality. All situation comedy inasmuch as it is concerned with discursive hierarchies is also concerned with sexuality, the latter being one of the dominant modes of manifestation of class difference. Sexuality is usually presented in its most highly domesticated form: the leading characters are married, have been married, or envisage marriage as a likely outcome in their lives. The discourse of sexuality in situation comedy constitutes it as necessarily heterosexual and necessarily unconsumable outside of matrimony. This is a discourse of sexuality as it is spoken in many of the dominant institutions of the present social formation. As Stephen Neale says, "Social comedy proper proceeds by mapping the field of a socio-discursive order, a field whose nodal points tend constantly to be those of class and sexuality (Neale, 1980: 24–25).

Sexuality as a discourse comes into contact with the discourse of class and each provides a means of manifestation to the other. The social class of the Cleavers in *Leave It to Beaver* is clearly indicated by the very proper relations between Mr. and Mrs. Cleaver, but also by the coming to sexual awareness of both Wally and Beaver in the most hackneyed boy-meets-girl terms. Indeed, in one episode in which Eddie Haskell gets Wally to talk to a girl who works at a movie theater, Wally's mother complains that she does not want Wally picking up girls at movie theaters because "this girl works," and is therefore of a lower social order. The same can be said of *Happy Days* or of *The Bob Newhart Show* or of *All in the Family*. In fact, the only way in which sexuality can be explicitly mentioned in situation comedy is in the tone of amused embarassment. To mention it is already to be funny. Shows in which there is no married couple have characters who wish they were *(Laverne and Shirley, Rhoda, Cheers)*, who have been married *(The Doris Day Show, Petticoat Junction, Andy Griffith)*, or for whom marriage is a natural possibility *(The Courtship of Eddie's Father, The Many Loves of Dobie Gillis)*. Always, sexuality bespeaks class origin. One of the most striking of recent examples is to be found in the character of the Fonz on *Happy Days*. The Fonz's sexual prowess is explicitly valorized not only by the fact that various women are perpetually at his beck and call but also by his manliness and knowledge of things technical (his motorcycle, his ability to make jukeboxes and telephones work on command). His overt sexuality is also a clear indication of his class origin. The Fonz is then slowly integrated into the camp of the "normal" kids on the show, into middle-class mores. Indeed, in the famous Christmas Day episode in which the Cunninghams invite the Fonz to spend Christmas Day with them so that he will not be alone, the show ends with the family gathered around the piano singing Christmas carols and the Fonz saying: "I love middle-class families." As he is integrated into middle-class values, his sexual potency undergoes a corresponding decline: he is seen to be not always successful, to be insecure, to be rejected by women who are as cool as he (Pinky Tuscadero), and finally, he too was married in the 1982–1983 season.

The "relevant" sitcoms also are organized in terms of the discourse of sexuality. Many of the characters of *MASH* have a relationship to sexuality that bespeaks their class origin. Radar's perennial virginity refers explicitly to his rural origin and innocence about the ways of the world. B.J.'s faithfulness to his wife is indissociable from his dream of one day owning property and consequently from his very proper middle-class background. The mutual lusting of Frank Burns and Major Hoolihan, as well as the Major's subsequent unhappy marriage, are manifestations of their somehow unseemly desire for class mobility. And of course Klinger's constant transvestism besides being a ploy to evade the army is also an expression of his inability, because of his ethnic and class background, to abide by the rules of an authoritarian institution. An enormous number of episodes of *Maude* were constructed around questions of sexual appropriateness, and of course the whole plot of *The Mary Tyler Moore Show* was dependent on the idea of a young woman setting out in the world in order to break sexual stereotypes. *Barney Miller* is forever parading cops in drag who are sent out to catch various muggers and rapists in the park, and the only women who appear on that show are either sexually repressed or sexually unsatisfied. It is one of *Barney Miller's* standby jokes to have a female cop be hurt because a rapist found the male cop in drag more appealing. And of course much of the story line of *All in the Family* was bound up with Archie's disapproval of his daughter's marriage to a man who was of a different ethnic and class origin. The humor was to be generated by the clash of their dissonant discursive hierarchies with their attendant highly divergent attitudes to politics, sex, religion, and so on.

In *The Beverly Hillbillies,* the discourse of sexuality is manifested literally as a crisis of gender identity, perhaps as a metaphor of their class identity crisis. Before proceeding, however, it is perhaps interesting to note that *The Beverly Hillbillies* in particular, and sitcoms in general, seem to contain all those elements—authority and sexuality—to which the television writing discussed earlier was trying to give shape. It is as if there were a continuity from television programs to television writing to this particular paper, with each attempting to give shape to class and sexuality in a particular manner.

Let us now consider the discourse of sexuality. To begin with, the very bodies of the hillbillies are visibly marked as different. Not only do they dress differently but they are almost freaks of nature. Elly May, for example, is designated as being excessively nubile: not only does she pop the buttons on her shirt but she is also consistently marked out as the most desirable woman on the show. Like Jethro, she is also remarkably strong. Jethro is not only unusually strong but he is also indicated as being unusually big for his age, and a prodigious eater. What he has in strength, however, he more than lacks in intelligence. As for Granny, she is not only tremendously old, having lived through the Civil War, but also incredibly spry and feisty. Jed is, in fact, the only one of the hillbillies to be unmarked by physical abnormality. And he is also the only one who comes to any understanding or appreciation of urban life and who tries to come to terms with it without compromising his values.

The crisis of gender seems to superimpose itself upon the physical difference of the hillibillies. Elly May, though she is nubile and a girl, also dresses and acts like a boy. In herself, she combines excessive nubility and affirmed boyishness. As for Jethro, he knows nothing about sex. Jed is constantly saying about him: "Some day I'm gonna have to have a long talk with that boy." Though he wants a girlfriend, he does not know how to get one (his attempts are invariably disastrous), and whenever a girl expresses a liking for him, he is mortified with embarassment. In himself, he combines great potency with utter impotence. He even crosses gender boundaries as he has a sister, Jethrine, who is in every respect similar to him and who is played, for obvious laughs, by the same actor.

Granny and Jed operate as inverse functions of each other. Though she has never remarried, Granny effectively occupies the position of surrogate mother, and though he is now widowed, Jed occupies the symbolic position of father, even to Jethro who is his nephew. Both combine parenthood with celibacy.

What appears to be spoken here is a discourse on the proper public conduct of sexuality, which is a combination of chastity and the denial of sexuality, something safe enough for even the most impressionable child viewer to watch.

The only other person whose body is visibly marked by signifiers of difference is Miss Jane Hathaway. She is, for all intents and purposes—by her association with the bank, her efficiency, insight, and intelligence—a man who just happens to be a woman. She combines within herself a pronounced feminine desire with all the traits of masculinity, right down to her manner of dress and comportment. Interestingly, she is the only one of the nonhillbillies who is specifically accepted by the others as a member of the family and who comes to understand and even love them. She is forever defending them and decrying her boss's schemes to dupe them. Significantly, she is the only nonhillbilly whose body undergoes physical change similar to that of the hillbillies. Whenever someone must wear a ridiculous costume, or submit to one of Granny's haircuts, or whatnot, it is she. Difference is written right on to her body and she thereby crosses over into the camp of the hillbillies. *The Beverly Hillbillies* is perhaps one of the most striking examples of the discourses of class and sexuality at work in sitcoms. But to a very large extent, the way in which these two discourses serve as manifestations of each other is to be found in all sitcoms. Sexuality is usually inscribed onto the very bodies of the characters as class difference, and class difference finds its expression in sexuality. It is never as accident, for example, that so many sitcom characters are spouseless despite their explicit desire not to be so. This allows for all the possible modalizations of sexual relationships within the confines of what the institution of television will allow. Hawkeye's spouselessness is no more suprising that Doris Day's in her show or Diane Carroll's in hers. It allows the expression of an attitude towards sexuality that is itself examplary of class origin.

So, from the mass of television writing to the content of situation comedy, the same themes recur: class, sexuality, authority, and modes of social interaction, but with markedly different emphases.

In *The Beverly Hillbillies,* the discourse of sexuality is explicitly signalled as

> the inscription of a disruption in the spatio-temporal scales governing the order of the "human" and of "nature," producing figures such as giants—be they animals or humans—or, alternatively, homunculi, dwarfs, and so on (Neale, 1980: 27).

In other words, were *The Beverly Hillbillies* not a situation comedy, that is to say a genre in which discursive hierarchies themselves constituted the disruption, we could well be dealing with another genre altogether in which variations of the scales of the human and of nature also occur: the fantastic or the horror genre. It is, therefore, the presence of the discourses of class and sexuality, and the status of discourses as the agent of disruption that specifies the situation comedy as a genre. In the fantastic or the horror genre, the discourse of class would be absent and would be replaced by a discourse of metaphysics.

Indeed, a metaphysical discourse is not entirely absent from *The Beverly Hillbillies.* Many objects, animals, and people are mistaken by the hillbillies for that which they are not. A pink flamingo is mistaken for a giant chicken, a croquet ball for an egg, and a camel for a horse. Spatiotemporal variations abound. Furthermore, Granny dabbles in black magic and on more than one occasion believes that she has transformed someone into an animal.

Besides the dominant discourses on class and sexuality, there are in *The Beverly Hillbillies* minor discourses on nature and on the metaphysical. It is perhaps the specificity of *The Beverly Hillbillies* that the discourses of class and sexuality figure not only the very disruption of the initial equilibrium but also that they are articulated across other minor discourses on nature and the metaphysical, and thence across spatiotemporal distortions. Other situation comedies could perhaps likewise be specified: through the specific weight given the discourses of class and sexuality and through their articulation across other minor discourses, which would have to be specified in each case. Generic cycles are then the relative recurrence of these minor discourses. Perhaps a generic cycle can be detected in sixties sitcoms such as *I Dream of Jeannie, My Favorite Martian,* and *Bewitched,* all of which deal with the order of the metaphysical and with magic. In these, the metaphysical is more pronounced than in *The Beverly Hillbillies,* but it is also allied with questions of sexuality, class, and correct behavior. Perhaps there is a general discourse of sixties sitcom that links the metaphysical to questions of class and sexuality. It might also be worthwhile to explore further the links between these themes and other television genres. It should not be overlooked that sitcoms such as *I Dream of Jeannie* explicitly link the metaphysical with technology, featuring both spaceflight and the genie's powers as two types of magic. What then could be the relationship between this and other genres more explicitly interested with technology (science fiction) and with the metaphysical (the fantastic)? And what then of other genres, such as news programming, which explicitly foreground their own technology and consistently display its limitless possibilities?

Perhaps we can also find another generic cycle more appropriate to the seventies that links a didactic and moralizing attitude to questions of class and sexuality. Perhaps on the basis of this one study, we can begin to identify other discourses at work in other genres and begin to see the perhaps surprising relationships between genres.

NOTE

1. For a few preliminary exceptions, one might consider various essays in Adler and Cater (1976), Newcomb (1974, 1982), and several of the journals cited in the references.

REFERENCES

Adler, Richard and Douglas Cater [eds.] (1976) Television as a Cultural Form. New York: Praeger.
American Film, various issues and articles.
Autrement (1982) "La tele, une affaire de famille. . . ." January, 36.
Barnouw, Erik (1975) Tube of Plenty. New York: Oxford University Press.
Barthes, Roland (1970) S/Z Paris: Seuil.
Bazin, Andŕe (1961) "Qu'est-ce que le cinéma? III," in Cinéma et Sociologie. Paris: Les Editions du Cerf, Collection 7e Art.
Bennett, Tony et al. [eds.] (1981) Popular Television and Film. London: British Film Institute.
Brooks, Tim and Earle Marsh (1979) The Complete Directory to Prime Time Network TV, 1946-Present. New York: Ballantine.
Brown, Les (1971) Television: The Business Behind the Box. New York: Harcourt Brace Jovanovich.

Brundson, Charlotte and David Morley (1978) Everyday Television: "Nationwide". London: British Film Institute.

Cahiers du cinéma (1981) "Television." Special Issue, Fall.

Cawelti, John (1970) The Six-Gun Mystique. Bowling Green: Bowling Green University Popular Press.

Ellis, John (1982) Visible Fictions. London: Routledge & Kegan Paul.

Esslin, Martin (1982) The Age of Television. San Francisco: W. H. Freeman.

Fiske, John and John Hartley (1978) Reading Television. London: Methuen.

Foucault, Michel (1969) Les mots et les choses. Paris: Gallimard.

Garnham, Nicholas (1978) Structures of Television. London: British Film Institute.

Genette, Gérard (1970) Figures III. Paris: Seuil.

Gerani, Gary with Paul H. Schulman (1977) Fantastic Television. New York: Harmony Books.

Gibson, William (1980) "Network news: elements of a theory." Social Text 3 (Fall).

Hall, Stuart (1971) "Television as a medium and its relation to culture," in Stencilled Occasional papers No. 4. Birmingham University, Centre for Contemporary Cultural Studies.

_____ (1973) "Encoding and decoding the television discourse," in Stencilled Occasional Papers No. 7. Birmingham University, Centre for Contemporary Cultural Studies.

Harris, Jay S. [ed] (1978) TV Guide: The First 25 Years. New York: Simon & Schuster.

Lasfargues, Alain (1982) "10 ans de télévision aux USA." Cahiers du cinema 331 (January).

Metz, Christian (1975) Le signifiant imaginaire. Paris: UGE, 1977. Reprinted as "Le signifiant imaginaire" in Communications 23. Paris: Seuil.

Mitz, Rick (1980) The Great TV Sitcom Book. New York: Richard Marek.

Morley, David (1980) The "Nationwide" Audience. London: British Film Institute.

Neale, Stephen (1980) Genre. London: British Film Institute.

Newcomb, Horace [ed.] (1982) Television: The Critical View. New York: Oxford University Press.

_____ (1974) TV: The Most Popular Art. Garden City, NY: Doubleday.

Quarterly Review of Film Studies (1983) "The economic and political structure of American television." 8(3).

Rovin, Jeff (1979) The Great Television Series. New Jersey: A. S. Barnes.

Schramm, Wilbur, Jack Lyle, and Edwin B. Parker (1961) Television in the Lives of Our Children. Toronto: University of Toronto Press.

Screen (1981) "TV issue." 22 (4).

Screen Education, various issues and articles.

Steiner, Gary A. (1963) The People Look at Television. New York: Alfred A. Knopf.

Surgeon General's Scientific Advisory Committee on Television and Social Behavior (1972) Television and Growing Up: The Impact of Violence. Washington, DC: Government Printing Office.

Televisions, various issues and articles.

Terrace, Vincent (1976) The Complete Encyclopedia of Television Programs 1947–1976 (2 vol). New Jersey: A. S. Barnes.

Todorov, Tzvetan (1970) Introduction à la littérature fantastique. Paris: Seuil.

Williams, Raymond (1974) Television: Technology and Cultural Form. London: William Collins and Sons.

Wright, Will (1977) Six Guns and Society: A Structural Analysis of the Western. Berkeley: University of California Press.

Chapter 10

FANTASY AMERICA
Television and the Ideal of Community

Thomas H. Zynda

FOR NEARLY ALL of the eleven years in which it was in production, *MASH* drew both the acclaim of critics and very large audiences. Its final episode, in February of 1983, was a two-and-a-half hour leave-taking with one of the largest audiences in television history.

The columnist Ellen Goodman found in this national attention a clue to the meaning of *MASH*. In the last episode, she wrote, "we'd all witnessed the breakup of a community." It was, she continued, "the community of a bunch of Army medical people in Korea; the community of a bunch of actors in Los Angeles; the community of a nation of viewers" (Goodman, 1983). For Goodman, *MASH* was not just one of the better television entertainments, but an inscription of communality overcoming time, distance, and sociological uncertainty.

Goodman's description of the television audience is of particular interest. It is easy to imagine those working at an actual combat hospital, individuals relying on each other in a common task amid a common danger, as a kind of community. Similarly, we can understand the writers, production people, and actors cooperating to produce the show as a community of workers on an extended project. Imagining the mode of sharing and identification among the audience members, however, is more problematic. Goodman justifies her vision in a rather stretched explanation. "Community," she writes, "is a group whose special interest is each other." "Television watching," she continues, "is a solitary experience, yet in some ways a shared one," since for viewers "the TV set is a shared text." This explanation does not resolve her inclusion of conflicting meanings within the single term, "community." It serves, though, as the avenue to her concluding image of "the community of a nation of viewers," of America united through the agency of a mass medium.

Goodman's employment of "community" in such an indiscriminate way indicates the talismanic power of the word; and of the meanings packed into her usage of it, none are unusual in a scholarly sense. In particular, finding community in the use of a common medium is a common rhetorical strategy for depicting a medium. In a recent essay on the state of American book publishing, for example, Samuel Vaughan employs a rhetorical strategy parallelling Goodman's. Vaughan refers to "the community of the book . . . those for whom the written word . . . is of the first importance" (Vaughan, 1983: 85). His description quietly requests us to understand a medium, the word, as the cement of communality.

Such conceptions rest upon a comparison of mediated communication to the directness of face-to-face communication. This comparison ignores the alienation of the receivers of mass-mediated messages from their senders, not to mention the content of what is printed or televised. It ignores, too, the overwhelming commercial circumstance of most mass communication, particularly television. These are large issues for writers, whether scholars or columnists, to overlook.

Considering their oversights, Vaughan's and Goodman's attribution of community to a communication medium points not only to an attempt to justify their respective media but also to an almost desperate search for some way of imagining America as unified, somehow ordered, somehow having a modus vivendi as a collective. This need is satisfied, in their explanations, through understanding the extensiveness of a medium as signifying an equivalently extensive sharing of ideas, values, and material circumstances.

Such explanations have deep roots in American culture. They are revealing of the persistence of an historical American problem of conceiving of a form of society fitted to the ideals and possibilities of a New World, and a tendency to envision pure communication as the solution to the problem.

THE HERITAGE OF "COMMUNITY"

The modern concept of community derives from sociology, especially from Ferdinand Tönnies's analysis of the shift in social organization from Gemeinschaft to Gesellschaft, or roughly, from community to society (Tönnies, 1983). These categories are ideal types rather than actual descriptions, and they can be given concrete meaning in different ways. In the American cultural vocabulary, "community" is a crucial and complex word. Its many dimensions of meaning and value can be seen in the ways in which it is employed in the interpretive routines of television news.

One of the most common usages is the designation of a small town as a "community." This usage is the rule in feature stories portraying rural America as the repository of traditional values; such stories illustrate "community" as peacefulness and absence of competitiveness. Another usage is the reference to groups not fully assimilated into the mainstream culture as "communities," as in "the Black community," "the Chinese community," and so on. In this case, "community" attributes to the named group a high degree of internal coherence and cooperation, leading to the implication that it is different but self-sufficient. In an allied usage in the idiom of network news, professionals can be "communities," as in "the medical community" or "the scientific community."

Generally, professions become communities when a problem of some kind calls for reassuring the audience. In headline stories of international crises involving the superpowers, for example, references will be made to "the diplomatic community." The phrase invokes the presumption of close communication and concern among the group's members, whom we are to understand as having things under control or as at least taking their responsibility for our welfare as seriously as possible. Rhetorically, this employment of "community" identifies a locus of order amid threatening uncertainty.

"Community" then is a perceptual category invoked to serve specific rhetorical functions in interpretations of the situation of America. The strategic character of the word's employment becomes most visible in cases in which it is not used. Commonly this occurs in news stories about some national damage for which a profession is held accountable. For example, in the context of a story about the unaffordability of hospital care, what would otherwise be "the medical community" is likely to become "the medical establishment." "Community" is a positive form of order, "establishment" a negative form connoting the insulation and indifference of institutionalized power. The concepts of order and beneficence are the core meanings of "community," and these in turn are understood as qualities opposite to the characteristics of the society at large. "Community" thus bears a large cargo of other values, such as self-reliance, competence, mutual aid, strength, concern, and civilization, which are attributed to the group to which the word is applied.

The term carries considerable honorific potential, with the power to legitimize groups as respectable components of society. Interestingly, "the medical community" includes doctors but not nurses, just as "the business community" includes the heads of the automobile companies but not the automobile workers. "Community," in short, designates a social network that is seen to form the society rather than to be formed by it, and which can thus be understood to be a stable reference, a pillar of the larger society. There is as well a certain status implied. Auto workers are members of a union, but union executives are "labor leaders" rather than "the labor community"; "community" honors a group as standing apart from self-interested partisanship, as above politics. Goodman's reference to "the community of viewers" exploits this honorific potential, using it to rhetorically coerce acceptance of the idea of an America unified in outlook on fundamental matters and, hence, politically unified.

As an explanation, Goodman's view of television lies within a long tradition of thought that has grown from Americans' experience with media. Alexis de Tocqueville, reporting on his visit of 1831–1832, remarked on the large number of newspapers he had found. He explained them as a necessity in a country where the population was dispersed, social ties weak, and political power decentralized. The political character of Americans' association was disclosed in the profusion of newspapers, "which bring to them every day . . . some intelligence of the state of their public weal." A newspaper survived, he understood, by "publishing sentiments or principles common to a large number of men," and hence "it always represents an association which is composed of its habitual readers (de Tocqueville, 1945: 121–122), who through it were able "to converse every day without seeing one another, and to take steps in common without having met" (de Tocqueville, 1945: 119–120). In de Tocqueville's view, the newspaper enabled Americans to achieve the shared outlook and coherence of community without physical community.

De Tocqueville's report describes the prototypic experience of media as the means to a new type of social cohesion, which has shaped the American understanding of communication and society. As a body of thought, this understanding was articulated as America underwent a cluster of drastic changes. By the late 1800s America was no longer the agrarian democracy de Tocqueville had toured; it was socially variegated, increasingly urban and industrial, and torn by class conflict. The fundamental American problem of democratic cohesion had reappeared.

At the same time, the means of public communication had developed and multiplied. The telegraph connected all areas, the mass press thrived in the cities, and national magazines had become established. The telephone was spreading across the country and, along with electrification in the cities, augured the mass media of the next century. In this provocative atmosphere of crisis and promise American thought on communication and society was born, in the work of John Dewey, Charles Horton Cooley, and Robert Park.

Perhaps because of their small-town backgrounds, their concern was with understanding the modern society in terms of cohesion. Their common theme is best suggested by John Dewey's often-quoted lines of 1915: "Society not only continues to exist *by* transmission, *by* communication, but it may be fairly said to exist *in* transmision, *in* communication." "Men live in a community by virtue of the things they have in common," he explained, "and communication is the way they come to possess things in common" (Dewey, 1966: 4).

Cooley likewise emphasized communication as "the mechanism through which human relations exist and develop." For him, society and culture, insofar as they are material, simply gave witness to this process, for "communication, including its organization into literature, art, and institutions, is truly the outside or visible structure of thought" (Cooley, 1962: 61). Park expressed a very similar idea in his explanation that "human society . . . is mainly a social heritage, created in and transmitted by communication" (Park and Burgess, 1969: 61).

Park's experience and observation of modern America may be characterized as those of a latter-day de Tocqueville. In many years spent as a reporter in the city he noted that ethnic groups maintained their cultures through their own press, and from this he developed a theory of how the urban press served to maintain society. In an idea very close to de Tocqueville's conception of the newspaper, Park explained that a mass medium represented an interacting group he called a public, which was the distinctive form of modern society. The newspaper "does not so much inform as orient the public," he explained, adding, in an echo of de Tocqueville, "giving each and all notice as to what is going on." It produces cohesion by stimulating discussion that "usually terminates in some sort of consensus or collective opinion—what we call public opinion" (Park, 1940: 677).

The work of Dewey, Cooley, and Park is an exposition of Americans' understanding of communication and social association. In it, society is not institutional structure but process, and institutions are understood as the evidence rather than the condition of communication. Communication itself is seen as a sharing of mind or outlook; society becomes, in effect, collective mind. To the extent that it is a

structure, society appears in their work as a disembodied communication network; physical proximity and shared material situation
are hardly even implied.

For these thinkers, communication offered a fulfillment of democracy, "for society to be organized more and more on the higher
faculties of man, on intelligence and sympathy, rather than on authority, caste, and routine," in Cooley's words. The media thus became of central importance, for they made possible the sharing of
"the higher faculties of man" without regard to distances of social
class or geography. They meant, in Cooley's vision, "the expansion
of human nature . . . of its power to express itself in social wholes,"
that is, the development of an America that would be a single vast
community of individuals united in a shared culture. For Cooley,
indeed, the whole world might eventually be included, as "the public
consciousness, instead of being confined . . . to local groups, extends . . . until wide nations, and finally the world itself, may be
included in one lively mental whole" (Cooley, 1962: 81).

Cooley's words may seem naive, but it is only the archaism of his
language that brackets his vision as utopian fantasy. In spite of, and
indeed because of, the chaos of recent history, we continue to explain
and justify media in terms of such a vision of unification and commonality, and better communication is something of a god-term for
Americans. On this basis we have celebrated photography, the telephone, film, radio, television, communication satellites, and the international free flow of communication. Within the more wieldy vision
of America itself, cable television was for years seen as a means to
participatory democracy.

In our understanding of communication, then, we focus another
vision, that of America itself. Communication, in the vision of Americans, is the means of creating a country of communal sharing of
values that obviates questions of class, power, and privilege. Communication, in short, is the American answer to politics, a way of
reinventing America as the community of de Tocqueville's visit.

THE TELEVISION COMMUNITY

The tradition of seeking national community and finding it in communication media informs Goodman's explanation of *MASH* and of
the social role of television. Television exerts a temptation toward
such a view in its programming, which is pervasively on the theme

of community. In television dramatic series of all genres, community is presented figuratively, in the metaphor of the workplace or professional family such as was featured in *MASH*.

In the workplace family, the characters have a material basis for their relationship through their employment in a common organization or task. Dramatically speaking, this conveniently establishes the relationships among the characters so that the show can focus on a plot and, in situation comedies, the accompanying repartee. Thematically, in this way television passes off the central problem of inequality that besets the capitalist society it claims to mirror, or at least it presents the problem as moot. Second, although the shared task is the material basis of the characters' association, dramatically speaking their association is explained by their shared outlook and their concern for each other. Third, conflicts among the members of the workplace family are resolved within the family, usually through a process of discussion leading to consensus. These conflicts, however, never question the basis of their association. Fourth, television workplace families have, in recent years, moved increasingly to positions of clear social utility; we find them in the press, in medicine, in police work. Finally, and most importantly, the workplace family bridges the tension between individualistic society and traditional community. The workplace family's members are there by choice, rather than accident of birth, and thus represent a normative role for the contemporary individual. Their unity is based on feeling, on liking each other, and on the shared outlook they derive from their commitment to their profession and its values.

The milestone in television's elaboration of the workplace family as a model of contemporary community is *The Mary Tyler Moore Show*, which remained continuously popular from its opening in 1970 to its end seven years later, and in much syndication since. *Mary Tyler Moore* justified the workplace family as a social form that resolved the fragmentation and confusion with which America had emerged from the 1960s. The show's characters formed a minicommunity whose members helped each other through all sorts of life crises, such as Mary's frequent self-doubts, her co-worker Murray's worries over middle age, and Lou's divorce by his wife. The little group provided Mary with the stimulation and the emotional support to develop her personality. Through the community, the pain of change became little more than initial embarassment, and usually change was presented as an increase in social equality that benefited all and cost none. The community's members demanded of each other only adaptability, acceptance, and openness, and they supported rather than attempted to control each other.

Mary's workplace family put no restrictions on her private life, but actually it absorbed her private life. Her hopes, her ideas of herself, and her romantic affairs provided the material of her relations with her co-workers, who thus really became her family. In this way the workplace family dissolved the tensions between personal independence and the need for belonging. The workplace family was presented as an alternative social form at least as good as the kinship family, and the new American community it represented to be better than the restrictive community implied by the domestic family of earlier television.

In the *Mary Tyler Moore* workplace family, the characters were associated because they earned their living together; this was and remains television's way of presenting America as a pluralistic society in which everyone has his or her share of the means of life. In keeping with the concept of community as mental unity, the "problems" the show's community dealt with were nearly all of a purely symbolic sort as well. What much of the celebration of *Mary Tyler Moore* has failed to see is that the issues of the episodes were usually simply thematic motifs on which were hung a set of characters and plots traditional to the sitcom. None of the problems dealt with were of the material sort that movements such as feminism responded to in the real world, and the show thus trivialized the concerns it purported to mirror.

In many ways the show's political blandness proceeds from American ideas of society. Membership in American society is not so much inherited as it is earned by economic productivity. The problem of achieving this economic membership has been left aside, in American thought, as an individual concern. In American social thought, membership in community has been more readily considered, then, as essentially a communication process, without attention to the implications of our society's economic basis. *Mary Tyler Moore* defined community as equality, mutual support, and cooperation rather than competition. The show's location of community in a television station attributed to it a veneer of usefulness, as well as lending it glamor and prestige—that is, celebrating it within the values of the noncommunal larger society.

MASH, which opened in the fall of 1972, developed the same community values but placed them in circumstances that justified community as a necessity of survival. The *MASH* community comprised a collection of compatible and conflicting personalities; united in the task of saving lives, even the oddest characters were accepted. The show's humor was directed at those who tried to assert control or their own superiority. Thus, Corporal Klinger received good-natured ribbing about the dresses he wore, but Burns and Winchester, officers who insisted on the privileges of rank, received Hawkeye's continual sarcasm. An approved form of authority was illustrated by Blake and Potter, who exercised a quiet command of the hospital unit by virtue of the respect they had earned of their subordinates. Thematically, this is how *MASH* illustrated democratic authority as a central distinction of community.

In the course of the show's development some characters became members of its community. Major Margaret Houlihan, for example, begins as an outsider, an officer afraid to be human. In these early years Hawkeye undercut her military dignity by naming her "Hot Lips," a reference to her sexual affair with Burns. In later episodes she dropped the mask of authority, earned the others' respect as an officer and a person, and was rewarded by Hawkeye's acceptance of her as fellow member of the community.

MASH differed from other television comedies of its era in the seriousness of its situation. The show depicted war, the field hospital, bloody bandages and surgical gowns; in some episodes, attractive characters died or suffered amputation. The shared outlook that unified the *MASH* community was black humor, the humor of men and women trying to keep going in a world that offered no evident hope. Burns and Winchester, the butts of Hawkeye's jokes, were absurd because they could not see that rank, a principle of order in society, was no longer relevant to survival. *MASH* in this way appealed to Americans' awareness of the danger to humanity posed by the social and political chaos of the world, and to our disenchantment with society's traditional institutions and values. It implied that traditional social, military, and sexual structures were the cause of mankind's problems, and community, which eliminated these structures, thus became compellingly attractive.

MASH carried the family/community from the limits of situation comedy to the broader relevance of drama. Following its success, this broadened relevance was further developed in straight drama series. Two of these series, *Quincy* (1976–1983) and *Lou Grant* (1977–1982), profitted by extending characters that their lead actors, Jack Klugman and Ed Asner, had originally developed in situation comedies. This was accomplished, in both cases, by transforming their previous comical bluster and insensitivity into the forcefulness required of them as community heads in their new shows.

The legitimacy of communal leadership versus formal authority was central to *Quincy,* as it had been in *MASH.* Quincy was technically subordinate to Asten, the coroner, but he constantly badgered and lectured him. Lieutenant Monohan handled relations between the police and the coroner's office, but, along with a police sergeant, actually served as Quincy's assistant. This blurring of lines of authority and of institutional boundaries was a way of suggesting equality and community cooperation across social boundaries. The *Quincy* community operated as a kind of meritocracy. Quincy's assistants obeyed him out of recognition of his expertise, and expertise, in turn, was displayed not as routine technical knowledge but as Quincy's unique superiority of knowledge, intuition, and ingenuity.

With such deserved leadership, Quincy involved police, doctors, and attorneys all over Southern California in his pursuits, all without bureaucratic procedure of any kind. He thus welded diverse professions into a single community that, in the series, became an illustration of core American values.

Lou Grant featured a community very similar to that of *Quincy,* except for its reverse depiction of professions. Whereas Quincy led a diversity of professionals, Lou Grant headed a community of journalists who, however, accomplished their work by enacting the capacities of detectives, police, social workers, counselors, and even lawyers. As in *Quincy, Lou Grant* showed how the personnel of a large, impersonal organization developed a personal commitment to each other as a workplace family. In both cases, their work was exposing social problems such as child abuse, graft, or mistreatment of hospital patients. Again, as in *Quincy, Lou Grant* united diverse personalities into a community that then extended its caring to the individuals of the atomized larger society. As the community head, Lou, like Quincy, was larger than his professional role. In addition to his professional leadership, he offered his youthful reporters knowledge of the world, wisdom about life, and emotional support. The gratification offered by *Quincy* and *Lou Grant* lay in the way their communities served as fonts of caring and justice in a larger society depicted as isolating, impersonal, and competitive.

In *Hill Street Blues* (1981–   ) and its derivation, *St. Elsewhere* (1982–   ), the environment that justifies community is more than simply competitive; as in *MASH,* it is actively hostile. These shows, too, locate their workplace families in life-and-death institutions: the police station and the hospital. These serve dramatistically as the vantage points from which the viewer is shown the larger world, which appears as a no-man's land of predatory, criminal individualism.

Against this setting *Hill Street Blues* presents the most developed and integral example of television's articulation of the workplace family as a national community. The show's group of regular characters refurbishes the melting pot theme common in 1950s war movies. Frank Furillo heads the Hill Street Precinct and its family, which comprises the ethnic and class mosaic of the urban Northeast. The social mix is more complex, however, than the WASP-Jew-Black-Worker-Southerner of the earlier stereotype. It includes, for example, Ray Calletano, a veteran officer who is Colombian, and Mick Belker, an undercover detective who, unconventionally, is Jewish. The most innovative character, Lucy Bates, is a young woman who, in effect, changes her gender to move from desk clerk to patrol officer to sergeant. As tough as any of the male cops, her thematic significance is conveyed by her contrast with Frank's ex-wife, Fay, whose 1960s-style liberalism and feminism are humored by the others. The characters' backgrounds, personalities, and political stances are too varied, however, for either a simple liberal-conservative ordering or a comfortable melting-pot trivialization of their differences.

Their contrasts are not just eccentricities, as in *MASH,* but real differences of class, race, politics, and personal style that produce real conflicts among them. Lieutenant Goldblume puts up with Lieutenant Hunter's conviction that Jews are somehow peculiar; Bobby has political battles with other black cops; Ray is fed up with being considered a Chicano; Washington calls it quits with his long-time partner, D.J., who has been showing up for work drunk. They have conflicts over promotions, assignments, girlfriends, and questions of ethical conduct. The resolutions impose costs; someone always loses. Goldblume becomes deeply resentful when, for political reasons, the department gives the promotion he was due to a less qualified black officer. At a party, Joe loses a sexy woman to Bobby when she sees that Bobby has a lot of money. Joe and Lucy agree to cover a serious infraction committed by another cop to whom they owe a favor, and as a result nearly lose their jobs.

Hill Street Blues is a major advance in the sophistication of television's analysis of community. In the face of the losses they endure from doing the right thing or simply from life's competition, the cops yet have a powerful cohesiveness. They share an unquestioned commitment, manifested in their sharing of the strict personal discipline and loyalty required of their work, to holding at bay the criminals that infest the city. They care for each other because they must depend on each other in the dangerous streets, and they extend this caring as help and sympathy to those struggling to survive in the city. As in

MASH, Quincy, and *Lou Grant,* the work of this community is that of maintaining civilization according to core American values.

Another recent series has placed the family in a more plausibly social workplace setting. *Cheers* (1982–   ), which is set in a bar of the same name, dramatizes community as refuge. The bar is located in a basement, a den of safety. Its owner, Sam, is a reformed alcoholic who now can help others. Diane, his sparring partner in the dialogue, came to Cheers by way of shipwreck: she was abandoned at the bar by a professor with whom she was eloping. Following this emotional trauma, she stayed to work at the bar and be restored with the help of Sam and the bar's patrons. Similarly Coach, a helper, is an aging former athlete who was broken by the pressure to perform. All the characters have had their confidence shattered by their experiences as individuals in the larger society. In Cheers they form a community to provide each other with practical help and emotional support for rebuilding their damaged selves. In *Cheers,* also, community is shown to be a necessity of survival, a crucial personal support in an exploitive and unforgiving world.

Another model of the social service community is presented in *Fame* (1981–   ), which is set in a high school of the performing arts. The young students work hard to meet the demanding, perfectionist standards of the theatrical world they aim to enter. They learn their potential and their limitations, and how to accept both. Most importantly, they form a community of concern for each other. In their competitive and individualistic milieu, they help each other to improve, to overcome failure, and to keep up determination. The continuous reference of the communities in recent shows such as *Fame, Cheers,* and *Hill Street Blues* to the larger society is a measure of their maturation from the insulated group of *Mary Tyler Moore.*

The workplace family in television, whether in situation comedy, situation tragicomedy, or more serious drama, is both a metaphor and a model for community. Metaphorically, the workplace itself represents the territorial place of the traditional community; it is where the characters find belonging. The organization to which they belong is usually one of clear social utility, corresponding to the economic basis of the traditional community and to the broader American conception of how individuals are "productive members of society." In this connection, television drama's portrayal of the workplace or the profession as a community corresponds to television news' reference to professions as communities.

The workplace communities also dramatize the mobility of American life. As much as the characters belong to them, their membership is subject to new opportunities. Sometimes characters leave, with the explanation of going to another city, and sometimes they leave to reappear in those other cities in their own shows. After the end of *Mary Tyler Moore,* Lou Grant reappeared as a Los Angeles newspaper editor in *Lou Grant; Mary Tyler Moore* had also previously generated *Rhoda* (1974–1978) and *Phyllis* (1975–1977). *Trapper John, M.D.* (1979–   ) was spun off from *MASH* in this way, and *AfterMASH* (1983–   ) appeared as a sequel. Series characters move not as actors but as community characters, and in their new shows and new communities they have elbow room to expand the identities established in their earlier shows, usually as heads of their new communities. When they move they achieve higher stations in life, both within their new show's community and also outside of it, in becoming stars with their own television series. Television in this way accounts for mobility as we do in actual life; one moves to take a better job.

The professional membership of characters such as Hawkeye, Quincy, Lou Grant, and Frank Furillo is one of the chief elements of their attractiveness. They are figures not only of strength but of trust, for we understand them to be acting not out of selfish competitiveness, but out of commitment to the values of their professions, which are the values, we see, of America as a civilization. By their position in crucial professions such as medicine, journalism, and law enforcement, they represent a fundamental stability and agreement in a society that seems otherwise unanchored and conflict-ridden. We see also, in their demonstration of superior professional competence, that they have earned their high social position meritocratically. The professional hero, in this way, validates the ideal of equality as reality.

The communities of television series are fantasies in more than one way; they adjust reality to meet our needs for dramatization of values and wishes. Actual communities do not fare so well in television depiction. Television news, with its bias toward the limits of the real world, documents actual communities of place almost purely in terms of their risks and costs. Directed at revealing to the audience "some intelligence of the state of their common weal," to use de Tocqueville's phrase, news stories of community stand in contrast to the benign view of dramatic series. They are almost invariably stories of catastrophe and psychological devastation. The catastrophes are produced by centralized forces, especially economic forces, and they befall those who chose to live in community among those with whom they were born and raised.

A list of evening news communities is a litany of suffering and despair: Love Canal and Times Beach, poisoned by chemical wastes;

Youngstown, Johnstown, Peoria, and Lorain, marooned by closed industries. Unemployment remains a frequent theme of community news stories partly because it is an actual problem, and also because, since employment is the primary index of membership in the larger society, it is a perfect theme for the documentary minidramas of the state of society that comprise the news. Thus, television's documentation of the stagnation and victimization of communities reflects reality, but it is more than objective reality reporting itself. These stories are fables of Americans' idea of personal catastrophe, which is not, as is often said, to be alone, but to be bound to a common fate with our neighbors, hence to be without options, without avenues to a larger world. Such stories seize our attention because, as Tony Schwartz argues, television works not by information but by resonance, by the fact that its images evoke in us what we already believe (Schwartz, 1982: 11–24). Community, in these news stories, exacts a cost of helpless dependence, an isolation from the sources of life in the economic drive of the larger society, and such places, we seem to believe, are asylums of the unfit. In a *New York Times* essay on dying farm towns, for example, the writer explains that "the ambitious kids, the ones needed most by [small towns], leave, while those on the other end of the scale stay around but contribute little" (Barada, 1983). In this statement the diagnosis of dying communities becomes a reaffirmation of the individualism and mobility of the larger society. Its writer's "scale" of social worth is that of ability to achieve membership in a community not of place but of profession, which has as its place the nation.

This is the understanding Americans have inherited and which we pragmatically reconfirm. We choose to live in the city, to live our lives as urban lives, with urban attitudes toward association with others, whether we live in Chicago or Oberlin. The urban nation we join is not a social but an economic nation, the Geselleschaft to which our functionality is relevant as traditional community ties are not. The problem of a social nation, of a common weal, however, remains.

TELEVISION AS A MEDIUM OF COMMUNITY

Television's increasing concern with the theme of community since *Mary Tyler Moore* parallels an expansion of this concern among Americans in the same period. Daniel Yankelovich, in *New Rules,* his survey of American attitudes in the 1980s, reports that "ten years ago roughly one-third of Americans felt an intense need to compen-

sate for the impersonal and threatening aspects of modern life by
seeking mutual identification with others based on close ethnic ties
or ties of shared interest, needs, background, age, or values." In the
decade since, he explains, the proportion "deeply involved in the
Search for Community has increased to 47 per cent" (Yankelovich,
1982: 248).

This search for community suggests both the appeal and the imaginative sources of programs such as *MASH* or *Cheers*. In such series
the depiction is realistic in some respects, while its overall strategy
is to mask the problem of community, to "solve" it by evading its
terms. The world of work, the basis of the community in most of
these shows, is represented by metonymies—characters with professional identification and dress, settings with the furniture and para-
phernalia of a line of work, factual details of professional knowledge—
that allow us to understand the representation as thematically faithful
to the real world we live in. The work situation is the dramatic
envelope of the characters; within it they find professional effectiveness and human engagement. They are in direct association, forming
an oral group, and what they share is the immediate and personal
rather than the remote and public; their interaction as workplace
associates is thus displayed as communal identification. The fullness
with which they engage each other's personalities and the casualness
of their access to each other suppresses the material basis of their
association, which is that of function. It is a depictive strategy of
showing Gesellschaft situations to fulfill the ideal of the Gemeinschaft. The depiction thus dramatistically closes out the political significance of the concern with community found by Yankelovich's
surveys. The motive in this depictive strategy, though, is less nefar-
iously political than artistic: drama requires characters related to each
other, forming some kind of community that enables their dramatic
engagement, beyond simple interaction, with each other.

The difficulty this requirement presents to television dramatists is
pointed to by a reflection of Stanley Cavell on the implications of
television's existence. Cavell notes "the fear or repulsion or anxiety
that I have found television to inspire in what I [call] educated circles."
This fear, Cavell explains, grows from the fact that television serves
essentially to monitor, and "what it monitors is the growing unin-
habitability of the world." What we thus perceive in television is "the
loss of our humanity" (Cavell, 1982: 90). The "growing uninhabita-
bility of the world" evokes most immediately the network news images of crime, pollution, and urban decay. But Cavell is referring to

our more extended perception, of the social character of our world, as offering no way to engage humanly with others.

Television series solve the contradiction between reality and the requirements of drama by converting the functional relations of the workplace, a conveniently credible group setting, into communal belonging. The requirements of drama take precedence in this equation not simply because the audience demands drama in exchange for attention; we demand drama because we make sense of our world as drama. Our need to imagine America as a community is a need to imagine it dramatically, a need to make sense of it. The fulfillment of this need may take our imagination some length, to viewing workplaces and professions as communities, or to understanding television's ubiquitousness as the demonstration of a national American community.

REFERENCES

Barada, Paul W. (1982) "It's called Rushville, but times are slow." New York Times (April 10): EY23.
Cavell, Stanley (1982) "The fact of television." Daedalus 111 (Fall): 75–96.
Cooley, Charles Horton (1962) Social Organization. New York: Schocken.
de Tocqueville, Alexis (1945) Democracy in America (The Henry Reeve Text as revised by Francis Bowen; Phillips Bradley, ed., Vol. II). New York: Vintage.
Dewey, John (1966) Democracy and Education. New York: Free Press.
Goodman, Ellen (1983) "A community breaks up." Washington Post (March 5): A23.
Park, Robert E. and Ernest W. Burgess (1969) Introduction to the Science of Sociology. Chicago: University of Chicago Press.
———(1940) "News as a form of knowledge." American Journal of Sociology 45 (March): 669–686.
Schwartz, Tony (1983) Media: The Second God. Garden City, NY: Doubleday.
Tönnies, Ferdinand (1963) Community and Society (C. P. Loomis, trans. and ed.). New York: Harper & Row.
Vaughan, Samuel (1983) "The community of the book." Daedalus 112 (Winter): 85–115.
Yankelovich, Daniel (1982) New Rules. New York: Bantam.

Chapter 11

TELEVISION AND MORAL ORDER
IN A SECULAR AGE

Victor Lidz

THE DENUNCIATIONS of television as an artistic wasteland leave the social scientist with a puzzle: How has television grown to such prominence in American cultural life? If television shows are so lacking in aesthetic worth, how have they captured so large a place in the life of the American imagination? The intent of this essay is to outline a partial solution to the puzzle. The solution is not an answer to the aesthetic attacks on television, for it presupposes them to be in key respects valid. But it does seek to understand how and why a vast American audience finds meaning in television shows despite their artistic shortcomings. My argument will be that television shows participate deeply in American *moral* culture. They are saturated with moral themes of individualism, strength of character, energetic activism, and commitment to freedom. However, in a manner that has descended from Puritan times, our popular moral culture tends to be inhospitable to frankly aesthetic cultural forms. The artistic possibilities of television are often overwhelmed by a deeply fixed emphasis on moral beliefs.

SECULAR MORALITY

Television has arisen in an age of secularized moral culture. In speaking of secularization, we need not presume that religious life is certainly and finally waning in our time or that, if yet active, it must

AUTHOR'S NOTE: An earlier incarnation of this chapter was presented at a conference, "Toward a Public Philosophy of Communication," convened by Trinity Institute of New York. I am indebted to Durstan McDonald and William Fore for an invitation to that conference, and to Dunbar Moodie, James Carey, and Gregor Goethals for insightful comments on and criticisms of my talk there. Barry Schwartz and Harold Bershady have also given me helpful critiques of the earlier paper.

be inauthentic, without spirit, or radically maladapted to the broader society (Parsons, 1979). The secularity of modern civilization is simply this: there has grown up since the Enlightenment a framework of secular moral culture that is independent of religion (functionally differentiated, in the lingo of sociologists) and that serves as the primary body of beliefs legitimating social institutions (Lidz, 1979). The same body of beliefs also provides ethical restraint over individuals who act with moral authority under the cover of the legitimate social order. The secular moral order encompasses our beliefs about the foundations of constitutional and legal order, economic ethics and practices, civil freedoms and duties, educational ideals, personal, familial, and community morals, and so forth. On these many matters, Americans share both agreements and certain patterns of disagreement, such as that between political liberals and conservatives, that are structured independently of religious commitments. Most issues of public deliberation, whether controversial or not, are broached primarily within the frameworks of secular moral belief. These frameworks were constructed largely at the founding of the republic and have evolved as common understandings about how public deliberations should be conducted ever since. If public discussion is to result in legitimate convictions about a need for change in policies or institutions, the secular moral order provides the necessary terms of conscientious judgment.

The secular order is a differentiated and specialized sphere of the moral life. It is therefore not fully self-sufficient, but related in various ways to religious institutions and spiritual life. The major concern of the secular moral order is with the world of practical affairs and with the legitimation of our principal social institutions. It appeals to the individual in terms of conscientious duty and the reciprocation of duty. To religious life it leaves the underpinnings of duty in the realm of faith. It leaves to religion questions of ultimate principles and identities, the sustenance of the spirit, and the resolution of existential dilemmas (Bellah, 1968). The secular order maintains a variety of civil rituals, but few that answer to the needs of the person or provide celebration of the life-course. Its ethics do not concentrate on dilemmas and problems of the individual life-world. Nor do they answer directly to the "problems of meaning" (Weber, 1963) generated by illness, poverty, failure, disappointment, loneliness, and sin, except insofar as they foster practical hopes or assign duties for meliorating undesirable conditions. In these respects, secular beliefs do not preclude a religious life—social action addressed to the sacred rather than the profane world—and perhaps they even leave individuals dependent upon it.

Television, however, has been aligned mainly with the claims of the secular order. The network audience during prime time is addressed in terms provided almost entirely by the secular culture. The God who is occasionally invoked is the curiously abstract figure conceived as a foundation of the "entire Judeo-Christian tradition" in the now conventional phrase. He is called upon through a precise etiquette only to frame a statement of moral commitment and underscore the good faith with which it is intended. The overt action of primetime, network television is enclosed within worldly concerns that focus on job, family, health, safety, neighborhood, law-and-order, skill, achievements, material well-being, success, fellowship, and loyalty to nation and way-of-life. Whether a drama is placed out in space and in the future, in the frontier of the Old West, in the dangerous streets of today's cities, in the offices of doctors, lawyers, private investigators, or journalists, or in one or another type of comic family situation, the overt concerns of the action remain secular and mundane. Life is depicted as largely enclosed within the realities of the secular order, as even comprehensible only within its prosaic terms.

And yet there is also a deeper, somewhat more covert aspect to the action of television. There is a mystification of character and motive, a dwelling on unseen ways in which mundane persons come to serve high callings, worldly conduct assumes qualities of a larger mission, or individual sacrifice becomes heroic devotion to duty—in short, in which activities in the everyday world figure the workings of a transcendental reality. On this plane of implied deeper meaning, television drama reflects the dependence of the secular order on certain modes of religious belief and symbolism. To understand penetratingly the events and characters of American television dramas, we must apprehend them against a background of long-established, essentially Puritan traditions of order, calling, duty, and motive. The secular order, prominent as it stands in the American view of values, concerns, and energizing interests in the make-up of civil society, is also a screen on which a characterology deriving from the Puritan sense of self and conscience is still projected (see Bercovitch, 1975).

The use of television to convey ritual and ceremony to the nation at large, one of its most vivid uses, confirms its strong relation to the secular morality. Most of the ceremonial occasions that have engrossed and sentimentally united large audiences have turned on secular events, for example, State of the Union Addresses, Presidential Inaugurals, the return of prisoners of war from North Vietnam, the landing on the moon and other space "missions." Certain recurrent secular celebrations are ritualized on television in palpable connection to themes central to American moral culture, for example, the Super Bowl and World Series, the Academy Award Presentations, even the Miss America contests. A number of complicated political events have been realized largely through television and its special capacity to dramatize their portents for the American destiny before the public as a whole, for example, the Army-McCarthy Hearings, events in the Vietnam War, especially the denouement of the Tet Offensive, the Watergate Hearings of the Senate Judiciary Committee, and the impeachment proceedings of the House Judiciary Committee. Television presentations such as these are concerned with secular events and framed in terms of secular beliefs, but are subtly saturated with themes of mission, portent, destiny, and fulfillment that are religious in origin. They show the American secular morality, despite its functional autonomy as a belief system, to be vitally connected to traditions of civil religion (Bellah, 1970). The continuing importance of religious thematics and attitudes within the context of American secular morality was especially apparent during the weekend of national mourning for President Kennedy, surely the most memorable of all televised rituals (Parsons and Lidz, 1967).

Were it to project its qualities of vivid presence centrally into the affairs of denominational religions, television would potentially be caught up with forces of social division. The growth of television as a civil institution has thus precluded denominational religion from a prominent role. Television, like radio, follows a model developed in the public print media, newspapers in particular, during the nineteenth century. Although many newspapers and journals directed to special religious readerships prosper, the central media of mass circulation address the public at large without denominational concern. Similarly, religious shows appear on cable television and on television stations unaffiliated with a major network, but infrequently address a large part of the primetime audience.

EPISODE AND CHARACTER

In arguing that television has become enmeshed in the relations between the secular moral order and values descended from Puritanism, I do not suggest that American ethical life has made an entirely comfortable accommodation with it. The controversies over the consequences of television for the American character signal that there is yet little comfort on this terrain. Down through World War II, the American intellect and imagination remained firmly within the reflective, analytic, inward-turning culture of intensive reading (Booth, 1982). Against this culture, the television experience has been a discomfitting change. The great volume of criticism from intellectuals, with their loyalties to print forms, indicates that the television experience threatens their habits of mind and imagination. It is threatening not only in its immediate qualities, but more basically as a challenge to reflection, character, and conscience. A story on television, unlike a novel, consists in radiant images and sounds, not more or less distantiated descriptions of or commentaries about them, and hence realizes its artistry more directly and fully through sensuous appeals. It is intrinsically disarming of the conscience and seductive. As television and its techniques have matured, and as color television has become the common type, the sensuous appeal has been accentuated more and more prominently (Goethals, 1981). The vivid presentations of television thus stand to the Puritan-derived lilterary tradition in much the same relation that the elaborate Catholic ritualism stood to early Calvinist asceticism of worship.

Moreover, television makes itself appear to the viewer in a constantly renewed present. A television story line unfolds in a sequence of events that must be apprehended, at least for initial interpretation, in their immediate connection with the viewer. One cannot halt the unfolding of the drama in order to move back and forth freely and questioningly in the construction of the plot so that its implications can be grasped on a basis of controlled, critical reflection. In this respect, television shows, like movies, but with deeper penetration into the routines of life, and unlike still photographs or paintings, do challenge the ascetic Protestant idealization of conscientious control over the conditions of experience. Thus, the American heritage is tied to an ambivalent attitude toward television: as technology, television serves the ideal of developing more effective resources because

it vastly extends communication; as sensuous medium, television sub-
verts a heritage of highly controlled relation to cultural life.

The traditional formatting of television shows responds to the sus-
picions that Americans may hold for a medium with sensuous appeal.
Shows are designed and plotted in ways that enable them to become
familiar cultural objects to national audiences. Typical shows of entertainment, whether household or family comedies, comedies of the
workplace, crime or crime-detection dramas, medical or courtroom
dramas, space fantasies, historical dramatizations, or Westerns, follow the episodic structure developed for early radio. The episodic
structure elaborates on a form used more crudely in heroic folktales,
for example, stories of Paul Bunyan or John Henry, and in the newspaper or comic book cartoons. In the ideal-typical case, the episodes
of a show, commonly presented weekly, are independent and complete stories in themselves. A series of episodes differs from a serial
story in that there is no direct carry-over of plot from one episode
to the next. The viewer can watch an episode and expect fairly full
understanding and expressional satisfaction despite being unfamiliar
with previous episodes. Yet, a deeper kind of carry-over from episode
to episode is intended to draw the viewer into an involvement with
an entire series as it continues from week to week. It is a carry-over
that explores an interesting character or set of characters on the one
hand, and an interesting human situation, ordinarily treated through
heavily symbolic typifications, on the other hand.

As we watch the series *Quincy* from episode to episode, we are
led to examine the character of Quincy and the workings of a met-
ropolitan coroner's office. The numerous episodes show us how a
personality with the virtues and shortcomings of Quincy will respond
to a variety of challenges. Over and over we are shown his exceptional
skill as physician and forensic investigator, his devotion to professional principles, his integrity where difficult moral judgments must
be made, and his concern to expose corruption, fraud, and foul play
on the part of others, especially people of wealth, power, and social
advantage. We also see that he has a strong temper, may be abrasive
when he disagrees with others, resents the authority of his bureaucratic superiors, and judges others hastily. At the same time, the
setting of a large medical examiner's office is also explored, usually
in highly idealized and simplified terms. We are shown its interesting
responsibilities to the law and courts, to the medical profession, and

to public health. Emphasis is placed on the theme that postmortem examinations can be beneficial to living people. Entanglements in politics and bureaucratic muddles are portrayed as chronic sources of difficulties for medical examiners who do their work with integrity. The viewer who sees a number of episodes of *Quincy* may be drawn symbolically into an intense relationship with the character of Quincy and the typical, indeed, repetitive, sorts of situated dilemmas he encounters. The expressional interest in watching additional episodes is to follow new exploits of a vivid character and see additional features of an intriguing setting. These matters have been carefully typified to encourage us to develop expectations about the kind of experience we may have if we view another episode of *Quincy*. There will always be suspense and surprise plotted into *Quincy* episodes, but within parameters that enable us to have an advance familiarity with the goings-on. While the formats of better television shows present greater varieties of experience and address more subtle qualities of human existence, they are similarly formulaic and calculable from episode to episode. Our typifications about the kinds of events that will be dramatized in any particular episode give us an attitudinal defense against the seductively sensuous qualities of television stories.

Traditional episodic shows are also plotted to keep certain dramatic features from carrying over from one episode to others. Kojak can be presented as a tough, street-wise cop who has been involved in many nasty situations. Somehow, though, the viewer is not brought to characterize him as a pathological killer even when he is seen shooting suspects in nearly every episode. Nor should the viewer experience Kojak's shooting of still another suspect as the foregone conclusion of a new episode and hence devoid of suspense. Some years ago Karl Malden sustained the character of a mild-mannered detective, dutifully reluctant to use his weapon, even though he was portrayed weekly as "having" to shoot malefactors. Television physicians encounter unusual diseases or complications, patients with improbable personal problems, and colleagues who violate basic medical ethics with a frequency that would be quite unbelievable in any actual career. Thus, the element of having a fresh start for the plot of each episode, though framed by continuing involvements with characters and situation, is a liberating convention for the story writers.

How pervasively television relies on episodic structure is suggested by the tendency to make even news and public information broadcasts conform to it (Gans, 1979; Schudson, 1982). Particular news shows tend on any day in which there have not been truly exceptional events—a disaster, a shift in a national policy, a sports championship—to present a similar mix of national, international, and regional or local stories. There tends also to be a standard mix of politics, economic conditions, matters of mass culture, advances in science or technology, and a "character" with a distinctive skill, service, or personal quality. There is generally a standard format for accentuating lead stories, grouping stories by topic, and interspersing news expected to hold the interest of viewers with advertisements. The episodic formulae differ for national news broadcasts and local news broadcasts, often leading to striking transpositions of materials between, for example, early evening and late evening news shows. Thus, news is reported in episodic molds in which the day's events are treated as variant exemplars of standard categories of what is newsworthy and how it should be regarded.

Episodic formulae make the viewing experience calculable in some specific respects and thereby help to stabilize it for the audience. The stability is conveyed through constancy in what a given show portrays, but obviously in relation to interesting variation. The episodic structure enables each episode to confirm certain principles about the character and situation being dramatized. Across sequences of episodes, which become very numerous over the years for an *I Love Lucy*, a *Gunsmoke*, a *Marcus Welby, M.D.*, or a *MASH* (or even the *CBS Evening News*), the implications of constant principles may be explored over wide ranges of materials. If Marcus Welby is presented as personifying the competent, compassionate, and supportive, yet stoic and activistically therapeutic physician, over many expisodes we can watch him confront intractable as well as quickly cured illness, patients who are recalcitrant as well as ones who dutifully adhere to their regimens, ones whose disabilities are stigmatizing in Welby's conventional culture, diseases that involve Welby's family or himself (as when he suffered a heart attack and needed to reduce his pace of work), and so forth. Such variation among episodes plays a large part in drawing viewers into close sentimental engagement with the principles of character dramatized in the show. It enables a show to realize the viewer's sense of identification in relation to central characters more fully, for it involves the viewer in a range of moral dilemmas that must be resolved with integrity if strength of character is to be portrayed authentically. It engages the viewer in a cumulating sense of the life-experience implied by the dramatized principles of character. In deciding to watch another episode of a familiar show, the prospective viewer affirms a certain kind of figurative but emotional identification with the life-experience to be portrayed. The identification has both retrospective and anticipatory qualities. It rests on involvement with the principles of action established in past episodes, but carries forward to an expectation that another interesting dilemma will be encountered in the next dramatization of a continuous life-experience.

More recent serial variations on episodic forms (e.g., *Dallas, Hill Street Blues, St. Elsewhere*) have broken the taboos on plot carryover—indeed they celebrate the old magazine, Saturday morning movie, and radio and television soap opera conventions of continuing serial action. But for present purposes sustained identification with the characters and situations of traditional episodic shows remains a form of sentiment on which large and constant audiences can be built. It is a commercial reality on which an industry has been gaining great wealth, but also a form in cultural life that has become a meaningful part of social routines over the last generation. Most American individuals and families now maintain notions of character and situation drawn from their experiences of many popular television shows as key typifications in their social lives and personal imaginations.

MIDDLE-CLASS MORALITY

However new its elaboration of episodic structure as a form of culture or its rise to control over a large part of American sentimental life, television dramatizes moral themes that are old and well established. Two sets of themes appear to be especially strongly emphasized, which I will call the Puritan and the democratic. Together they comprise what I speak of as the "middle-class morality": our conventional, mundane, eminently practical, sternly disciplined, yet sentimentally expansive moral sensibility.

The middle-class morality can already be recognized in de Tocqueville's account of the pragmatic mediocrity of American social standards in the 1830s (de Tocqueville, 1948). As de Tocqueville understood, it is intimately connected with the relative absence of fixed—ascriptive—grounds of association in American society. Indeed, many kinds of association in the world of practical affairs are commonly established on quite impersonal grounds. Individuals and groups often must decide whether or not to trust one another and establish ties of common association even though they cannot assess each other through relations of mutual familiarity. Americans frequently have to calculate the degrees to which they can depend on others whose origins, background, and character they cannot know reliably and in circumstantial detail. Reciprocally, they often face the task of having to show themselves to be trustworthy in settings where others cannot know their qualities of character. Not only are situations requiring impersonal judgments of character and reliability a practical reality with which Americans have to cope without leaving their interests open to exploitation, but they are also valued and idealized. They are commonly viewed as fair arrangements that extend opportunities to all who wish to improve their status in society. The middle-class morality, then, affirms the ideology of universalistic opportunity while providing standards for the subtle interplay by which citizens warrant their own characters while assessing the characters of others. Specific standards of characterological assessment vary considerably from situation to situation. They are different in the academic world as compared with the industrial world, in the financial world as compared with the world of marketing and advertising, in the snobbish world of country clubs as compared with the world of community service associations, and so forth. Yet, the middle-class morality also has a unity of common emphasis on honesty, hard work, development of skill, self-improvement, performance of duty, and the trustworthiness of promises.

Given the importance that American society attaches to judgments of character based on the middle-class morality, it should not surprise us that television exhibits a veritable cult of character. Heavy emphasis falls on depicting the practical benefits, for the individual and for society, to be derived from principled character. The viewer is drawn sentimentally into relations of respect for characters who maintain authentic integrity in situations that tempt and test them severely. Dramatic emphasis may also be placed on matters of inherent abilities, skills, training, or knowledge, but usually in ways that give priority to the moral commitment to develop and use one's personal talents methodically. Exceptional ability can thus be portrayed as in essence a manifestation of strong character. A tendency to heroize admirable abilities as signs of disciplined character is probably the most persistent moral "argument" of American television. It pervades the broadcasts of sports events of all kinds, but especially of the sports most engrained in American culture—baseball, football, and basketball. It is highlighted on shows that portray the socialization and education of youth, for example, *Fame,* with its elaborations on themes of personal promise for the future. Shows focusing on physicians, especially surgeons, and on scientists dwell on the long, disciplined hours of education and training and on virtuosities of knowledge and skill that must be displayed. Even shows with more humble settings, detective shows, westerns, even shows depicting office work, underscore uses of exceptional abilities. Given the widespread conviction that the "work ethic" is no longer respected in America, it is noteworthy that popular television stresses that ethic so relentlessly to an audience so large.

The dramatization of character on television also emphasizes the importance of association with others and capacity for teamwork. Character is made evident through reliability and trustworthiness and through dependable devotion to collective ends. The praiseworthy athlete is not only skilled but reliable in doing his or her part on a team, will be cooperative and selfless in devotion to teamwork, and will make the sacrifice of playing with pain. Telecasts of football games are tireless in reiterating these moral points and in self-consciously emphasizing their relevance to other spheres of life. But the same lessons are dramatized in the surgery of *MASH,* the detective work of *Hill Street Blues,* or the stages and studios of *Fame.* More deeply, the involvement of individuals in cooperative teamwork tends to be portrayed as having larger purposes. Cooperation in the laboratory follows from a devotion to science. Physicians are depicted as ideal paradigms of cooperation because lives depend on their teamwork. Television shows that portray conflicts on hospital staffs quickly become dramas of life-and-death; and documentaries on doctors and hospitals take care to show the absence of conflict or deny its importance. Patriotism and civic spirit are depicted as the grounds of teamwork in shows about spies, diplomats, the military, or political leaders.

American dramas rarely portray groups, teams, or associations as indissoluble wholes—as, for example, they are shown in Japanese films such as *The Magnificent Seven* or *High and Low.* American television dwells on the prominent characters who make up a group and assume responsibilities for spheres of the collective action. Sports teams are televised with concentration on their stars and on the ways in which the stars do or do not accept the discipline of teamwork. The surgery of *MASH* is similarly a cooperative field for the action of vivid figures, as are the courtrooms of *Perry Mason*, the laboratory of *Quincy*, the New York streets as shown in *Kojak*, and the newspaper cityroom of *Lou Grant*. For American television, collective action provides occasions for examining the conscientious conduct of autonomous individuals as they commit themselves to shared purposes and procedures. If members of a group are not suitable for dramatization as vivid and usually heroic individuals, television is unlikely to take an interest.

The tenuous portrayal of the reality of groups has a complement in television's emphasis on self-reliance. The westerns and private-eye shows, which so often culminate in life-and-death confrontations between a single hero and a villain or group of villains, are the genres most consistent in depicting individuals as ultimately alone and de-pendent on their own resources. Many kinds of adventure story typ-ically arrive at denouements that turn on tests of individuals who must confront their difficulties by themselves, however. Spy stories tend to heighten the issue of self-reliance by placing the hero quite alone or with support of doubtful reliability in a setting dominated by enemies. Dramas placed in everday situations may also rest on the theme of self-reliance. When emphasis falls on the qualities of character needed to develop successful careers, times and situations that test a central figure are likely to be shown in ways that highlight the value of self-reliance. The time of test may follow the death of a mentor, a divorce, or betrayal by a colleague. Figures in positions of high authority or on whom many others may depend for their well-being are especially likely to be portrayed as essentially alone when difficult responsibilities must be discharged. Historical and docu-mentary television is emphatic in depicting presidents and generals in this fashion, as are political advertisements.

The Puritan sources of television portrayals of character become more evident when we look into the nature of the obligation on individuals to live up to high standards or withstand demanding trials. Television often highlights a duty to perfect oneself as an instrument of higher principles or purposes. Given the secular temper of our times, entertainments addressed to the public at large rarely highlight divine inspirations or ordainments of valued conduct, although they do portray religious people. The final source of moral obligation is usually left implicit, rather mysterioiusly taken for granted. Yet, the principles of our secular moral order may be treated as ineffably transcendent, genuine grounds of action that establish categorical rather than contingent imperatives. Secular principles that are transcendental in this fashion may take on certain religious colorations. Thus, American television shows are preoccupied with secular "missions," as are news reports. The American way of life as a whole, with its devotion to freedom of the conscience and political liberty, is regarded as a grand mission (Bellah, 1970). Stories about the protection of that way of life, especially from Nazi or Communist armies or agents, become saturated with senses of mission. Advancing the qualities of American civilization in sciences or the arts, perfecting the principles of popular democracy, or contributing to the material welfare of the citizenry may be protrayed as forms of mission. Matters as worldly as conspicuous success in business or even athletics are commonly interpreted on television shows as favorable outcomes of missions. Thus, the human condition as dramatized on television is shown to be filled with higher principles, missions, and ordainments in a fashion that remains Puritan-like. However secularized contemporary American world-views, life would seem flat, purposeless, lacking in fascination and marvel were its portrayals empty of implications of mission. In this respect, the tradition of Puritanism has passed through the process of secularization without succumbing to the utter disenchantment of the world that Max Weber feared (Weber, 1963).

The Puritan tradition has also contributed to television's culture of character a tendency to treat the individualistic presuppositions of its moralism as ontological. In almost any setting of action, television selects out the involvements of focal individuals as the ultimate matters of concern. The dramatic fascination with missions comes to dwell on the dilemmas of conscience that individuals must confront in order to fulfill higher duties. The outcomes of stories are presented as reportage on the fates of the individuals whose efforts at conscientious conduct have been dramatized. The drama of episodic shows is dominated by particularly vivid individuals who are elevated above the others with whom they interact. As the episodic formats have evolved over the past few decades, the drama has focused ever more completely around vividly highlighted persons—Marshal Dillon, Elliot Ness, Marcus Welby, Hawkeye Pierce, Archie Bunker, Kojak, Lou Grant, and so forth. As Puritan conduct reduced culturally to dilemmas of the conscience, so the action dramatized on television reduces to stories of vivid characters.

The democratic element in the middle-class morality shows up on television in the variety of situations that are dramatized and in their modes of symbolic connection to American society. The settings of television shows often reflect ordinary features of American life, although they may do so through idealized typifications. The customs and routines of television characters may be presented as depicting common practices in American communities. Shows that focus on occupational roles often dramatize work that has a firm status in practically every locality. Thus, television often dramatizes situations that will be familiar to us in outlines, at least. We see homes, schools, hospitals, fire stations, town halls, shops, offices, and so forth that are like ones in our own communities, even if they appear newer, better equipped, and better cared for. We see teachers, firemen, policemen, doctors, politicians, lawyers, shopowners, and bureaucrats who seem to be typified after and intended as comments upon people we commonly encounter.

Sometimes we are shown figures who are "representative" in another sense, not as typical but as approximating what is the "best" in America—dutiful, able youth, tenaciously honest public servants, teachers devoted to the futures of their students, surgeons who are bold, yet calm, and virtuosos of the scalpel. Figures who represent excellence are connected to a popular audience by the values that their exemplary performances may reinforce. Viewers who appreciate their special qualities have been moved to respect their principles of conduct. Where the action of television occurs in exotic settings that cannot be portrayed as representative, it is often dramatized from a standpoint that is very ordinarily American. Dramas of World War II, even when they relate exceptionally harrowing and heroic experience, tend to be peopled with a set of "types" that together represent America—the Texas cowboy, the Brooklyn Jew, the WASP New Englander with Ivy League education, the Iowa corn farmer, and so forth. A story of the German concentration camps is likely to be related by a subsequent immigrant who gives it a location in American experience. The crew of a space rocket set centuries in the future, as on *Star Trek* or *Battlestar Galactica,* will on television consist of several recognizably American types whose reactions to their experiences confirm our conventional judgment.

Beyond these basic ways of democratizing their moral import, television shows use some special devices for broadening their sentimental appeals to a mass audience. One common device is the designed use of a humble setting. It is employed most consistently in comedy shows, where much of the humor turns on a familiar relation between the dramatis personae and viewers. It has been used in many episodic shows situated in families, from *Ozzie and Harriet* to *All in the Family* or *The Jeffersons*. It has also been used on many comedies located in ordinary workplaces, from *Duffy's Tavern* to *Barney Miller* or *Alice*.

A notable example, *The Honeymooners,* dates back as long as 25 years, but continues to be popular in many parts of the country through reruns. Its focal character, played in the vaudeville tradition of exaggerated gestures by Jackie Gleason, was a bus driver frustratingly trapped in a life of poverty despite harboring fantasies of wealth and success. Most of the action was set in Ralph Kramden's sparsely and poorly furnished, cramped and seedy New York apartment. The show's set for the apartment was designed in the naturalistic tradition to convey the emptiness of poverty more graphically than, to my knowledge, it has otherwise ever been portrayed on television. Typically, the action involved the bus driver's relations with his loyal, though outspoken, wife Alice—the couple had no children—and his closest friend Ed Norton, a sewer worker, and Norton's wife. Many episodes turned on the appeals of a get-rich-quick opportunity or scheme, not always an honest one, which would stimulate the hopes of Ralph and his friend despite the misgivings of common sense voiced by their wives. After the men invested effort and savings as well as hopes, the scheme would turn sour and leave them more hopelessly trapped in poverty and dependent on their tiresome jobs. While loud recriminations usually ensued, the resolutions of the stories generally involved the husbands and wives reaffirming mutual love and the two men renewing their friendship.

The Honeymooner episodes and especially their endings were as lavishly sentimental as the setting of action was materially austere. The sentiment projected to the audience a moral that poverty and ill-rewarded, unappreciated work were difficult to endure in America, the land of successes, but also that, with love, they could be endured and were best endured through responsible involvement in one's calling and family life. The moral was thoroughly in line with respectable middle-class convention. Yet, it was given a setting so humble and stories so melodramatic that the sentimental appeal could hardly "pass over" any class within the active television audience. The bus driver's and sewer worker's circumstances may have been depicted as so poor and their conduct as so childish to assure that members of the working class, while identifying with the characters, could also feel themselves, by comparison, superior in conscience and more successful in material condition.

Another form of appeal to democratic sentiment involves dramatizing matters of current moral concern. In recent years, many shows have presented episodes that moralize on problems of drug use among youth. Kojak, the officers of *Hill Street Blues,* Lou Grant and his colleagues, Quincy, Dr. Welby, the teachers and kids of *Fame,* and many other television worthies have tried to assist with the much publicized "drug crisis." Devoting episodes to what are regarded as real problems in American society—whether the drug crisis (see Lidz and Walker, 1980), the crime on the streets crisis, the mental health crisis, the "warehousing" of the elderly crisis, the child abuse crisis, the police corruption crisis, the mediocre schools crisis, or the shoddy work on the assembly line crisis—is presented as marking the show's authenticity. Such episodes give viewers the assurance that the characters of the show, police, journalists, doctors, or whatever, are engaged with American society in all of its actuality and with all of its serious problems. Although episodes dealing with "touchy" problems, mental illness, rape, or child-molestation, tend to be self-conscious about being venturesome, they are typically cautious in conveying only the moral conclusions currently being voiced by authoritative experts (or people deemed to be such). Television can be profuse with sympathy for individuals and families caught up in serious problems, such as drug use, but it tends to be firm in prescribing the kinds of conduct deemed "right" as solutions. Often the problems are portrayed as having their sources in underlying difficulties in family life and as having remedies in action that can be taken by ordinary citizens. In the context of an "entertaining" show, then, a problem may be depicted as typically existing within the neighborhoods of viewers and its solution as resting largely on viewers' having the consciences to act. The democratic element in this moralistic stance lies in the universalism of the conscientious appeal addressed to the audience as a whole.

A third means of democratizing a moral appeal is to dramatize kinds of action with which members of the audience can be presumed to identify. Some of the identities taken as a basis of dramatic involvement are fairly concrete and familiar. Patriotic sentiments are involved in the depictions of GIs fighting in World War II that continue to be popular. Given the controversies over the Vietnam War, television producers have needed a number of years to devise dramatizations of it that do not offend viewers by their treatments of patriotic sentiments. Presentations of most scientific or medical work can also presume widespread identification with their underlying missions, usually treated as betterment of the human condition in a material fashion. Yet, there is also a genre, presented at times on television though more popular in movies, of Frankenstein-like science fiction depicting mad or evil scientists plotting harm against humankind. It tells us that there is enough ambivalence that large audiences can identify negatively toward science. Human missions are also projected into fantasies of a future where conflicts between good and evil, often between the American way and a Communist-like threat to it, can be depicted as cosmic and cataclysmic.

Many shows have been set in an expressional midground between the domains of the familiar and the domains of fantasy. Most spy stories, especially ones about Free World-Communist World conflicts, take place in a frame constructed out of special literary, movie, and television genres that mix references to real characters, events, and locations with quite fantastic matters and eschatology. Stories set in the Old West, whether emphasizing conflicts beween settlers and Indians, homesteaders and ranchers, hard working townspeople and bands of outlaws, or sheriffs and gunslingers, also take on a semblance of actuality largely from long-evolving popular genres. Shows of these types, for example, the durable *Gunsmoke,* also act on viewers' identifications with valued endeavors of the past—civilizing new territory, making the land productive, ridding towns of vice, upholding law and order. Popular in their sentimental frames, they reinforce old moral understandings about the legitimation of venturesome and risky conduct. By dramatizing that moral principles are worth the devotion of a life's work or the risk or even sacrifice of a life, they support conventional American beliefs. The moralization flows less from the daring adventures, the challenges few of us will ever experience, than from the ordinary ideals to which we presume one another to be committed and which are shown to be served by true heroism. Heroic or fantastic missions are thereby related in sentiment to the routine lives of viewers.

Through the Puritan focus on character and the democratic embrace of the commonplaces of American life, the middle-class morality is projected over television to a vast audience that it exhorts and integrates. To be sure, network television has been set up primarily to entertain. However, given the ethical traditions of America, not least its venerable distrust of the expressionally immediate and sensuous, entertainments must be thoroughly moralized if they are to be culturally acceptable. Moreover, they must be popularly moralized. Television is thus the heir of Puritan sermonizing, of the revival mentality, of popular self-improvement literature, of mass readership newspapers, of the radio shows that devised the weekly episode, and of the Hollywood film industry with which it is now so closely joined.

THE EXAMPLE OF *MASH*

The extraordinary success of *MASH* as a television show highlights some rather interesting ways in which the middle-class morality shapes an episodic series and its reception by a mass audience. An exceptionally well-sustained commercial success, *MASH* has also become a celebrated part of contemporary American popular culture. Its characters (and the actors portraying them) are widely known and talked about. Critics of television and popular culture have been nearly unanimous in their enthusiasm for the show. Self-consciously bizarre in its humor, although more restrained than the novel and movie it followed, it has not lacked courage to delve into matters involving intense moral sentiments for an American audience.

The setting for *MASH* seems at first an improbable scene for comedy and too removed from present-day concerns to be made popular. *MASH* is set in a small military surgical hospital, a hospital of tents, just behind the front lines of the Korean War. Its main characters are two young surgeons whose presenting qualities are dislike for the war and alienation from military discipline. They are in many respects dramatized as modern anti-heroes, being comic in dress, personal manners, and characteristic motives. However, these qualities are given more serious texture by their imaginative efforts to dissociate themselves from the war and army in which they are caught up. The plots of most episodes turn on events that transform the comic anti-heroes into true heroes displaying exceptional integrity and fortitude under duress. They show uncommon skill as surgeons, ideal physicianly compassion for the wounded, fellow-feeling for a member of the hospital staff in personal difficulty or, beneath their anger toward the military, a finer patriotism. Their attitudes toward war and the military are never undermined (even if stated more moderately in the late episodes), but are connected to personal virtues widely admired in American culture: willingness to work hard, creatively, and selflessly; devotion to duty, comrades, and nation; technical skill, personal integrity, and compassion.

Portrayals of other characters in the series serve to accentuate the qualities shown by the two young surgeons. Initially, they are set off against another surgeon who covers over his professional incompetence and lack of commitment to patients with a veneer of aggressive, intolerant, self-serving patriotism; a commanding officer who is bumbling as a leader and unwilling to accept the responsibilities of authority, yet ambitious to please superiors; a sexy but capable chief nurse whose strongest concern is to advance her army career; a compassionate and dedicated company clerk whose inexperience and naivete makes him dependent on the hero-surgeons for guidance; a well-intended, cooperative, though other-worldly and often ineffective, Catholic chaplain; an orderly who resorts to transvestism in a desperate effort to win discharge from the army; and, more occasionally, a paranoid intelligence officer who finds Communist plots in everyday events, a psychiatrist whose expressions of sympathy by psychotherapeutic formula offer meager relief from the burdens of wartime, and various generals whose vanity makes them easily gulled and ineffective. In later episodes, the incompetent colleague is replaced by a surgeon of exceptional skill, but whose upper-class snobbery and professional ambition strain the fellowship of the hospital staff. The commanding officer in the late episodes is a career colonel who represents military discipline more favorably, but who wisely tempers it out of respect for the personal needs of his staff, especially the surgeons, whose skill and devotion he appreciates.

The cast of characters is a parody of the "e pluribus unum" variety of figures that commonly appear in American dramas about national causes. These characters exhibit variety, but largely as a variety of personal failings. They are often seriously divided against themselves, caught up in egocentric jealousies, peeves, and competitive ambitions that break down the cooperation necessary in a hospital. The humor developed in the antic playing on human weaknesses highlights characteristically American deficiencies: ambition, self-centeredness, intolerance of the unfamiliar, self-interested abuse of higher principles, vanity, and so forth. When the surgeon heroes galvanize this morally fragmented group into effective cooperation and mutual respect, the surpassing nature of their qualities is dramatized strongly. The comedy of *MASH* is exploited methodically for didactic moralism. As self-consciously innovative as its humor may be, it retains a footing in the familiar middle-class culture of character and calling.

The popularity of *MASH* has yet another key source. The wide-spread conviction that it was an especially meaningful show rested on a crucial symbolic device: its setting in Korea was a moderately transparent substitute for the war of its own times in Vietnam. By using an apparent setting in the Korean War, *MASH* could become a popular vehicle for the antiwar, antimilitary, antinationalistic attitudes of the opposition to the Vietnam War. Moreover, it could dramatize these attitudes in ways that reassuringly connected them with traditionally recognized virtues of character. The critique of war, the military, and fervent nationalism was united with traditional social criticism of ambition, egocentrism, incompetence, and lack of feeling. Had *MASH* been set overtly in Vietnam, such morally and sentimentally serious matters could not have been addressed. The affront to Americans who served in Vietnam and/or backed the war policies would have been too direct. Only a storm of disapproval could have resulted. However, the temperate effort to show the grounding of war-criticism in traditional moral culture, giving it broader legitimacy in American life, could not have been undertaken either. It would have seemed overly compromising and lacking in integrity. Yet, the audience for *MASH* could not miss the point that Korea was a tasteful stand-in for Vietnam. Much of the culture, not least the style of humor and the slang, but at times material objects and even items of medical technology, was taken from the era of the Vietnam War, not the Korean War. The events of *MASH* existed in their own world with typical features of their own. They could not have happened in Korea or Vietnam. But by matters of cultural style they commented with only slight ambiguity on Vietnam.

MASH can provide an occasion for considering the relevance of routine television forms to more serious sources of order and common commitment. *MASH* was presented to its audience as an "entertainment," not as a didactic treatment of an ideology or religion. Its success was realized through its ability to "entertain" an audience embodying most of the ideological and spiritual diversity of the nation. In experiencing an "entertainment," its audience was engaged with a form of popular art that ordinarily maintains an attitudinal distance from serious dilemmas and controversies. The satire of *MASH* often had serious themes or overtones, but viewers were allowed to remain in the experiential frame of enjoying entertainment. Had the audience felt that the satire amounted to ideological proselytization, it would likely have rejected *MASH* as an inappropriate exploitation of the television format of a "show." At least, the success of *MASH* as a show of general appeal would have been jeopardized. We may also speculate that more diffuse and overtly critical satire could not have been sustained at a high level for the long run of *MASH*, at least not within its episodic formulae.

Many of the themes in *MASH* are utterly typical of the way in which the secular entertainments of American television participate in the middle-class morality. *MASH* presents us with vivid heroes who display skill, dedication, compassion, bravery, conscientiousness, and so forth. Their missions and activities reverberate in our senses of national identity. They are surrounded by figures who represent a wide range of the types that compose the American community. The show's persistent concern with the horrors of war dramatizes what may be America's greatest social problem. More deeply, *MASH* gave its huge audience a healing mediation between the antiwar culture of the Vietnam War years and many long-established values of the middle-class morality. In doing so, it served American civilization more penetratingly and venturesomely than most television has dared to attempt. It endeavored to provide a culture of reconciliation to resolve strongly felt social and cultural divisions. Here, *MASH* took up a higher calling than just continuing to dramatize conventional moralism. It adopted a stance of respectful criticism as well as a stance of affirmation. By uniting these stances in a continuing drama, *MASH* reached a moral and spiritual fulfillment to which television has not often aspired.

CONCLUSION

The American middle-class morality, ever since it crystallized as a major force through early nineteenth century nondenominational evangelism, has been an ethic of social integration (Miller, 1965; Ryan, 1982). In styles varying from Tom Sawyer's Aunt Polly to the bus driver's wife in *The Honeymooners,* it has upheld the values of a trustworthy way of life that can unite a diverse and mobile people. However different Americans are from one another and however unknown they may be to one another, they hold a basis of mutual trust in their common displays of conformity to an elaborate ethic of conventional behavior. From early in American history, mass media preaching conformity to conventional standards have complemented our traditions of individualism.

The sensuous, captivating, even hypnotic qualities of television would appear to clash with the ascetic emphases of American culture. However, the television industry has developed the cultural forms—particularly in the episodic shows focusing on character and on situations of popular concern—that bring its vast expressional capacities into concord with the middle-class morality. Television today has become—implicitly, yet relentlessly—a national medium of expression for middle-class moral conventionalism. Day and night it addresses diverse sectors of its national audience with one or another mode of expression of the common ethic. The audience addressed by television is essentially the social whole, Americans, conceived as ethically and conventionally alike as subjects of morality. Pluralism of ethnic background, region of the country, job or calling, and socioeconomic circumstance may be ritually acknowledged, but generally as additional means of dramatizing the claim of the common ethic over all and its appeal to all who are essentially conscientious. The controversies over the ways in which Blacks, Hispanic-Americans, Native Americans, women, homosexuals, and other disadvantaged groups are shown on television have turned mainly on the right to be portrayed as equally respectworthy in the terms of middle-class morality. The legitimacy of its conventional claims have been largely presupposed. In this respect, the controversies may themselves be evidence of the integrative efficacy of the American middle-class ethic.

To be emphasizing the respects in which television has remade a vast and diverse country into a "national village" may seem to be belaboring a cliche of television criticism. The cliche, however, has portrayed the national village as growing out of the lavish deployment of television's technology. I emphasize rather the middle-class morality as a factor controlling the expressional use of television, especially its dramatic formats. I argue that it has been television's standing as an agent of conventional moralism that has made it so meaningful within the routines of daily life as well as integrative of popular social experience as a whole. Its efficacy in contemporary social life cannot be grasped unless its role as scion of a moral tradition stemming from the popular strains of Puritanism is understood. The vitality of television in American popular culture must be seen as an historical derivation, for secularized society, of the mass-oriented, moralistic religious movements that flourished in the early decades of the Republic.

REFERENCES

Bellah, Robert N. (1968) "Religion, the sociology of." International Encyclopedia of the Social Sciences. New York: Macmillan.
_____ (1970) "Civil religion in America," in Beyond Belief. New York: Harper & Row.
Bercovitch, Sacvan (1975) The Puritan Origins of the American Self. New Haven, CT: Yale University Press.
Booth, Wayne (1982) "The company we keep: self-making in imaginative art, old and new." Daedalus (Fall).
de Tocqueville, Alexis (1948) Democracy in America. New York: Alfred A. Knopf.
Gans, Herbert (1979) Deciding What's News. New York: Pantheon.
Goethals, Gregor T. (1981) The TV Ritual: Worship at the Video Altar. Boston: Beacon.
Lidz, Charles and Andrew Walker (1980) Heroin, Deviance, and Morality. Beverly Hills, CA: Sage.
Lidz, Victor (1979) "Secularization, ethical life, and religion in modern societies," in H. M. Johnson (ed.) Religious Change and Continuity. San Francisco: Jossey-Bass.
Miller, Perry (1965) The Life of the Mind in America. New York: Harcourt Brace Jovanovich.
Parsons, Talcott (1979) "Religion in postindustrial America: the problem of secularization," in Action Theory and the Human Condition. New York: Free Press.
_____ and Victor Lidz (1967) "Death in American society," in E. Schneidman (ed.) Essays in Self-Destruction. New York: Science House.
Ryan, Mary (1982) The Cradle of the Middle Class. New York: Cambridge University Press.
Schudson, Michael (1982) "The politics of narrative form: the emergence of news conventions in print and television." Daedalus (Fall).
Weber, Max (1930) The Protestant Ethic and the Spirit of Capitalism. New York: Scribner.
_____ (1963) The Sociology of Religion. Boston: Beacon.

ABOUT THE CONTRIBUTORS

PAUL ATTALLAH is a McConnell Fellow at McGill University, currently completing doctoral research on film and television.

JOHN FISKE is Senior Lecturer and Acting Head of the School of English, Western Australian Institute of Technology. He is a coauthor of *Reading Television,* which combines a theory of the cultural role of television with a semiotic-based method of analysis.

JOHN HARTLEY is a Lecturer in Mass Communication and Cultural Studies, Polytechnic of Wales. He is a coauthor of *Reading Television.*

PAUL M. HIRSCH is a Professor of Sociology in the Graduate School of Business, University of Chicago. He has written widely on various issues in communication, social and organizational theory, and he is the author and editor of many works, including *Reader in Public Opinion and Mass Communication* and *Strategies for Communication Research* (Volume 6 of this series).

JOLI JENSEN is an Assistant Professor in the Department of Rhetoric and Communication Studies, University of Virginia, where she teaches media history, theory, and content analysis from a cultural studies perspective. She has written on country music as a cultural forum and is interested in problems of culture production, genre definition, and social groups in American life.

ALBERT KREILING is Chairman of the Department of Communication Arts, Johnson C. Smith University, Charlotte, North Carolina. His interests include communication history, the black press, and popular culture.

VICTOR LIDZ is a Lecturer in Sociology at Haverford College and the University of Pennsylvania. He has published a number of essays on secular moral culture, the sociology of religion, and general sociological theory. He is a co-editor of *Explorations in General Theory in Social Science.*

HORACE M. NEWCOMB is a Professor of Radio-TV-Film, the University of Texas, Austin. He has written extensively on the relationship between media and popular culture, and is the author, coauthor, and editor of several books, including *Television: The Critical View* and *The Producer's Medium: Conversations with Creators of American TV.*

GERTRUDE JOCH ROBINSON is Professor and Director of the Graduate Program in Communications, McGill University. She is interested in the cultural aspects of television news coverage and is the author of several volumes, including *News Agencies and World News* and *Tito's Maverick Media.* Her work reported in this volume is part of a larger study, the results of which will be published in the 1984 *McGill University Working Papers in Communication* series.

WILLARD D. ROWLAND, Jr. is Associate Dean in the College of Communications and Associate Professor in the Institute of Communications Research, University of Illinois. He has written on American broadcasting, telecommunications policy, public broadcasting, and communications reform, and is the author of *The Politics of TV Violence.*

THOMAS STREETER is an Assistant Professor in Communication Arts, University of Wisconsin, Madison. He received an undergraduate degree in semiotics from Brown University and is completing his doctoral work in speech communications at the University of Illinois. He has written on telecommunications policy, as well as cultural studies.

JOSEPH TUROW is an Associate Professor in the Department of Communication, Purdue University. He has written extensively on issues related to the institutional nature of mass media and is the author of three books, including *Entertainment, Education, and the Hard Sell: Three Decades of Network Television* and *Media Industries: The Production of News and Entertainment.*

BRUCE WATKINS is an Assistant Professor in the Department of Communication, University of Michigan. He has written on media effects on children, socialization, and problems of qualitative methods. He is currently a Congressional Science Fellow, working with the staff of the U.S. House of Representatives Subcommittee on Telecommunications, Consumer Protection, and Finance.

THOMAS H. ZYNDA is an Assistant Professor in Theatre and Communication Arts, Memphis State University. The paper in this volume grows out of a series of presentations on family and society in drama, and he is currently working on a cultural study of the police/detective genre in television.

DATE DUE

30 9 '86			
30			
3 0			
DEC 3 0			
FEB 8 '89			
NOV 30 90			
MAY 30			
SEP 1 4 '9			

DEMCO 38-297

MAR 3 - 1986